LPC CASE STUDY:
CIVIL LITIGATION

FOR OUR PARENTS

LPC CASE STUDY: CIVIL LITIGATION

Michelle Robson LLB, Solicitor

Senior Lecturer, University of Northumbria at Newcastle

and

Tim Clarke LLB, Solicitor

First published in Great Britain 1994 by Blackstone Press Limited, Aldine Place, London W12 8AA.
Telephone: 0181-740 2277

© M. Robson and T. Clarke, 1994

ISBN: 1 85431 697 4

First edition 1994
Second edition 1995
Third edition 1996
Fourth edition 1997

British Library Cataloguing in Publication Data
A CIP catalogue record for this book is available from the British Library.

Typeset by Montage Studios Limited, Tonbridge, Kent
Printed by Ashford Colour Press, Gosport, Hampshire

All rights reserved. No part of this book may be reproduced or transmitted in any form or by any means, electronic or mechanical, including photocopying, recording, or any information storage or retrieval system without prior permission from the publisher.

CONTENTS

Preface   ix

Acknowledgments   x

How to Use This Book   xi

Personal Injury Action: *George Martin* v *Easyshop Ltd*   1

Introduction   1

The documents contained in this case study are as follows:

Document 1: Note of Client's Appointment	2
Document 2: Accident Questionnaire	3
Document 3: Road Traffic Accident Questionnaire (Extract)	5
Document 4: Factory Accident Questionnaire (Extract)	6
Document 5: Attendance Note: First Interview with Client	7
Document 6: Client Correspondence	9
Document 7: Green Form	11
Document 8: Legal Aid Letter	13
Document 9: CLA1	17
Document 10: Legal Aid Certificate	26
Document 11: Proof of Evidence — The Client	29
Document 12: Letter to Client — Draft Proof of Evidence	33
Document 13: Letter Before Action	34
Document 14: Letter to Health and Safety Executive	39
Document 15: Letter from Defendant's Insurers	41
Document 16: Letter to Defendant's Insurers	42
Document 17: Letter from Defendant's Solicitors — Authority to Accept Service	43
Document 18: Letter to Defendant's Solicitors — The Accident Report Book	44
Document 19: Letter to Client's Employer	46
Document 20: Letter to Client — Medical Examination	48
Document 21: Consent Form for the Release of Medical Records	49
Document 22: Letter to Client's GP — Disclosure of Client's Medical Records	50
Document 23: Letter to Oldcastle General Hospital — Disclosure of Client's Medical Records	51
Document 24: Letter from Defendant's Solicitors — The Accident Report Book	52
Document 25: Proof of Evidence — Gina Wright (Witness)	53
Document 26: Attendance Note — Medical Expert	54
Document 27: Letter of Instruction to Medical Expert	55
Document 28: Medical Report	57
Document 29: Writ	61
Document 30: Letter to Oldcastle District Registry — Issue of the Writ	67

CONTENTS

Document 31: Letter to Defendant's Solicitors — Service of Proceedings	68
Document 32: Statement of Claim	69
Document 33: Letter to Expert	74
Document 34: Letter from Defendant's Solicitors — Intention to Defend	75
Document 35: Acknowledgment of Service	76
Document 36: Letter to Client — Medical Examination	79
Document 37: Letter to Defendant's Solicitors — Conditions for Medical Examination	80
Document 38: Attendance Note — Advice to Client	81
Document 39: Instructions to Counsel to Advise on Quantum	82
Document 40: Defence	85
Document 41: Letter to Defendant's Solicitors — Issue of Summons	87
Document 42: Summons: RSC Ord. 29, r. 10	88
Document 43: Letter from Defendant's Solicitors Admitting Liability	90
Document 44: Letter to Defendant's Solicitors	91
Document 45: Letter from Defendant's Solicitors — Payment In	93
Document 46: Notice of Payment In	94
Document 47: Letter to Client — Payment In	96
Document 48: Letter to Defendant's Solicitors refusing Payment In	99
Document 49: Affidavit in Support of Application under RSC Ord. 29 (Interim Payment)	100
Document 50: File Note	105
Document 51: Attendance Note — Hearing of Applications for Summary Judgment and Interim Payment	106
Document 52: Order — Summary Judgment	110
Document 53: Order — Interim Payment and Directions	112
Document 54: Letter Instructing Second Medical Expert	113
Document 55: Attendance Note — Medical Expert	114
Document 56: Client's Witness Statement	115
Document 57: Letter from Defendant's Solicitors — Without Prejudice Meeting of Experts	120
Document 58: Brief to Counsel to Attend the Assessment Hearing	121
Document 59: Letter to Expert — Advising of Hearing	124
Document 60: Letter to Process Server	125
Document 61: Subpoena	126
Document 62: Attendance Note — Assessment Hearing	128
Document 63: Bill of Costs and Legal Aid Taxation Certificate	130

Contract Action: *Rent-A-Tent Ltd* v *Hawthorn Ltd*   147

Introduction   147

The documents contained in this case study are as follows:

Document 1: Letter Before Action	148
Document 2: Default Summons	150
Document 3: Particulars of Claim	153
Document 4: Attendance Note — First Interview with Client	156
Document 5: Initial Letter to Client	161
Document 6: Client Care Letter	163
Document 7: First Letter to Plaintiff's Solicitors	168
Document 8: N9 (Form of Admission, Defence and Counterclaim)	169
Document 9: File Note	171
Document 10: Client Correspondence	172
Document 11: Client Correspondence	173
Document 12: Client Correspondence	174
Document 13: Automatic Directions	175
Document 14: Letter to Client — Company Search	179
Document 15: Proof of Evidence (Anne Francis)	181

CONTENTS

Document 16: Defence and Counterclaim — 186
Document 17: Letter to Plaintiff's Solicitors — Service of Defence and Counterclaim — 190
Document 18: Letter from Plaintiff's Solicitors (Reply to Document 17) — 191
Document 19: Letter to Plaintiff's Solicitors (Reply to Document 18) — 192
Document 20: Notice of Application — 194
Document 21: Letter to Chief Clerk Enclosing Notice of Application — 195
Document 22: Letter to Plaintiff's Solicitors — Service of Notice of Application and Affidavit — 196
Document 23: Letter to Oldcastle County Court — 197
Document 24: Affidavit of Thomas Arthur Wood — 198
Document 25: Order (Security for Costs) — 202
Document 26: Letter from Plaintiff's Solicitors — Service of Request for Further and Better Particulars — 203
Document 27: Request for Further and Better Particulars of Defence and Counterclaim — 204
Document 28: Letter to Plaintiff's Solicitors — Time Extension — 206
Document 29: Letter from Plaintiff's Solicitors — Service of Reply and Defence to Counterclaim — 207
Document 30: Reply and Defence to Counterclaim — 208
Document 31: Further and Better Particulars of the Defence and Counterclaim — 209
Document 32: Third Party Notice — 211
Document 33: Notice of Application for Leave to Issue — 214
Document 34: Order Giving Leave to Third Party Directions — 215
Document 35: Letter of Instruction to Expert — 216
Document 36: Defence to Third Party Notice — 219
Document 37: List of Documents — 221
Document 38: Witness Statement of Anne Francis — 226
Document 39: Letter to Plaintiff's Solicitors — Exchange of Witness Statements — 233
Document 40: Letter to Plaintiff's Solicitors — Service of Witness Statements — 234
Document 41: Letter to Client — Interrogatories — 235
Document 42: Letter to Plaintiff's Solicitors — Exchange of Expert Reports — 237
Document 43: Letter to Plaintiff's Solicitors Serving Interrogatories — 238
Document 44: Interrogatories — 239
Document 45: Instructions to Counsel to Advise — 241
Document 46: Notice to Admit Facts — 246
Document 47: Witness Summons — 249
Document 48: Writ of *Fieri Facias* — 253
Document 49: Affidavit for Oral Examination — 257
Document 50: Order for Oral Examination — 259
Document 51: Bill to Client — 263

Pre-Action Relief — An Application for an Anton Piller Injunction: *Hawthorn Ltd v Sidney Diamond and Plank Ltd* — 267

Introduction — 267

The documents contained in this case study are as follows:

Document 1: Writ — 271
Document 2: Notice of Motion — 274
Document 3: Order — 277

PREFACE

Our aim in writing this book is to provide students with a practical guide to civil litigation by three illustrated case studies. You will follow the case studies through from the moment the client walks through the door of the solicitor's office to the final resolution of the action (two successful, the other not so successful). Like a civil litigation file, the book is document based. We have tried to demonstrate a wide range of procedural matters and we provide explanation by way of notes and commentary on the documents and steps taken.

The first case study is a personal injury claim proceeding in the High Court. We depart from the usual road traffic accident scenario and follow a supermarket accident claim. The plaintiff is legally aided, therefore we provide commentary on the procedural aspects of a legal aid action. The study also illustrates that summary judgment is not only for a debt action. We also discuss the usefulness of an application for an interim payment.

The second case study arises from a commercial dispute. The solicitor in this action represents a privately-funded defendant. This enables us to look at the issue of costs and the privately paying litigant. It also demonstrates that the defendant's solicitor is as important as the plaintiff's solicitor in determining the shape and course of the action, by invoking such procedural tactics as a security for costs application and interrogatories. We illustrate an extensive use of pleadings and consider the role of the expert whose evidence can be decisive. In this case study we have also introduced a third party claim.

In this fourth edition we have introduced a new third case study, retaining one of the parties and a firm of solicitors from the commercial dispute, to illustrate that sometimes lawyers and the courts can move extremely quickly if the circumstances demand it. This scenario follows initial instruction through to an application for an Anton Piller injunction, obtaining the order and its execution all in the same day, providing detailed commentary on the strict procedural requirements which have recently been updated to provide safeguards given the intrusive and potentially oppressive nature of this form of relief.

Please note that it is impracticable to demonstrate every attendance note, letter, fax etc. in each matter; however, we hope there is enough here to give you an understanding of what a solicitor's file could (or dare we say, should!) look like.

Finally, we would like to thank a large number of people without whom this book would never have made it to the publishers. In no particular order (other than the order we remember them!) our thanks to Peter Maughan, Murray Heining, Mrs Carole Stockdale, Dr Andrew Chaplin and Dr Richard Smithson for advice of a medical nature, William Leith, Smithson & Co., Professor Hugh Brayne, Charles Morgan colleagues at the University of Northumbria at Newcastle, namely Michael Stockdale, Fiona Boyle, Christina McAlhone and to Margaret Bell and Diane Lightburn for their help in the preparation of the manuscript.

A special thanks must go to Edna Brown of the Newcastle-upon-Tyne Legal Aid Area Office who once again never failed to assist in times of need!

Last, but not least, thanks go to Blackstone Press, in particular to Mandy Preece who always retained her sense of humour in the face of great adversity, to Paula Doolan, who has been responsible for the last three editions and to our latest victim, Amanda Crook, who has been involved in the preparation of this edition.

ACKNOWLEDGMENTS

Permissions to use the following forms are gratefully acknowledged:

Documents reproduced by kind permission of the Legal Aid Board are the Green Form, CLA1 and the Legal Aid Certificate.

Reproduced for educational purposes only by kind permission of The Solicitors' Law Stationery Society Ltd are the Acknowledgment of Service of Writ of Summons, Subpoena ad test. and the *Praecipe* for Writ of *Fieri Facias*.

Reproduced by kind permission of HMSO are N2 (Default Summons), N9 (Admission, Defence and Counterclaim), N450 (Automatic Directions) and Legal Aid Taxation Certificate.

Crown copyright is reproduced with the permission of the Controller of HMSO.

HOW TO USE THIS BOOK

You will see that each case study is divided into steps corresponding to steps in the action. These are followed by the relevant documents accompanied, where appropriate, by notes explaining the document and a commentary which explores some of the wider issues and other matters linked to this step. Please note that the notes in the text refer to the superior figures which appear in the documents.

The book is designed to be read in sequence, but should a student wish to just look at a particular stage of the action, this can be achieved by cross-referring to any other documents as necessary.

You should follow each case study through its various steps and in doing so we hope you will gain an understanding of the wider context in which each step arises. Once you have become familiar with each case study we hope you will be able to utilise this book as a reference guide in the successful pursuit of your qualification.

Abbreviations to the rules of court procedure are:

RSC — the Rules of the Supreme Court, to be found in *The Supreme Court Practice* (commonly referred to as *The White Book*) governing practice in the High Court.

CCR — the County Court Rules, to be found in *The County Court Practice* (commonly referred to as *The Green Book*) governing practice in the county court.

PERSONAL INJURY ACTION:
GEORGE MARTIN v EASYSHOP LTD

Introduction

This case study follows a personal injury action. The case begins with the initial interview and consideration of the accident questionnaire. To avoid the usual road traffic scenario the plaintiff in this instance is claiming against a supermarket for damages after falling over in the store.

What follows is just an example of how the case would progress and does not reproduce the entire file. There would be more letters to the client informing the client of the progress of the case, and far more attendance notes of numerous telephone conversations.

You will see at the onset of the case study the solicitor addresses the client formally but very soon after they are on first name terms. This is a matter of style and will of course depend on how the relationship between the solicitor and client develops. Our own view is that, dependent upon the circumstances of the case (and client), it is better to dispense with needless formality at an early stage.

GEORGE MARTIN v EASYSHOP LTD

STEP 1

Meg Davis is a solicitor in the civil litigation department of Watkins & O'Dwyer of 17 Sycamore Avenue, Oldcastle. On 4 March 1997 her secretary passes to her the following note:

Document 1

> George Martin rang. He wishes to see a solicitor who handles personal injury claims. He said that he had a claim against the local supermarket, as he slipped on something on the supermarket floor and hurt his back badly. His address and telephone number are as follows:
>
> 33 Cherry Street, Oldcastle, OL3 4LL, tel no: 231 1366
>
> He asked that someone contact him as soon as possible.
>
> I have made an appointment for him to see you on 7 March and this is in your diary. Do you want me to send him the standard accident questionnaire?
>
> Date: 4 March 1997

Meg writes to George enclosing a copy of the accident questionnaire. She asks George to complete it and bring it with him to the meeting on 7 March. She additionally sends him the firm's standard client care letter (see contract case study for an example of this at page 161).

Note: We have reproduced the completed questionnaire which will be referred to later on in the case study.

GEORGE MARTIN v EASYSHOP LTD

Document 2

<table>
<tr><td colspan="1" align="center">ACCIDENT QUESTIONNAIRE</td></tr>
</table>

Name: George Martin Address: 33 Cherry Street, Oldcastle, OL3 4LL
Telephone number: Work: Home: 231 1366
Marital status: Married Children: Two
Date of birth: 30.7.51   Age: 45
Occupation: Chartered accountant
Gross weekly earnings: £832.50 Net weekly earnings: £493.25[1]
Employer's name and address: Smythes & Co., 44 Highway, Oldcastle, OL4 3TY Date and time of accident: 2 Feb 1996 at about 6.45 p.m.
Place of accident: Easyshop supermarket at Unit 7, Beech Court, Oldcastle
Injuries received: Back injuries
Returned to work?: No. I was unable to work due to the injuries I sustained and I left my employment on 17 May 1996
Name and address of General Practitioner: Dr Shipley, Merrywell Medical Centre, 21 Barnett Grove, Oldcastle, OL12 4QL
Hospital where treated and hospital record number: Oldcastle General Hospital; 2221XC
Name of hospital doctor: I was treated by a Mr Goode in hospital and then Mr Astley as an out-patient
Local DSS Office: Oldcastle, Central[2]
National Insurance Number: NM56TY789
Previous accidents/injuries: None
Any existing medical condition:[3] No, although I was told at hospital that I had a weak back and it may become progressively worse.
Name and addresses of witnesses: I don't know the name of the woman who rushed up to me at the time of the accident.
Name and address of person/company responsible for the accident: I hold Easyshop entirely responsible for the accident, in fact looking at the letter they sent to me it seems that they have admitted as much.
Name and address of the insurers of the person/company responsible for the accident: Don't know.

GEORGE MARTIN v EASYSHOP LTD

Was the accident reported and if so to whom: I think it was by the woman who rushed up to me when I fell.
Is the client receiving disablement benefit: Yes
Losses and expenses to date: I have been forced to leave my job because of my injuries and therefore I have dropped from earning £40,000 a year to live on income support. I have spent a considerable amount on travel to hospital for physiotherapy and I can obtain details of all my visits to my physiotherapist and my GP together with details of my prescription charges.
Description of how the accident occurred (and sketch plan if of assistance):[4] I was walking through the shop buying a few groceries. I had just reached the aisle with the oils and sauces and was reaching for a bottle of olive oil when the next thing I knew I slipped and fell on the base of my back. I felt terrible pain and then I can't remember any more because I think I fainted with the pain.
Dated 7 March 1997   Signed George Martin

NOTES: QUESTIONNAIRE

It is a good idea to send to the client a questionnaire to complete before the initial interview. By doing this the client will know what to expect of this interview and it will concentrate the mind on the accident and the issues involved.

Listed above is an example of what might be sent to the client. It is self-explanatory but the following points should be noted:

(1)   Earnings. Meg will be writing to the client's employer at a later date to get exact details.

(2)   DSS Office and National Insurance Number. Meg will need this information to obtain details of benefits paid to the client which the defendant will ultimately have to repay to the Compensation Recovery Unit, see note (5) at page 35.

(3)   It is important to ascertain whether the client had any pre-existing injuries or condition at the time of the accident. If yes then his present condition may not be due solely to the accident and therefore his damages may be reduced accordingly.

(4)   The accident. Check that you fully understand how the accident occurred. This is why a sketch plan may be appropriate.

The questionnaire above is fairly basic. We set out below what additional questions may be asked if the accident was (1) a road traffic accident and (2) a factory accident. We have also included a short commentary on each.

GEORGE MARTIN v EASYSHOP LTD

Document 3

ADDITIONAL QUESTIONS ON A ROAD TRAFFIC ACCIDENT QUESTIONNAIRE
Name and address of the driver responsible for the incident:
Name and address of owner of vehicle responsible for the accident:[1]
Vehicle responsible: 　Reg No: 　Make: 　Insurers:[2] 　Extent of cover:
Client's vehicle: 　Reg No: 　Make: 　Insurers:[3] 　Extent of cover:[4]
Police station accident reported to:
Notice of intended prosecution served:[5]
Seat belts fitted and worn by the client:[6]
Previous convictions and endorsements:
Extent of damage to the client's vehicle:
Estimated cost of repairs or pre-accident value:[7]
Towage charges:　　　Hire charges:
Where client's vehicle is stored and can be examined:
Storage charges and other losses and expenses to date:

NOTES: ROAD TRAFFIC ACCIDENT QUESTIONNAIRE

(1) You should clarify whether the car driver and the car owner are one and the same. Often the driver is the employee or agent of the owner and therefore your claim will be directed against both under the principle of vicarious liability or agency.

(2) If you know the identity of the defendant's insurers then you can write a letter to them direct enclosing a copy of the letter before action you have sent to their insured. See the letter before action at page 34.

(3) The defendant's insurers will want to know the identity of your client's insurers as they may agree between themselves to cover their insured losses under a 'knock for knock' agreement.

(4) It is important to ascertain what cover the client has on his/her own policy, i.e., is it comprehensive or not. Remember that if the client has made a claim on his/her own insurance then the insurers, under their right of subrogation, are entitled to pursue the claim in respect of the insured's loss (albeit

GEORGE MARTIN v EASYSHOP LTD

in the name of the insured). You should in this case write to your client's insurers to obtain their agreement to your pursuing the whole claim, i.e., insured and uninsured losses. They may want their own solicitors to pursue the claim.

(5) It may be that the other side will be prosecuted. If the client has been warned to attend as a witness then it is likely that there will be a prosecution. The police accident report will not be released, however, until the prosecution has taken place.

(6) If there were seat belts fitted in the client's vehicle and they were not worn then the client's damages may be reduced by up to 25 per cent for contributory negligence: see *Froom* v *Butcher* [1976] QB 286.

(7) The client must obtain estimates of the costs of repairs. If the vehicle is beyond repair then obtain a pre-accident value.

Note: In the two questionnaires above you could also include a question as to whether the plaintiff is a minor and who is his next friend.

Document 4

ADDITIONAL QUESTIONS TO BE ASKED IN A FACTORY ACCIDENT
How long employed in the factory: Current job title:
How long engaged in that particular job:
What is client's status *vis à vis* other employees:
Who is in immediate authority over the client:
Was protective clothing available: If so give details:
Details of previous or similar accidents:
Dates of earlier relevant complaints to employer:
When was accident reported and to whom:
Was the accident reported in the accident report book:[1]
What is manufactured/undertaken in the premises:
Did the injury occur during a routine job:
How experienced is the client in this line of work:
Was the employer on notice as to the risk of injury. If yes, in what way:

NOTES: FACTORY ACCIDENT

(1) The employer has a statutory duty to maintain an accident report book. If there have been earlier accidents of a similar nature which the client or his colleagues reported then these will be relevant. The client can argue that the employer was aware of the danger but failed to take any steps to try and prevent it.

6

Note also the Management of Health and Safety at Work Regulations 1992 (SI 1992 No. 2051) as amended by the Management of Health and Safety at Work (Amendment) Regulations 1994 (SI 1994 No. 2865) which implement EEC Directive 391 and came into force on 1 January 1993. Now it is the duty of every employer to make a suitable and sufficient assessment of the risk to the health and safety of other workers likely to be affected. Hence it may be prudent to request disclosure of these records. See further page 10, note 2(a).

Commentary: Questionnaire

If the client is receiving industrial injuries disablement benefit, check whether the client appealed against the award. If he did there may be medical opinions on record which will be particularly important. It is important to check that the client is claiming all benefits for which he is eligible, e.g., severe disablement allowance and reduced earning allowance to name but two.

STEP 2

Meg meets with George Martin on 7 March 1997. An attendance note of the meeting is reproduced below.

Document 5

Watkins & O'Dwyer

Attendance Note

Your name   Meg Davis   Date 7 March 1997

Client's name   George Martin

Person attended   Client

Time start 10.30 a.m.   Time finished 11.35 a.m.

Attending George Martin in connection with his personal injury claim against Easyshop Ltd.

Took personal details from Mr Martin and established that he was eligible for Green Form advice. I then explained that he may be eligible for legal aid and explained to him the effect of the statutory charge. I handed him forms CLA1 and CLA4B together with explanatory leaflets *Legal Aid — What Happens Next*, *The Statutory Charge* and *Paying Back the Legal Aid Board*, and the firm's standard letter on legal aid. I asked Mr Martin to complete the legal aid forms as soon as possible and to read through the other documentation. I told Mr Martin that if he understood the contents of the legal aid letter then he should sign it and return it to me in the post.

I explained to Mr Martin that today I could only take a preliminary statement from him; I could not take any further steps until I knew he was eligible for legal aid.

We then went through the accident questionnaire which Mr Martin had completed. Mr Martin explained he wished to sue Easyshop, the local supermarket. On 2 February 1996 Mr Martin had just finished work and was making his way home. He thought he would call in at Easyshop for some groceries. Nothing extraordinary happened until he reached the aisle with the sauces and oils. All he can remember is walking with his basket towards the shelf with the olive oil and the next thing he knew was that he slipped and could not prevent himself from falling badly on the base of his spine. He tried to get up and found he could not move, and felt an excruciating pain in his back. A woman shopper rushed up to him and he believes she said 'You've slipped on that oil. I told them that they should clean it up immediately, it's no wonder that someone slipped. At the very least they should have put up a barrier.' Mr Martin, however, did not know the name of this woman.

GEORGE MARTIN v EASYSHOP LTD

Mr Martin then informed me that he was in such pain that he thinks he fainted because the next thing he knew he was in bed at Oldcastle General Hospital. I referred to the questionnaire which indicated that Mr Martin had sustained back injuries. Mr Martin said he remained in bed for two days. He had several x-rays and scans and was told by Mr Astley, his treating consultant, that he had a serious back injury (Mr Martin thinks he was told by Mr Astley that he had an entrapped nerve in his lower spine) which would not improve. Mr Martin was also informed that he may have already been suffering from a weak back. When Mr Martin left hospital he had to walk with a stick and was constantly visiting his GP for painkillers. He underwent intensive physiotherapy under the care of Mr Goode. After 12 sessions of physiotherapy he could walk short distances without his stick. He has, however, now been told by the physiotherapist that there is very little that he can do for him and unfortunately he will continue to suffer some pain and discomfort throughout his life. Mr Martin continues to have one physiotherapy session per week to try and keep his back supple. I told Mr Martin that at some stage it would be necessary to contact the hospital and his GP to obtain his medical records for the purposes of instructing a medical expert.

I referred Mr Martin to the section on medical conditions in the questionnaire. Mr Martin told me that until the accident he had had no back problems. Now he fears he may end up in a wheelchair and is certain that he will no longer be able to do all the things he enjoyed such as playing squash, football and badminton. He was an active member of his local sports club, but, however, has not been there since the accident.

Mr Martin told me that his whole lifestyle has changed dramatically. He is now virtually housebound as he cannot drive because of the pain and his wife doesn't drive. His relationship with his wife has suffered and they are no longer intimate. This is due largely to the fact that Mr Martin's physical condition has deteriorated drastically as he can no longer play sport, and he now weighs 17½ stones as opposed to 14½ stones before the accident. In addition, his whole personality has changed and he is often irritable and depressed largely because of the constant pain he is in.

Mr Martin fears that his relationship with his children will suffer. He can no longer play games with them, take them to scouts and brownies, and the family holidays to Wales and Scotland have had to be abandoned.

As a result of the accident Mr Martin has lost his job. At first his employers, Smythes, a firm of chartered accountants, were very understanding. However, when he had to take one afternoon a week off for physiotherapy, could not sit in his chair for more than an hour at a time, and as a result failed to meet his billing targets, and additionally fell behind schedule on a number of projects, it became clear that his employers' patience had run out and they asked him to leave. They explained that whilst they were sympathetic, the situation would not improve and they had no option but to terminate his employment. As a gesture of goodwill Smythes gave Mr Martin £10,000; however this money has now been used up as Mr Martin had no savings.

Since leaving Smythes Mr Martin has been trying to find part-time accountancy work that he could perhaps do at home but has had no success. He has had three interviews but on each occasion has been told that he is unemployable because of his health. Up to now he has managed financially because he had received an ex gratia payment from his employers. He has also been claiming disablement benefit and is now on income support. He is extremely worried as to how he will now meet his financial commitments such as his travel expenses to hospital etc. I stressed once again how important it was that he complete his legal aid forms. I took a list of all Mr Martin's expenses as a result of the accident [note this has not been reproduced here but see the special damages schedule at page 70].

About a month after his release from hospital he received a letter from Easyshop which he had brought with him. As far as he could make out they seemed to be saying that the accident was their fault. Included with the letter was £20 worth of gift vouchers to spend at the store. I said I would review the letter as it could amount to an acceptance of liability which would help our case.

GEORGE MARTIN v EASYSHOP LTD

I told Mr Martin that if we were to obtain legal aid and take his case that it could take a considerable time to bring to a conclusion. I told him that we had to commence proceedings by 1 February 1999 for limitation purposes. For the time being I asked him to continue to keep a diary of all expenses or losses incurred as a result of the accident in addition to those he had listed on the questionnaire. He should also keep a diary of his continued pain and suffering.

I concluded the interview with Mr Martin by agreeing that I would prepare an attendance note of our meeting, send it to him and, provided he was happy with the details of the accident, this note would then be sent with his completed legal aid forms to give details of his claim. I explained that until he was granted legal aid that I could take no further action on his behalf.

Document 6

CLIENT CORRESPONDENCE

Easyshop Limited
Unit 7
Beech Court
Oldcastle
OL8 3MN

23 February 1996

G Martin, esq
33 Cherry Street
Oldcastle
OL3 4LL

Dear Mr Martin

We refer to your unfortunate fall in our store on 2 February 1996. We hope that you are now making a full recovery and we would like to take this opportunity to apologise for the incident. We do hope that you will continue to shop with us and by way of a get well gift we enclose £20 of gift vouchers with our compliments. We hope that it is not too long before we see you in our store.

Yours sincerely

Mr D. Mills
Manager

Commentary: Attendance Note

See comments on attendance notes in contract case study at page 160.

1. It is important to take a full statement from the client as soon as possible. The Law Society *Civil Litigation Guide* 1990, paragraph 1, states that from the first interview the solicitor should obtain from the client sufficient information:

(a) to enable preliminary advice to be given on liability;

(b) to identify all the parties who might be involved in the matter;

(c) to form a basic view as to the quantum of damages.

2. From the initial statement it is clear that George may have a claim against Easyshop Ltd for negligence and/or breach of Occupiers' Liability Act 1957, s. 2(2) and it may be that the letter amounts

GEORGE MARTIN v EASYSHOP LTD

to an admission of liability. It would be prudent to do some preliminary research at this point into the nature of the duty of care owed by the supermarket to the plaintiff. It is not the purpose of this book to give detailed explanations of case law but in order to illustrate what investigatory steps Meg should take we will digress a little.

(a) The plaintiff will not establish negligence simply by proving he fell. However, once the plaintiff proves there was something on the floor which ought not to have been there he may be able to rely on the doctrine of *res ipsa loquitor* or in other words have a prima facie case of negligence (see *Ward v Tesco Stores Ltd* [1976] 1 All ER 219). It was held in that case that the onus was on the defendant to show the accident had not arisen from want of care. Pursuant to the Occupiers' Liability Act 1957, s. 2(2) whether Easyshop took reasonable care will involve considering the nature of the danger, the length of time the danger was in existence and the likelihood of injury occurring because of the danger, weighed against the cost of eliminating the risk.

Further consider the Workplace (Health and Safety and Welfare) Regulations 1992 (SI 1992 No. 3004) which apply to new workplaces from 1 January 1993 and to existing workplaces from 1 January 1996. Regulation 12(3) provides 'so far as is reasonably practicable; every floor in a workplace and the surface of every traffic route in a workplace shall be kept free from obstructions and from any article or substance which may cause a person to slip, trip or fall'.

Whilst a breach of these regulations would not automatically give rise to civil liability it would seem evident that failure to comply with them would amount to a breach of the common law duty of care.

(b) Considering the above it appears that Mr Martin has a good case. Meg will want to establish what exactly caused Mr Martin to slip, how long the substance was on the floor by hopefully interviewing the woman who rushed up to Mr Martin and any other witnesses and perhaps consulting the accident report book. It may be possible to interview one of the employees of the shop to establish what methods were used to guard against spillages and how quickly they were cleaned up. An employee may also be able to testify that there was oil on the floor and it was not cleaned up for some considerable time, and there were no warning barriers. There is after all no property in witnesses. However, it is unlikely that an employee will wish to give evidence against his/her employer.

(c) Quantum is more difficult to establish given the nature of Mr Martin's injuries; however, from the completed questionnaire we should be able to estimate the amount of special damages incurred so far. Meg can also, by consulting authorities such as *Kemp and Kemp, Current Law, Halsbury's Monthly Review* and *Guidelines for the Assessment of General Damages in Personal Injury Cases*, obtain an estimate as to the going rate for Mr Martin's injuries.

(d) Note Meg should always be aware of any limitation problems, e.g., does the writ have to be issued quickly to protect the limitation period? In a personal injury case the limitation period runs three years from the date of the accident or the date the plaintiff knew he had a cause of action (see the Limitation Act 1980, s. 11).

3. It is a breach of professional good practice for a solicitor to fail to advise on the availability of legal aid and the effect of the statutory charge (see *Civil Litigation — Guide to Good Practice*, prepared by the Law Society, 1990). To assist the solicitor there are three leaflets to help explain the effects of legal aid (see *Legal Aid — What Happens Next, The Statutory Charge* and *Paying Back the Legal Aid Board*, published by the Legal Aid Board). In addition, most firms now have a standard legal aid letter, illustrated immediately below at pages 13 *et seq.*, which in this instance Meg has handed to the client. The notes on the legal aid letter are set out at page 15.

GEORGE MARTIN v EASYSHOP LTD

Green Form

To be used by solicitors with NO franchise contract which covers the category of work into which this green form falls

GF 1 Key Card
LEGAL AID BOARD LEGAL AID ACT 1988

Legal aid account no: **B130P**

Ref: **SPECIMEN**

(Copy from extension authority before sending claim)

► If you have a franchise contract covering the category of work into which this claim falls, complete form GF7.
► If you give advice and assistance about making a will you must submit form GF4 with your claim.
► You should keep a copy of the entire green form.

Client's details *Please use block capitals* *Delete the one which does not apply*   Male/~~Female~~*

Surname: **MARTIN**   First names: **GEORGE**
Address: **33 CHERRY STREET, OLDCASTLE**
Postcode: **OL3 4LL**
National Insurance No: **NM 56 TY 78 9**   Date of Birth: **30.7.51**

Capital details
(give these details even if the client gets income support, income-based Jobseeker's Allowance, family credit or disability working allowance)

How many dependants (partner, children or other relatives of his/her household) does the client have? **3**

Give the total savings and other capital which the client has (and if relevant his or her partner)

Client: £ **975.00**
Spouse (or person living as if a spouse of the client): £ —
Total: £ **975.00**

SPECIMEN

Income details

Does the client get Income Support, any income-based Jobseeker's Allowance, Family Credit or Disability Working Allowance?

[✓] Yes: ignore the rest of this section   [ ] No: give the total gross weekly income of

The client: £ _____
The client's spouse (or person living as if a spouse of the client): £ _____
Total: £ _____

Calculate the total allowable deductions:
Income tax: £ _____
National Insurance contributions: £ _____
Spouse (or person living as if a spouse of the client): £ _____
Attendance allowance, disability living allowance, constant attendance allowance and any payment made out of the Social Fund: £ _____

Dependent children and other dependants: Age   Number
Under 11 _____ £ _____
11 to 15 _____ £ _____
16 to 17 _____ £ _____
18 and over _____ £ _____

Less total deductions: £ _____
Total weekly disposable income: £ _____

Client's declaration

I confirm that:
► I am over the compulsory school-leaving age (or, if not, the solicitor is advising me under Regulation 14(2A) Legal Advice & Assistance Regulations 1989);
► I ~~have~~/have not *(delete whichever one is not correct)* previously received help from a solicitor on this matter under the green form; and
► I understand that I might have to pay my solicitor's costs out of any property or money which is recovered or preserved for me.

As far as I am aware, the information on this page is correct. I understand that if I give false information I could be prosecuted.

Signed: **G. Martin**   Date: **7 / 3 / 97**

96/11/14

11

GEORGE MARTIN v EASYSHOP LTD

Attach a completed Form GF3 as proof of every financial extension

Category of problem *Please tick the relevant box:*

☐ Personal injury *(G)* ☐ Debt *(E)* ☐ Housing *(D)* ☐ Welfare benefits *(H)* ☐ Crime *(C)* ☐ Immigration *(I)* ☐ Employment *(F)*

☐ Consumer/general contract *(K)* ☐ Matrimonial/family: *please also tick one of the following boxes:*

☐ Other *(L) specify in the summary*

(A) ☐ Petitioner in divorce or judicial separation
(M) ☐ Respondent in divorce or judicial separation

(N) ☐ Child support assessment
(B) ☐ Other family matters *(please specify in the summary)*

Solicitor charge

Has any money or property been recovered for the client? ☐ No: go on to the next section ☐ Yes: please give details:

Summary of work

Has a legal aid certificate or order been granted or applied for? ☐ No ☐ Yes: give the reference: _____

Please give below a brief summary of the work done:

SPECIMEN

Breakdown of work done

Please give a breakdown of the work done. If an extension has been granted, record below only the carry forward total times spent, and any subsequent work undertaken. Complete in chronological order, continuing on a separate sheet if necessary.

FEE EARNER'S INITIALS	DATE D M Y	TRAVEL Hrs Mins	ATTENDANCE Hrs Mins	PREPARATION Hrs Mins
Totals carried forward from any extension(s) granted:		:	:	:
		:	:	:
		:	:	:
		:	:	:
		:	:	:
		:	:	:
		:	:	:
		:	:	:
		:	:	:
		:	:	:
		:	:	:
Time old rate		:	:	:
Costs old rate		£	£	£
Time current rate		:	:	:
Costs current rate		£	£	£
Total costs		£	£	£

Letters and Telephone Calls *(not telephone advice calls)*

		Number	£
Letters written	old rate:		
	current rate:		
Telephone calls	old rate:		
	current rate:		
	Total		

Details of disbursements

	£	VAT
Counsel's fees:		
Mileage:		
Other disbursements:		
Totals		

	Claimed	Area office use only Assessed
Profit costs: £		£
VAT on profit costs: £		£
Total disbursements: £		£
VAT on disbursements: £		£
Total claim: £		£

▶ I certify that all the information given in this claim is correct: I have not claimed and will not otherwise claim for the same items from the Legal Aid Fund and I have held a valid practising certificate throughout the conduct of this matter.

Solicitor's personal signature: _____ Date: ___/___/___ Sol ref: _____

Name & address of firm/office: _____

October 1996

Commentary: Green Form

1.   Other than taking an initial statement from the client there is very little a solicitor can do until full legal aid is granted. As the Green Form scheme only provides for two hours of free legal advice the solicitor should stress to the client the importance of completing the legal aid forms as quickly as possible. Obviously if the solicitor must act urgently, e.g., the limitation period is about to run out (something that must be considered in every action), then apply for an extension of the Green Form limit. Trigger this when 1 ½ hours of the 2 hours have elapsed.

2.   Remember that the Green Form scheme does not cover representation.

3.   The current financial limits for Green Form advice are a disposable capital of £1,000 or less and a disposable income of £77 per week or less for an applicant without dependants. An applicant will automatically qualify on income if in receipt of income support, income-based jobseeker's allowance, family credit or disability working allowance. Contributory Green Form advice was abolished on 12 April 1993.

Document 8

Watkins & O'Dwyer
Solicitors

17 Sycamore Avenue
Oldcastle OL10 1BR
Tel. 011-111-1111
Fax 011-111-1111
DX Oldcastle 1000

Partners: J. Watkins
A. O'Dwyer

7 March 1997

G Martin, esq
33 Cherry Street
Oldcastle
OL3 4LL

Our ref: MD/JR/144.346

Dear Mr Martin

<u>Re your claim against Easyshop</u>

I refer to our recent meeting and write to confirm that you have been handed the appropriate form for completion in order to apply for legal aid together with explanatory leaflets *Legal Aid — What Happens Next*, *The Statutory Charge* and *Paying Back the Legal Aid Board*.

With regard to the forms:

GEORGE MARTIN v EASYSHOP LTD

1. Financial Application Form

Please ensure that you complete this in full, to include the appropriate details for your partner. It is very important that you read the form carefully and answer all the questions.[1]

2. Statement of Case Form

Only complete the parts relevant to yourself. If you are at all unsure about any particular question then please contact me before completing it. Do not complete the section marked 'Statement of Case'.

When you have completed these forms they should be returned to me. Until I have received these forms I cannot make your application for legal aid.

On the return of these forms, I will check through them prior to submitting them to the Legal Aid Board. If there are any difficulties then I will have to return the forms to you because if they are submitted to the Legal Aid Board without being properly completed then they will simply return them to me.[2]

When the Legal Aid Board receives the forms, they will assess your financial means and this may result in you receiving enquiries from a department of the DSS to undertake this assessment on behalf of the Legal Aid Board. Please deal promptly with any enquiry or otherwise this could lead to a delay in your application being processed.

[After their consideration of the application, the Legal Aid Board may grant you a certificate without contribution, or otherwise make an offer to you of a Legal Aid Certificate with a contribution, that contribution being determined by your financial means. You can either then accept or reject the offer.]

If you are granted a Legal Aid Certificate then it is very important that you bear in mind the following points:

[1. If the Certificate is subject to a contribution then you must make sure that you make all payments required under the contribution promptly. If you do not do so this may lead to your Certificate being discharged.]

2. You must inform the Legal Aid Board of any change in your financial circumstances. If you are at all uncertain as to whether any matter should be notified then the safest course is to inform the Legal Aid Board who will then decide whether it is relevant. A change in your financial circumstances may again lead to your certificate being discharged.

3. The effect of the statutory charge.[3] Whilst you will not be required to pay any money [apart from any contribution payable on the Certificate] towards the costs incurred under the Legal Aid Certificate during the action, in the event that you recover [or otherwise preserve any property, to include] money [or other assets,] then the Statutory Charge will take effect and the Legal Aid Board will look to that money [or other property so recovered or preserved] to discharge the costs incurred under the Certificate. This will occur in the event of the money [or property] being recovered [or preserved] pursuant to any final judgment of the court or otherwise under the terms of any settlement you reach with the other side. Whilst I will therefore ensure you are aware of this point when discussing terms of settlement, you should always bear it in mind when considering the overall settlement and the costs which will be taken out of the money [or value of the property] recovered [or preserved]. In this event it is perhaps better to regard legal aid as a loan rather than as a free benefit.

I have mentioned above circumstances in which your Certificate may be discharged.[4] The Certificate may also be discharged if, at any stage in the proceedings, the Legal Aid Board consider that, as a matter of merit, the case should no longer be pursued and they are therefore not prepared to fund the action any longer.

In the event of the Certificate being discharged then (subject to the effect of the Statutory Charge) you will not be required to pay any costs arising prior to the date of the discharge but any further costs we incur in acting for you will be your own personal responsibility and payable by you to this firm. I will provide details of those costs in the eventuality.

As opposed to being discharged, circumstances may lead to the Certificate being revoked. This will usually only occur when the Legal Aid Board consider that there has been some misrepresentation of the position to them, either on merit or with regard to your financial circumstances, so that if they had been aware of the true position at the outset, they would not have granted you legal aid. In the event of revocation then the Legal Aid Board will be entitled to look to you for a refund of all costs incurred under the Certificate prior to revocation. After the date of revocation you will again be personally responsible and liable for our costs and I will again provide you with full details in the eventuality.

A legally aided party will only be required to pay costs of the other side pursuant to any Order if the court has been requested and has carried out an enquiry into the financial circumstances of the legally aided party and has decided that, notwithstanding the assessment made when legal aid was granted, the means of that party are now such as to justify allowing enforcement of the costs Order.

If there is anything raised in this letter upon which you require further clarification or otherwise wish to discuss with me then please do not hesitate to contact me.

Yours sincerely

Meg Davis

NOTES: LEGAL AID LETTER

Many firms now have a standard legal aid letter which they send out to the client dealing with all the possible queries the client could raise. Whilst being of benefit to the client, this is also of benefit to the firm in that it operates as their insurance policy should the client allege that something was not explained. It is always advisable to have a detailed record of what was said to the client re costs.

Below we list some of the more important points that arise from the letter.

Note those sections in square brackets in the legal aid letter are not applicable to this case because (a) George is on income support and will therefore qualify without contribution and (b) he is looking to recover any money by way of damages, not to recover or preserve property.

(1) It is likely that the legal aid forms were explained to the client at the first interview, but as it is of vital importance that the client completes them correctly then it is worthwhile repeating this in the letter.

(2) The letter then goes on to explain to the client what happens to the completed forms once the solicitor receives them. The client would otherwise be speculating as to why the solicitor could not immediately proceed with the action. (The letter emphasises that it is the client's obligation to ensure that any financial contribution is paid promptly and any decision on whether to accept the offer is up to the client. The Law Society's *Civil Litigation Guide* states at Appendix A that a solicitor must inform the client of his obligation to pay a contribution and of the effect of failing to do so.)

(3) Again, the statutory charge and issue of costs will have been dealt with at the first interview but they should be repeated in a letter format. The Law Society's *Civil Litigation Guide* at Appendix A states that the client must be informed:

GEORGE MARTIN v EASYSHOP LTD

(a) of the effect of the statutory charge on his case. When describing the effect of the statutory charge it is a good idea to use words such as loan. This the client can easily understand.

(b) that if he loses the case he may still be ordered by the court to contribute towards his opponent's costs even though his own costs are covered by legal aid. This is very important. Clients are often under the impression that because they are legally aided no financial demands can be made of them other than the contribution. However, the penultimate paragraph of the letter reassures the client that in the event that a costs order is made against him it will not be enforced without the leave of the court. Note also the recent decision *Wraith v Wraith* (1997) *The Times*, 14 February. In this case the plaintiff's action had been struck out for want of prosecution and the usual costs order was made against a legally aided party under s. 17 of the Legal Aid Act 1988. The plaintiff then sued his former solicitors and obtained an indemnity in relation to potential costs. As the plaintiff was now in funds the defendant sought and successfully obtained an order for leave to enforce the costs order; the plaintiff's argument that he was protected under s. 17 failed. The Court of Appeal held that the plaintiff was no different to a 'formerly impecunious litigant who had won the pools'. Furthermore, funds obtained from the settlement of the action could be taken into account though the Court acknowledged that the source of the funds would not be irrelevant in all cases.

(c) that even if the client wins his opponent may not be ordered to pay the full amount of his costs and may not be capable of paying what he has been ordered to pay. Again very important — this point reminds the client that if all of the costs are not recovered then the shortfall will have to be made up from his award of damages. (Note that this is not covered in this letter, but see the client care letter on page 163.)

(4) The letter then goes on to explain the difference between the revocation of the certificate and discharge. This is very important. The client should be made aware that if his financial circumstances change or the case no longer has merit then the certificate could be discharged and he will then have to personally fund the action. More importantly the client is again told of the consequences of trying to mislead the Legal Aid Board and the penalties he could incur if his certificate is revoked.

Note: Normally the legal aid letter would contain a reference that the L17 form should be completed by the client's employer; however, as George is no longer employed we have omitted this section.

STEP 3

Meg receives the completed legal aid forms from George. She attaches the attendance note to the section 'statement of case' and sends it off to the Legal Aid Board.

GEORGE MARTIN v EASYSHOP LTD

PAGE 1 Please complete in block capitals

Application for Legal Aid

CLA 1

Non Matrimonial Proceedings

LEGAL AID BOARD LEGAL AID ACT 1988

Use this form for all non-matrimonial cases. Applications relating to proceedings under the Children Act 1989 (as well as adoption or wardship or proceedings under the Child Abduction and Custody Act 1985 or Child Support Act 1991) should be submitted on forms CLA5 and CLA5A. Use form CLA2 for matrimonial proceedings and Children Act applications dealt with in family proceedings.

General Guide to Legal Aid application forms

form	proceedings	statement of means form required?
CLA 1	Non-matrimonial proceedings - not including free-standing Children Act proceedings	yes
CLA 2	Matrimonial proceedings - including Domestic Violence and Matrimonial Proceedings Act 1976 and Domestic Proceedings and Magistrates' Courts Act 1978 but **not** including free-standing Children Act proceedings, adoption, wardship and assault and trespass. You should use it for proceedings in the Family Proceedings Court but not for Child Support Act proceedings	yes
CLA 5A	Special Children Act proceedings where the applicant is the child, parent or person with parental responsibility, and the application to the court is for secure accommodation (child only), care or supervision, child assessment, emergency protection, or extension or discharge of an emergency protection order	no
CLA 5	All other free-standing Children Act proceedings, wardship, adoption, proceedings under the Child Abduction and Custody Act 1985 and under Sections 20 or 27 Child Support Act 1991	yes
ABWOR 1	ABWOR approval for proceedings in the Family Proceedings Court, Mental Health Review Tribunal proceedings, disciplinary proceedings before a prison governor/controller, Discretionary Lifer Panel proceedings and appeals under the Fire Precautions (Miscellaneous Provisions) Act 1971	no

Applicant's details

SPECIMEN

Surname: Mr/~~Mrs~~/~~Miss~~/~~Ms~~ __MARTIN__

First names: __GEORGE__

Date of birth: __30__ / __7__ / __51__   Occupation: __CHARTERED ACCOUNTANT__

Permanent address: __33 CHERRY STREET__

__OLDCASTLE   OL3 4LL__

Correspondence address: _____
(If different from above)

Name of next friend or guardian ad litem if relevant (a person applying on behalf of the applicant): _____

Solicitor's details

Individual solicitor to be nominated: __MEGAN DAVIS__

Legal Aid account no: __B130P__

Name & address of firm: __WATKINS & O'DWYER, 17 SYCAMORE AVENUE, OLDCASTLE__

Dx no: __17113__   Fax no: __011-111-1111__

Tel no: __011-111-1111__   Ref no: __MD/JR/144.346__

Crystal Mark Clarity approved by Plain English Campaign

Please tick which proceedings this application relates to *(tick one box only)*:
- [x] Personal injury
- [ ] Debt
- [ ] Housing
- [ ] Welfare benefits
- [ ] Immigration
- [ ] Employment
- [ ] Consumer/general contract
- [ ] Other

17

GEORGE MARTIN v EASYSHOP LTD

PAGE 2
General Questions

Please complete this page in all cases.
The Area Office will not be able to enter into correspondence about this application.
The merits of the case must therefore be clear from the information provided. If there is insufficient information,
Legal Aid may be refused.

Previous Legal Aid

SPECIMEN

1 Have you ever applied for Civil Legal Aid?

☐ Yes   ☑ No   ☐ Don't know

2 If you ticked 'yes', please tell us the reference numbers of the Legal Aid certificates or applications if you can and whether they were for the same matter:

3 If you do not know the reference numbers please tell us when Legal Aid was applied for and which town or county the submitting solicitor's office was in:

4 If your surname at the time was different from your present one, please give the old one:

Other people

5 Does any other person stand to gain anything if these proceedings are successful?

☐ Yes   ☑ No   ☐ Don't know: Please say why you are unsure:

6 If anyone does stand to gain anything, will they be involved in the court proceedings?

☐ Yes   ☐ No   ☐ Don't know

7 If you ticked 'yes' to boxes 6 and 7, please give details:

Help from other sources

8 Is any other person or body (*e.g. Motoring Organisation, Insurer, Trade Union*) willing to help out with any or all of the legal costs?

☐ Yes   ☑ No   ☐ Don't know

9 If you ticked 'don't know', please check whether you qualify for help from another source and on what terms before you continue with this application.

10 If you ticked 'no' but you have a policy or membership which provides for legal help, please give details of why you do not want to take it up or why it is not available to deal with this case:

11 If you ticked 'yes', please give details:

Please go on to page three

GEORGE MARTIN v EASYSHOP LTD

PAGE 3

Please complete this page in all cases

The opponent

SPECIMEN

1 Opponent's full name: EASYSHOP LIMITED

2 Opponent's occupation
    (if known): SUPERMARKET

3 Is the opponent insured against the client's claim (if relevant)?

☑ Yes   ☐ No   ☐ Don't know

4 If you cannot answer questions 2 and 3, or you have answered question 3 by stating that your opponent is unemployed, please tell us any information you have about your opponent's financial resources and why you think that he or she will be able to pay any damages which the court orders to be paid to you. For example, the opponent may have more than one property or other valuable items which could be sold to pay the claim (all property is relevant):

5 Has your opponent applied for legal aid in these proceedings?

☐ Yes   ☑ No   ☐ Don't know

If you ticked 'yes', please give the Legal Aid reference number if you know it:

Costs and merits (1)

To be completed by or on behalf of the nominated solicitor only:

1 Based on your knowledge of the case, which of the following best describes the prospects of a successful outcome?

☑ **A** Very good (80% +)   ☐ **B** Good (60-80%)   ☐ **C** Average (50-60%)

☐ **D** Below average   ☐ **E** Impossible to say. Seeking a limited certificate.

2 If you are estimating the chances of success as below average, please say why you believe Legal Aid should be granted:

3 If you have *not* ticked box E above, please estimate your likely final costs, including disbursements. Your estimate will need to take account of your view of likely settlement. (2)

☐ Less than £1,500   ☐ £1,500 - £2,500   ☑ Over £2,500

4 If you *have* ticked box E above, please say what work needs to be done under a limited certificate and at what cost:

I need to carry out the following work:

_____ at an estimated cost of: £ _____

Please go on to the rest of this form

GEORGE MARTIN v EASYSHOP LTD

PAGE 4

Personal injury actions

Please complete this page if you sustained or caused personal injury in any kind of accident (including medical negligence). If this page does not apply, please go on to page five.

1   Please tick whether you are the:

☑ Plaintiff   ☐ Defendant   ☐ Other Party

2   Have the proceedings started?

SPECIMEN

☐ Yes   ☑ No   ☐ Don't know

If 'yes', please make sure you enclose copies of all relevant court documents. If you do not, we might refuse your application.

3   Please describe clearly what injuries were sustained:

BACK INJURIES, NOTABLY AN ENTRAPPED NERVE

4   Please give the date when the personal injuries were sustained: 2 / 2 / 96

5   If the injury was caused by a 'pavement trip', or tripping over something else, please give the exact height of the obstacle that tripped you up in inches or centimetres:

☐ inches   ☐ centimetres

6   Please give the value of the claim being made by or against you: £ IN EXCESS OF £50,000 (2)

7   Please now write a statement of case on page seven, making clear why the opponent named on page three was at fault or stating why you have a defence to the action. It may help to bear in mind the following points:

➤ Please describe events in the order that they occurred. Photographs and medical reports, if available, are helpful.

➤ If there were witnesses, say whether they agree with what you say. Send statements if available.

➤ If the accident happened at work, try to show whether the employers may have operated an unsafe system or machinery or did not provide competent fellow employees.

➤ Draw a diagram or picture of the scene of the accident if it helps explain what happened. If you have a photograph, please enclose it.

➤ If the level of damages is in dispute, state the extent of the disagreement and say what evidence there is to support your view.

➤ If the police were involved, please give details of any prosecutions and enclose the police report if available.

Please go on to page seven and write a statement of case

GEORGE MARTIN v EASYSHOP LTD

PAGE 5

Breach of contract or faulty goods and services actions

Please complete this page if you are making a claim or defending an action for breach of contract or faulty goods and services. If this page does not apply, please go on to page six.

SPECIMEN

1 Please tick whether you are the:

☐ Plaintiff ☐ Defendant ☐ Other Party

2 Have the proceedings started?

☐ Yes ☐ No ☐ Don't know

If 'yes', please make sure you enclose copies of all relevant court documents. If you do not, we might refuse your application.

3 Please describe briefly an outline of the agreement entered into (if relevant):

_____
_____
_____
_____
_____
_____

4 Otherwise, please say what goods or services are alleged to be faulty:

_____
_____
_____
_____
_____
_____

5 Please give the date of any agreement and enclose a copy of it: ____ / ____ / ____

6 Please give the date when the goods or services were bought (if relevant): ____ / ____ / ____

7 Please give the value of the claim being made by or against you: £_____

8 Please now write a statement of case on page seven, making clear why the opponent named on page three was at fault or stating why the applicant has a defence to the action. It may help to bear in mind the following points:

➤ Please describe events in the order that they occurred.

➤ If possible, state what specific area of law is being relied on.

➤ If a written contract is available, please enclose a copy.

➤ Photographic evidence can often help us, e.g. in building disputes.

➤ If an expert's report is available, please enclose a copy.

Please go on to page seven and write a statement of case

GEORGE MARTIN v EASYSHOP LTD

PAGE 6

All other non-matrimonial actions

If your case was not covered by pages four or five, please complete this page.

1 Please tick whether you are the:

☐ Plaintiff   ☐ Defendant   ☐ Other Party

2 Have the proceedings started?

SPECIMEN

☐ Yes   ☐ No   ☐ Don't know

If 'yes', please make sure you enclose copies of all relevant court documents. If you do not, we might refuse your application.

3 Please give the value of the claim being made by or against you (if relevant): £——————————

Please tick the box that is relevant to your case and read the guidance on what the statement on page seven should include:

4 Landlord and tenant

Housing disrepair   ☐

Please give details of defects and the causes, if known. Please also give details of complaints to the landlord and how you have been affected.

Possession   ☐

Please provide a copy of the lease or agreement and say why you have a defence or why you need representing.

5 Property dispute

Jointly owned property ☐

Please give details of the basis on which you seek or oppose a sale, together with the value of the property and the amount of the mortgage.

Claim to an interest
in property   ☐

Please give details of ownership, why the interest is claimed or denied and the value of the property, together with the amount of the mortgage.

6 Assault/Trespass

☐

Please give details of recent incidents and say if an injunction is required.

7 Probate and inheritance

☐

Please give details of the size of the estate, details of other beneficiaries, the grounds for the claim (e.g. dependency) and provide a copy of the will.

8 Other

☐

Please give details of the proceedings:

_____

_____

_____

Please give full details of why you have a valid claim or defence and provide all relevant documents.

Please now provide a statement of your case on page seven, taking into account the guidance given above

GEORGE MARTIN v EASYSHOP LTD

PAGE 7

Statement of case

Statement (3)
Please type or write clearly

See attached attendance note dated 7/3/97

SPECIMEN

If you need more space, please attach a separate sheet to the inside of this form.

Please now turn to the back page

GEORGE MARTIN v EASYSHOP LTD

PAGE 8

Declaration to be signed by the applicant

This page must be completed

I have been given my own copy of the Legal Aid Board's leaflet about the legal aid statutory charge and this has been explained to me by my solicitor.

I have been given a copy of the Legal Aid Board's leaflet which explains what happens next.

I understand that

➤ even if I win I may have to pay all or some of my Legal Aid costs;

➤ if my means or marital status change I must report this and my contribution may be reassessed;

➤ my Legal Aid certificate could be cancelled and I might have to pay the costs in full if I do not deal promptly with Legal Aid Board requests; and

➤ if I make a false statement I may be fined or put in prison (or both) as well as losing my Legal Aid

As far as I know, the information I have given is true.

I understand that the Legal Aid Board may use any information about my case to carry out any of its functions under the Legal Aid Act 1988 but that my name and other personal details which could identify me will be kept confidential.

Signed _____ G. Martin _____ Date: _11_ / _3_ / _97_

Statement by or on behalf of the nominated solicitor   SPECIMEN

I certify that

➤ the statutory charge has been explained to the applicant and he or she has been given the Legal Aid Board's leaflet about the legal aid statutory charge;

➤ the applicant has been given the Legal Aid Board's leaflet which explains what happens next;

➤ the applicant has been told about his or her obligations including changes of means or address;

➤ the information requested on page 3 of this form relating to the costs and merits of this case has been provided and that the information is as accurate as possible; and

➤ the nominated solicitor holds a current practising certificate and will not act or delegate the conduct of this matter while not certificated.

Signed by or on behalf of the
nominated solicitor: _____ M. Davis _____ Date: _11_ / _3_ / _97_

To the solicitor: *Please complete the following. It will help us to process the application more quickly:*

1   Please tick this box if it is a possible multi-party action and state what it is about (e.g. give the name of the drug) ☐

_____

2   Please tick this box if the applicant's opponent is his or her spouse or cohabitee ☐

3   Please tick the boxes confirming that: ☑ page 3 has been completed in full   ☑ there is a statement of case on page 7

4   The enclosures sent in support of this application are:

_____ ATTENDANCE NOTE DATED 7/3/97 _____

_____

_____

5   The financial forms sent with this application are:

☐ CLA4A - all applicants (unless another form below applies)

☑ CLA4B - if the applicant or his or her partner gets income support

☐ CLA4C - if the applicant is resident outside the U.K.

☐ CLA4F - if the applicant is a child under 16 with no means

☐ L17 for applicant

☐ L17 for applicant's partner

☐ wage slips (if the application is made with an emergency application)

☐ accounts or other documents listed on page 4 of CLA4A

October 1993

24

GEORGE MARTIN v EASYSHOP LTD

NOTES: CLA1

Generally see the Civil Legal Aid Applications Checklist in the *Legal Aid Handbook 1996/97*: Sweet & Maxwell, page 563.

(1)   Costs and merits. Think carefully before stating that the case has a below average chance of success. Whilst you have a duty not to mislead the Legal Aid Board, it is unlikely that the Legal Aid Board will grant legal aid to a case which has very limited prospects of success. In any event if you feel this about the case then perhaps you should be advising your client not to pursue the matter.

When asked to estimate the costs of the case bear in mind that it is very easy to run up costs in a personal injury matter. You will need, at the very least, one medical report, therefore err on the generous side.

(2)   Personal injury actions — the estimate of the value of the case. This is very difficult at this stage; however you will not be penalised should you get it wrong. This question is linked back to the section dealing with costs and merits. If the estimate of costs is greater than the amount of damages likely to be awarded then legal aid will almost certainly not be granted.

(3)   With regard to the section headed 'statement of case', whilst it is possible to complete that section perhaps the easiest thing to do to save time is simply to attach the client's draft proof of evidence or the first attendance note. Both of these documents will outline the case.

Note: We have not exhibited the CLA4B; however this would be sent with the CLA1 to the Legal Aid Board.

Commentary: Legal Aid Application

1.   On receiving the completed legal aid forms the solicitor should check that they are completed correctly, signed and dated. Any mistakes or blank spaces and the Legal Aid Board will undoubtedly reject them. If a section does not apply then write 'n/a'.

2.   If the applicant is in employment then stress to the client that the employer must be asked to complete the L17 as quickly as possible without which the application will not be processed.

3.   Once the forms are completed they will be sent to the Area Office. Assessment Officers of the Benefits Agency specialise in civil legal aid cases and carry out the assessment of means. The assessment officer will assess the applicant's disposable income and capital and the contribution payable, if any.

Note that if the applicant's means change, a further assessment may be carried out. Hence, you must remind the applicant that a change of circumstances must be notified without delay.

4.   With regard to merits, essentially the applicant must show that he/she has reasonable grounds for commencing the claim. For further detail see the *Legal Aid Handbook 1996/97*: Sweet & Maxwell, paragraphs 7-01–7-06 and the Civil Legal Aid (General) Regulations 1989, Part IV.

5.   The legal aid application will take about three to four weeks to process, although this period will vary from area to area. Note that at point (2) in the legal aid letter Meg has indicated to the client what happens when she receives the completed application forms.

STEP 4

Meg receives a Legal Aid Certificate from the Legal Aid Board stating that George has been granted legal aid limited up to but excluding setting down. She writes to George telling him that she will now progress his case (copy letter not reproduced).

GEORGE MARTIN v EASYSHOP LTD

Document 10

CIVL_FC1 - 6

LEGAL AID BOARD
LEGAL AID ACT 1988

LEGAL AID CERTIFICATE

Reference No
08/01/97/27344/G
Assisted Person Mr GEORGE MARTIN

Solars A/C No
N181Q

Case Code
2762

MR GEORGE MARTIN
33 CHERRY STREET
OLDCASTLE
OL3 4LL

This certificate is financially
linked with the legal aid reference
number shown below.

Linked with reference Number.

This is to certify that the above-named has been granted legal aid as specified below subject to the above mentioned Act and Regulations made thereunder and subject also to the conditions and limitations (if any) specified below.

1. DESCRIPTION OF LEGAL AID
   To take proceedings for damages for Personal Injuries against Easyshop Limited (1)

2. CONDITIONS AND LIMITATIONS (IF ANY) (2)
   Limited to all steps up to but excluding setting down for trial but including obtaining Counsel's opinion at that stage.

SPECIMEN

3. A DETERMINATION OF FINANCIAL RESOURCES HAS BEEN MADE AS FOLLOWS:- (3)

   Disposable income £ Nil   Disposable capital £ Nil   Contribution Nil

The Solicitor is   M. DAVIS

                (4)

Signed   K. STUBBS
Authorised Signatory Legal Aid Area No 08

Solicitor reference   MD - 1321

WATKINS & O'DWYER
DX 17113
OLDCASTLE

Address
No. 8 (EASTERN) AREA
HOBART HOUSE
HIGH STREET
OLDCASTLE
OL3 4LL

Date 28-Mar-97

26

GEORGE MARTIN v EASYSHOP LTD

NOTES FOR THE SOLICITOR

1. Original legal aid certificates must be filed at court.

2. It is your responsibility to explain to your client the potential effect of the statutory charge.

3. The nominated solicitor must hold a valid practising certificate at all times while conducting this case.

4. You must inform the area office forthwith of any money and/or property recovered or preserved for your client and await instructions (see Part XI of the Civil Legal Aid (General) Regulations 1989).

NOTES FOR THE APPLICANT

EMERGENCY LEGAL AID

5. Unless you are on income support your income and savings will be assessed by the Benefits Agency. We will tell you if you have to pay a contribution towards your legal aid.

6. You must co-operate with the Benefits Agency even if the emergency has ended and/or proceedings have finished.

7. You will have to pay personally the costs of your case if:-
   (a) you do not qualify for legal aid on financial grounds,
   (b) you do not co-operate with the Benefits Agency
   (c) you fail to accept an offer of legal aid after your income and savings have been assessed.

8. You must tell the Legal Aid Board if you change your address.

LEGAL AID CERTIFICATE

9. You must supply any further information about your income and savings to the Legal Aid Board if you are asked.

10. If your income or outgoings change, or your capital increases, write and tell the Legal Aid Area Office immediately.

11. If you or your partner are self employed and have not sent in copies of your accounts you should do so as soon as they become available. Please send them to the Benefits Agency, Legal Aid Assessment Office, Albert Edward House, 3 The Pavilions, Ashton on Ribble, Preston, PR2 2PA quoting your full name and reference number.

12. You must tell the Legal Aid Board:-
    (a) if you receive any other financial help towards the cost of this case;
    (b) if you change your address, or
    (c) if you get married or start to live together as man and wife or get divorced.

13. You may get your contribution back if you are successful and your costs are paid by the otherside. If they are not paid then the Board can recover your costs from your contribution and, if appropriate, from any money or property you recover or preserve as a result of the case. This could happen even if you had no contribution to pay at the start.

14. If you are unsuccessful then your costs will be recovered from your contribution. Any excess will be returned to you.

15. If you have a certificate covering emergency protection care or supervision proceedings taken under the Children Act 1989 which was not means tested you need only report changes in your address and not in financial circumstances. If you are in any doubt as to your obligations to report a change you should ask the Area Office.

GEORGE MARTIN v EASYSHOP LTD

NOTES: LEGAL AID CERTIFICATE

(1) Generally the certificate will cover only one action, cause or matter and cover only one assisted person.

It is up to the solicitor and, if instructed, counsel to make sure that the certificate covers all the work that needs to be done. If the wording is incorrect it could affect the claim on the Legal Aid Fund.

(2) It is very common in personal injury cases to find that the certificate is limited, for example to obtaining counsel's opinion, which means that only preparatory work necessary to go to counsel can be carried out by the solicitor, and the papers must be sent to counsel for his opinion. The effect of the limitation is that payment will not be made out of the Legal Aid Fund for work done outside the scope of the certificate unless the area office has granted an amendment. So, for example once counsel's opinion is received, it will be sent to the Legal Aid Board who should then remove the limitation from the certificate before further work is undertaken. (Note that this will only happen if counsel's opinion is favourable.)

In this case the certificate is limited to all steps up to but excluding setting down for trial; therefore once Meg reaches this point she will have to apply for an amendment of the certificate, having obtained counsel's opinion.

Even with a full certificate be wary of taking any unusual/expensive step without first seeking the authority of the Legal Aid Board, e.g., instructing a particularly expensive expert. You should seek prior authority, submitting an estimate from your expert. See *Turner* v *Plasplugs Ltd* (1996) *The Times*, 1 February which held that a costs order may be made against a legally aided party if he issues proceedings when his legal aid certificate is limited to all steps up to settling proceedings. He will not be afforded any protection under s. 17, Legal Aid Act 1988.

(3) As the Legal Aid Board have assessed that George does not have to pay a contribution they have issued a certificate immediately. If a contribution had been payable the area office would have sent an offer of a certificate. If George accepted the offer, this would then be followed by a certificate. Note that an applicant will automatically qualify for civil legal aid free of a contribution if in receipt of income support or income-based job seeker's allowance.

(4) Note that the certificate specifies an individual nominated solicitor and a firm of solicitors. If either change an amendment of the certificate will be necessary. However, Meg can leave the case to be run by a competent or responsible representative of hers who is either employed in her office or otherwise under her immediate supervision (Civil Legal Aid (General) Regulations 1989, reg. 65(2)).

Commentary: Legal Aid Appeal

1. Although not an issue in this case it is possible for the client to appeal if refused legal aid. There are four grounds for refusal:

(a) financial eligibility — there is no right of appeal (though there is a right to ask for a detailed breakdown and ask for reassessment);

(b) the proceedings are of a nature for which legal aid is not available;

(c) no reasonable grounds have been made out for being a party to the proceedings;

(d) it is unreasonable in all the circumstances of the case.

See generally the Civil Legal Aid (General) Regulations 1989, regs 34–39 and the *Legal Aid Handbook 1996/7*, paragraphs 4-12–4-14.

Usually the appeal will be made via written representations. It is possible for the solicitor to attend in person but note that this is not covered by the Green Form scheme and usually the solicitor will only be allowed five minutes to make representations. Whatever method is adopted the submissions should be as full as possible and should deal with the reason for refusal.

GEORGE MARTIN v EASYSHOP LTD

STEP 5

Meg prepares the draft proof of evidence and sends it to George for his comments. She also writes a letter before action to Easyshop Ltd.

Document 11

PROOF OF EVIDENCE[1]

I George Martin of 33 Cherry Street, Oldcastle, OL3 4LL, Chartered Accountant will say as follows:

1. I am 45 years old and my date of birth is 30.7.51. I am married and I have two children, a boy aged 13 and a girl aged 9.[2]

2. On 2 February 1996 I was on my way home from work when I thought I would call in at Easyshop, my local supermarket, at Unit 7, Beech Court, Oldcastle, for some groceries. I parked the car in the store car park and went in. It was about 6.30 p.m.[3]

3. I picked up a basket and proceeded around the supermarket. The supermarket is divided into a number of aisles and I walked up and down each aisle.

4. Nothing extraordinary happened until I reached the aisle with the sauces and oils. I had at this stage only three items in my basket; I think I had a tub of yoghurt, some lentils and some sweets for the children. I wanted some olive oil as I thought I would make a dressing for the salad that evening. I wasn't in a particular hurry as I knew the children would not be back home until 7.30 p.m. as they were visiting their grandparents. I walked towards the shelf with the olive oil, when suddenly my feet slipped on something and I fell heavily landing on my back.

5. I remember feeling tremendous pain at the base of my back and when I tried to sit up I found I could not move.[4]

6. I also remember that a woman rushed up to me and I think she said, 'Are you OK? You've slipped on that oil. I spoke to the manager about five minutes ago about it. I told them they should clean it up immediately, it's no wonder that someone slipped. At the very least they should have put a barrier up.' I do not know the name of this woman.

7. I really cannot remember any more because I think I fainted due to the pain. The next thing I knew I was in Oldcastle General Hospital under the care of Mr Astley. I was in acute pain. Mr Astley sent me to be x-rayed and then I was sent to have a scan. Mr Astley told me that I had a serious back injury. I think he said I had an entrapped nerve in my lower back. Mr Astley said there was not much he could do and I would continue to suffer pain for the rest of my life. Mr Astley also told me my back may have already been in a weak condition.

8. I stayed in hospital for two days to rest my back. Mr Astley then referred me to Mr Goode in the outpatients' clinic for a course of physiotherapy. Mr Astley recommended that I undergo several sessions of physiotherapy as it may relieve the pain in my back. When I left hospital I was walking with a stick; however after 12 sessions of physiotherapy with Mr Goode over six weeks I was able to walk short distances without my stick.

9. I am still undergoing physiotherapy once a week. Mr Goode has told me that there is nothing more he can do for me and that I will continue to suffer pain for the rest of my life. The physiotherapy does relieve a little of my pain for a day or so, but it is true I am always in constant pain. I visit my GP, Dr Shipley, at least once a fortnight for check-ups and painkillers. My GP is also concerned about my blood pressure, as since the accident I can no longer take regular exercise and my weight has risen from 14½ stones to 17½ stones (I am 5ft 11in tall).

GEORGE MARTIN v EASYSHOP LTD

10. About one month after the accident I received a letter from Easyshop apologising for the accident and enclosing £20 worth of gift vouchers. I was enraged. I have not been back to the shop since.

11. I was off work for a total of six weeks after the accident. When the accident happened my employer Smythes & Co. of 44 Highway, Oldcastle OL4 3TY, a firm of chartered accountants, were very understanding and kept me on full pay. However, when I returned to work on 18 March 1996 I found that I could no longer sit at my desk for more than an hour at a time and I also had to have one afternoon a week off for physiotherapy. During this time my employer said that as I could not work for long periods at a stretch they would not pay me for the time I took off for medical treatment. As I could not do much work I agreed. Eventually, after about two months, it became clear that my employers wished me to leave. They called me in and my senior partner, Mr Foscoe, said that my billing was about an eighth of what it should be and that I was behind schedule on a number of projects. Mr Foscoe said that he was very sympathetic but as the situation would not improve I should leave. As a gesture of goodwill Mr Foscoe handed me a cheque for £10,000. I left work on 17 May 1996.[5]

12. I feel very frustrated that my career has been cut short. I graduated in 1972 with a 2:2 degree in Accountancy and have worked for Smythes since 1985. I had achieved the position of senior accountant and I fully expected to be made a partner in the next two years. At the time I was dismissed I was earning £40,000 a year.[6]

13. Since leaving Smythes I have written numerous letters for jobs. However I have only managed to obtain three interviews and on each occasion I was told that because of my ill health they could not offer me employment.[7]

14. Because of the accident I am now virtually housebound. I can no longer play squash and badminton which I used to play regularly at my local sports centre and Mr Astley tells me that it is highly unlikely that I will ever play again. I can no longer play football, golf with my brother-in-law nor cricket with the local team.[8]

15. My children now have no time for me. I can no longer play games with them and because of my condition I am constantly irritable.

16. In addition, family holidays are now curtailed. My wife does not drive, and I cannot drive because of the pain. Therefore I am unable to take my children to scouts, brownies and away for day trips, and all family holidays to Wales and Scotland have been abandoned.

17. My marriage is in serious difficulties. My wife and I are no longer intimate and we are constantly arguing because of my moods and depression.

18. As a result of the accident I am now registered unemployed. I have been able to manage financially over the last few months because of the payment from Smythes; however this has all been used up and I have no savings. All of my money that I saved when I was employed was spent on the house. I now claim income support and disablement benefit.

19. I am now finding it very difficult to manage financially. As a result of the accident I have incurred the following expenses:

Loss of earnings[9]

1 half day for 8 weeks (18 March–17 May 1996) = £281.34

Travelling expenses

12 Feb–18 March 1996
12 sessions of physiotherapy at £3.00 per journey = £36.00

GEORGE MARTIN v EASYSHOP LTD

18 March–28 August 1996
23 sessions of physio at £3.00 per journey = £69.00

28 August 1996–to date
14 sessions of physio at £3.00 per journey = £42.00

5 Feb 1996 – to date
43 visits for check-ups and prescriptions at £2.00 per journey = £86.00

7 March 1997
1 visit to solicitor = £5.50

Damaged clothing
1 suit = £275.00

Prescription charges
5 February 1996–31 January 1997 = £475.00

Signed   Dated

NOTES: PROOF OF EVIDENCE

(1)   You should not confuse the terms 'proof of evidence' and 'witness statement'. We have called the preliminary statement from George the former to distinguish it from a witness statement which will be exchanged at a later date (see page 115). The proof of evidence will be a record of the client's version of events. The principal difference from a witness statement is that it will contain evidence, including opinion evidence and perhaps material that may be deemed irrelevant which Meg will exclude from the final witness statement. Note, however, that hearsay evidence is now admissible in the final witness statement (see further page 118).

(2)   The proof begins with George's personal details, i.e., name, address, occupation, age, date of birth, marital status and number of dependants.

(3)   The proof then proceeds to give the date of the accident, what happened and who was responsible. It may seem as though much of the information is irrelevant, e.g., how many items George had in his shopping basket. However, the initial proof should contain as much information as the client can remember. The irrelevant material and opinion evidence will be edited out when the witness statement is prepared for exchange (see RSC Ord. 38, r. 2A). The initial proof should contain all the information to hand to enable the solicitor to investigate the case. Likewise counsel will want to know everything the client can recollect about the accident to prepare for a hearing/the trial. Therefore, if the accident happened in a factory the proof should outline what machinery was involved, what work was undertaken, what instructions were given etc.

In this case Meg wants to know what George was carrying and whether he was in a hurry so as to establish if there was any contributory negligence.

(4)   The proof then continues to say what happened as a result of the accident. This is logical — it has given details of how the accident occurred, now it must outline the result. This should be recorded in as much detail as possible — how long was George in hospital, how long was he off work etc.

(5)   The proof then continues by setting out the effect of the accident on George's career. This is obviously required to enable counsel to see what is his loss of earnings, both present and future.

(6)   Paragraph 12 of the proof links back to paragraph 11. It is included so that counsel can see what would have been likely to happen if George had continued in employment. It illustrates that George had

GEORGE MARTIN v EASYSHOP LTD

a promising future and a good work record. Therefore, he may have a substantial claim for loss of future earnings.

(7) Paragraph 13 demonstrates that George attempted to mitigate his lossses by seeking other employment.

(8) Paragraphs 14–17 recount the effect the accident has had on George's family life. The proof should include details of how the injuries affected his social life, hobbies and sports, his relationship with his family, and generally how his everyday life has changed. All this will go to determine his loss of amenity claim.

(9) Finally, the special damages calculation. It will only be approximate. Bear in mind that George will have to show the reason for the expenditure and prove it. Note that the prescription charges are only shown up to 31 January 1997. After this date George was receiving income support and did not pay for his medication. See further RSC Ord. 18, r. 12A and page 70.

Commentary: Proof of Evidence

1. From the above you will see why it is important to take a detailed attendance note. From the attendance note Meg has prepared the proof of evidence. It will of course be updated on several occasions; however, it is essential that Meg has as much information as possible at the outset of the action.

2. As for format, use short numbered paragraphs. It should also be signed and dated by the client. Note, however, that if the client is not able to give evidence at trial, the statement will still be admissible pursuant to the Civil Evidence Act 1995 as hearsay evidence. A signed and dated statement will also act as the solicitor's insurance policy (see commentary, paragraph (f), page 160).

Note: Refer also to the notes on the affidavit re interim payment at page 102.

Document 12

Watkins & O'Dwyer
Solicitors

17 Sycamore Avenue
Oldcastle OL10 1BR
Tel. 011-111-1111
Fax 011-111-1111
DX Oldcastle 1000

Partners: J. Watkins
A. O'Dwyer

28 March 1997

G Martin, esq
33 Cherry Street
Oldcastle
OL3 4LL

Our ref: MD/JR/144.346

Dear Mr Martin

Re your claim against Easyshop

I now enclose your proof of evidence for your consideration. The proof of evidence (a statement) sets out your version of the accident and therefore should be as accurate as possible. Please make any alterations or any additions you think fit.

If you make an amendment then it should be initialled in the margin. I have enclosed an additional copy of the statement for your own retention; however I should be grateful if you could return the other in the pre-paid envelope, signed and dated. If a number of amendments are required I will prepare a fresh copy.[1]

Finally, I have today written to Easyshop Ltd notifying them of your claim and enclose a copy of that letter for your information.[2]

Yours sincerely

Meg Davis

NOTES: LETTER TO CLIENT

(1)   Meg sends the proof of evidence to George for his approval and to check that it is correct and perhaps prompt further recollections. It is important that George makes any amendments that he considers necessary.

(2)   One of the simplest ways of keeping the client informed of your progress is to send him copies of your correspondence with the other side; hence Meg has enclosed a copy of the letter before action.

GEORGE MARTIN v EASYSHOP LTD

Document 13

Watkins & O'Dwyer
Solicitors

17 Sycamore Avenue
Oldcastle OL10 1BR
Tel. 011-111-1111
Fax 011-111-1111
DX Oldcastle 1000

Partners: J. Watkins
A. O'Dwyer

28 March 1997

The Manager
Easyshop Ltd
Unit 7
Beech Court
Oldcastle
OL8 3MN

Our ref: MD/JR/144.346

Dear Sirs

<u>George Martin</u>[1]

We act[2] on behalf of the above named who was injured whilst shopping on your premises on 2 February 1996. Mr Martin sustained serious back injuries caused by falling heavily on his back after slipping on a substance on the shop floor. We consider that there has been negligence and/or breach of statutory duty pursuant to Occupiers' Liability Act 1957, s. 2(2), in that the premises were not safe for visitors.[3]

We have advised our client to make a claim for damages against you. Presumably you will have reported Mr Martin's fall to your insurers but if you have not already done so we should be obliged if you would acknowledge receipt of this letter and forward it directly to your insurance company,[4] providing us with particulars of the company and policy number so that we may contact them directly.

Finally, to enable your insurers to contact the DSS Compensation Recovery Unit our client's details are as follows:[5]

NAME: GEORGE MARTIN

DATE OF BIRTH: 30.7.51.

EMPLOYER'S NAME AND ADDRESS: SMYTHES & CO.
44 HIGHWAY
OLDCASTLE OL4 3TY

PAYROLL NUMBER: GM/1093

NATIONAL INSURANCE NUMBER   NM56TY789

Note that Mr Martin was forced to leave his employment on 17 May 1996 due to his injuries.

We look forward to hearing from you. If we fail to hear from you within 14 days of the date of this letter we will advise our client to commence proceedings without further delay.[6]

Yours faithfully

Watkins & O'Dwyer

NOTES: LETTER BEFORE ACTION

(1)   The letter should always have a heading. Remember that the insurers may have several claims of the same nature. Try to make sure that it is addressed to the person who is handling the claim and always give correct references.

(2)   Try to begin the letter with 'we act' rather than 'we are instructed by'. The former phrase gives a sense of permanence and suggests that the client is an old established customer; the latter sounds as though the client has just walked off the street.

(3)   As discussed below in the commentary the letter should be short, sharp and concise. Bearing in mind that it is the insurers we will be dealing with ultimately, there is little point in writing a complex letter to the supermarket. Similarly, there is little point in asking Easyshop, or for that matter the insurers, to admit liability at this juncture, when at best they will only have a few details on file and will not have investigated the case. Remember, time is money — there is no point in giving an abundance of detail if liability has not been admitted.

(4)   If you already know the name of the insurers then it is possible to write to them direct quoting the reference number and policy number, if known, with a copy letter sent to their insured.

If you know a party is being represented in the matter by a solicitor then the letter should be addressed to them. It is a breach of professional practice to contact the opposing client directly if they are legally represented. However, in this case it is unlikely that they will have involved a solicitor, known to you, at this early stage.

(5)   The new Social Security (Recovery of Benefits) Act 1997, replacing Part IV of the Social Security Administration Act 1992, has made significant changes to the provisions regarding the clawback of benefits, though note the new scheme will not be operational until 1 October 1997. As you will be beginning your studies at this time, however, it is thought more appropriate to refer to the new regime under the 1997 Act.

Where the defendant (the compensator) makes a payment in respect of damages for personal injury to the plaintiff (the claimant) then the following provisions apply:

(a)   The relevant period over which a benefit is paid begins the day after injury or accident, or in the case of disease, on the first day benefit is claimed. The period ends five years later or whenever the last compensation period is paid (s. 3(1)).

(b)   Within 14 days of notification of the plaintiff's claim the defendant's solicitor must notify the Compensation Recovery Unit (CRU) by sending a form CRU1. The form will give personal details of the plaintiff, i.e., date of birth, address, details of the accident. These details should be supplied to the defendant's solicitor when the plaintiff's solicitor notifies him of the claim, hence the letter above. The form will be acknowledged by the CRU and it will keep a record of all benefits paid. When the compensator is ready to make an offer of total payment then he will apply to the CRU for a certificate of total benefit. This certificate is valid for eight weeks and then will require renewal.

GEORGE MARTIN v EASYSHOP LTD

(c) When the compensator makes the payment to the claimant he will deduct the amount specified from the payment and pay this amount to the CRU within 14 days (see s. 6). Therefore, the obligations of the compensator are threefold:

(i) no payment must be made until the compensator has been notified of the amount of benefit to be deducted by the CRU,

(ii) the compensator must deduct the said sum and pay it to the CRU, and

(iii) the compensator must notify the claimant of the amount so deducted. See s. 9, paras (a) and (b).

Note that under the 1992 Act the benefit payment was deducted from the whole of the compensation sum. Additionally, payments of £2,500 or less were exempt from the clawback provisions. However, under the 1997 Act the clawback provisions will not apply to that part of the award in respect of pain and suffering and future loss, and further the small claims limit of £2,500 is abolished, which removes any incentive the plaintiff had to settle at this amount or less to avoid the clawback provisions. Now the clawback provisions will apply to all compensation awarded for loss of earnings, cost of care and loss of mobility up to the date of the final compensation payment made in discharge of the claim.

(d) The benefit that is recoverable is that which has been paid 'in consequence of any accident, injury or disease' (see s. 1(1)(a)).

The following benefits that will be deductible include:

(i) attendance allowance;

(ii) disability working allowance (from 6 April 1992);

(iii) incapacity benefit (from 13 April 1995);

(iv) income support;

(v) invalidity pension and allowance;

(vi) jobseeker's allowance;

(vii) mobility allowance;

(viii) reduced earnings allowance;

(ix) severe disablement allowance;

(x) sickness benefit;

(xi) unemployment benefit.

Note that for statutory sick pay the Statutory Sick Pay Act 1994 amends Part 1 of the Social Security (Contributions and Benefits) Act 1992, abolishing the right of employers to recover 80 per cent of statutory sick pay paid to their employees from their remittance of national insurance contributions (see Statutory Sick Pay Act 1994 (Consequential) Regulations 1994 (SI 1994 No. 730)).

(e) Under s. 11 an appeal can be lodged against the amount claimed by the CRU on the grounds that the benefit is not attributable to the accident, injury or disease. However, the appeal can only be lodged after the certificate has been honoured by repayment to the Secretary of State.

What happens, however, when the victim was already receiving benefit at the date of the accident? This point was considered in the case of *Hassal* v *Secretary of State for Social Security* [1995] 1 WLR 812. The claimant had been receiving income support prior to his accident in August 1990. From August 1990 until February 1991 he received income support because he was sick and unfit and unable to work. The claimant argued that he should not have to repay the income support he received during this period because he would have in most probability continued to receive income support in any event. The settlement he had received related only to pain and suffering, not loss of earnings.

The Court of Appeal held that the post-accident benefits recouped were clearly paid as a direct consequence of the accident. Recoupment is not limited to the loss of earnings element. Additionally, not only was the claimant's benefit to be recouped but also the portion in respect of family members also had to be recouped.

The Court however were not oblivious to the injustice of this decision and said the benefits which had to be recouped in circumstances such as these could form part of the claim for damages by the claimant against the persons at fault. Therefore a claim should be made for the lost benefits which would not, but for the accident, have had to be recouped. Any solicitor who fails to make such a claim may well be negligent.

Note that the outcome of *Hassal* may well have been different had the new 1997 Act been in force.

(f)   In any event the following are not deductible:

(i)   Redundancy payments unless they relate to incapacity to work;

(ii)   Private accident insurance;

(iii)   Public/private benevolence;

(iv)   Pensions whether contributory or non-contributory;

(v)   Other earnings unless they were obtained whilst off work and would not otherwise have been earned.

For further information on the deduction of benefits contact the Compensation Recovery Unit of the DSS, Reyrolle Building, Hebburn, Tyne and Wear, NE31 1XB.

(6)   See notes on the letter before action in the contract case study at page 149. However, as a reminder remember that it is a breach of professional practice to say you will do something if you have not yet obtained the client's instructions, e.g., do not say that you will commence proceedings if the other side fail to reply within seven days unless you have instructions from the client to do so. If in doubt, say that you will advise the client to do something if the other side don't reply.

Commentary: Letter Before Action

1.   The first letter that is written to the other side is known as a letter before action. As the name suggests its purpose is to give the other side notice of the claim before commencing proceedings. It may also prompt negotiations and thereby avoid litigation.

2.   The first letter will be brief because within a few weeks the defendant (or their insurers) should come back confirming their interest. There is an argument that perhaps the letter should be exhaustive, but this is debatable as you will have to set out the allegations in full so that they can be investigated — however, have you completed your investigations yet?

GEORGE MARTIN v EASYSHOP LTD

3.   In a road traffic accident it is of vital importance that you either notify the defendant's insurers either before or within seven days of commencing a claim (i.e., issue a writ/summons) in court in accordance with the Road Traffic Act 1988, ss. 151 and 152. Providing the plaintiff does this, then any judgment can be enforced against the insurers notwithstanding the fact that they may be entitled to avoid their insured's policy. The plaintiff's solicitor should either send a letter to the other side on the day he issues the writ/summons or notify the other side in the letter before action by the words 'we intend to commence proceedings'. Similar provisions apply where the defendant was uninsured and the claim is being brought against the Motor Insurers' Bureau (MIB), the main difference being that within seven days after commencement of proceedings written notice *must* be given to the MIB or to the defendant's insurer, notwithstanding the fact that notice may have been given before commencement.

4.   A litigant who commences proceedings without writing a letter before action may find that even if he is successful, the court will disallow some or even all of the costs (*R* v *Inland Revenue ex parte Opman International UK* [1986] 1 WLR 568). See also *Rockett* v *Rotherham Health Service Trust* (unreported), 26 April 1996, which held that the defendant's insurers must be given an adequate opportunity to settle.

STEP 6

Meg receives the proof of evidence from George signed and dated. She writes to the Health and Safety Executive.

She also receives a letter from Easyshop's insurers, Marlowe Insurance Group plc, to which she replies.

Document 14

Watkins & O'Dwyer
Solicitors

17 Sycamore Avenue
Oldcastle OL10 1BR
Tel. 011-111-1111
Fax 011-111-1111
DX Oldcastle 1000

Partners: J. Watkins
A. O'Dwyer

4 April 1997

Health and Safety Executive
22 Crookshank Way
Oldcastle
OL6 7RT

Our ref: MD/JR/144.346

Dear Sirs

Re Accident at Easyshop Ltd on 2 February 1996

We act for George Martin in connection with an accident in which he sustained personal injuries at the premises of Easyshop Ltd of Unit 7, Beech Court, Oldcastle, OL8 3MN on 2 February 1996.

Please confirm whether or not the accident was investigated and if the company was subsequently prosecuted.

Yours faithfully

Watkins & O'Dwyer

Commentary: Letter to Health and Safety Executive

1. This is often the first letter the solicitor should write when investigating liability. The Health and Safety Executive report will contain statements of witnesses, photographs of the scene of the accident and obviously their report (though this will not be released at this stage). The release of information by the Health and Safety Executive (or the Environmental Health Department in any local authority) is governed by s. 28 of the Health and Safety at Work Act 1974.

A number of documents may be released without a court order and these include:

(a) Relevant factual materials observed during the investigation such as the nature/condition of the floor (relevant to this case), name of the machine examined etc. Note that these reports should be treated with some caution. What the inspector sees and reports on may not be as it was at the time of the accident, e.g., spillages may have been cleaned up, machines may have been repaired.

GEORGE MARTIN v EASYSHOP LTD

(b)   Relevant drawings and/or sketches.

(c)   The results of tests or samples taken (though this would not include any interpretation of them).

(d)   Relevant photographs.

(e)   Relevant advice sent before or after the accident.

(f)   Any relevant witness statements where the witness consents to disclosure.

All of these documents, however, would not be released until civil proceedings had been commenced and when pleadings had closed. (For commentary on the close of pleadings, see page 107 (paragraph 2).) The inspector/enforcing authority will usually require a copy of the writ/summons together with the statement/particulars of claim to determine which documents are relevant.

Documents would not be released, however, if they involved or related to criminal proceedings or industrial tribunal proceedings, commercial or medical confidentiality or national security. Additionally, documents would not be released until any criminal proceedings are complete (which can take considerable time).

Any documents, other than those specified above, would require a court order for release, i.e., an order for discovery.

Note that enforcing authorities may charge for the release of information. However, in many instances, insufficient information may be recorded to be of value to applicants (even though the incident was investigated). Applicants should enquire as to the amount of information available before seeking copies of all relevant documents.

Additionally, if the shop had been prosecuted Meg could obtain a certificate of conviction from the magistrates' court.

2.   Note that if the incident occurred in the workplace and the solicitor is arguing that there was an unsafe work practice, the Health and Safety Executive produces a number of publications on industrial good practice which can be good evidence when arguing that there was an unsafe system of work.

3.   In a road accident case the first report a solicitor should obtain is the police accident report which, like the Health and Safety Executive Report, will contain statements of witnesses, photographs of the scene etc. and, most importantly, details of the defendant's insurers and whether the defendant has been convicted of a criminal offence. This can be obtained by writing to the Chief Superintendent of the area where the accident occurred and enclosing the appropriate fee, currently £46 for a full accident report. If criminal proceedings are still pending, the report will not be released until they are completed.

4.   Finally, in a workplace accident think about writing to the Factory Inspector in addition to the Health and Safety Executive. In addition to providing a statement of the accident they could provide a description of any machinery involved and how it works.

GEORGE MARTIN v EASYSHOP LTD

Document 15

> *Marlowe Insurance Group plc*
> *Grays Court*
> *Kings Street*
> *Oldcastle*
> *OL3 4JP*
>
> 8 April 1997
>
> Watkins & O'Dwyer
> 17 Sycamore Avenue
> Oldcastle
> OL10 1BR
>
> Your ref: MD/JR/144.346
> Our ref: GTH/PI/ESP 7361
>
> Dear Sirs
>
> <u>Claim No. ESP 7361 Easyshop Ltd v George Martin</u>
>
> We act as insurers to Easyshop Ltd.
>
> We refer to your letter of 28 March 1997 and note your interest. We are proceeding to investigate your client's claim. We appreciate that it may take some time to obtain a medical report but wonder whether you can let us have a copy of this together with a list of all other damages your client is claiming.[1]
>
> We look forward to receiving your reply but you should note that whilst our investigations are continuing, all correspondence is without admission of liability.
>
> Yours faithfully
>
> Marlowe Insurance Group plc

GEORGE MARTIN v EASYSHOP LTD

Document 16

Watkins & O'Dwyer
Solicitors

17 Sycamore Avenue
Oldcastle OL10 1BR
Tel. 011-111-1111
Fax 011-111-1111
DX Oldcastle 1000

Partners: J. Watkins
A. O'Dwyer

11 April 1997

Marlowe Insurance Group plc
Grays Court
Kings Street
Oldcastle OL3 4JP

Your ref: GTH/PI/ESP 7361
Our ref: MD/JR/144.346

Dear Sirs

<u>Claim No. ESP 7361 Martin v Easyshop Ltd</u>

Thank you for your letter of 8 April 1997. We shall be happy to comply with your request providing that you undertake to pay our reasonable copying charges.

Finally, unless we hear from your solicitors to confirm authority to accept service of proceedings, then when we issue proceedings these will be served directly upon your insured.[2]

Yours faithfully

Watkins & O'Dwyer

NOTES: CORRESPONDENCE BETWEEN WATKINS & O'DWYER AND INSURERS

(1)   As expected the insurers have replied on behalf of Easyshop. The request they have made is not unreasonable; however always ensure that they will be responsible for your costs (i.e., reasonable photocopying charges) if you agree. Remember that proceedings have not yet commenced, therefore Meg wants to ensure that costs will be paid by the other side. At the moment they have no incentive to settle and the best way forward for the plaintiff is to issue proceedings as quickly as possible (see pages 56 *et seq.*). It is not unusual that they have requested a medical report. Given that Meg will need to obtain a medical report before she commences proceedings (see RSC Ord. 18, r. 12(1)(A)), then this should not place her under any undue burden.

If the request for copy documents came from solicitors there is an implied obligation that they will be responsible for your reasonable photocopying costs.

(2)   It is almost inevitable that the insurers will authorise solicitors to accept service but ensure you have written authority from those solicitors — don't rely simply on the insurers giving you their solicitor's details.

STEP 7

Meg receives a letter from Ritson & Co., solicitors, confirming that they have authority to accept service of proceedings on behalf of Easyshop.

Document 17

Ritson & Co.

27 Lonsdale Terrace
Oldcastle
OL7 7PP

21 April 1997

Watkins & O'Dwyer
17 Sycamore Avenue
Oldcastle
OL10 1BR

Your ref: MD/JR/144.346
Our ref: NP/BB/OK/133.1

Dear Sirs

<u>Re Martin v Easyshop Ltd</u>

We act for Marlowe Insurance Group plc and have been passed your letter of 11 April. We confirm that we have authority to accept service of any proceedings.

Yours faithfully

Ritson & Co.

Commentary: Correspondence with Insurers

1.   Here Meg intends to issue proceedings rather than negotiate with the insurers. It will be a matter of experience as to whether to negotiate with insurers or not. In this case where damages are likely to be large and the insurers are unlikely to agree quantum it is probably better to issue proceedings as soon as possible. Before proceedings are commenced the insurers have no incentive to settle, and therefore will probably delay matters as long as possible. Bear in mind that interest will begin to run on general damages from the date of service of proceedings. If you have delayed issuing proceedings in the hope of the insurers agreeing quantum and six months later an agreement has not been reached your client probably won't be pleased.

2.   If matters are more clear cut, i.e., both on liability and quantum, then it may be worthwhile negotiating with the insurers and possibly asking for an interim payment (see page 89). The insurers will of course want details of the plaintiff's claim. Only agree to this if the insurers agree that if the matter is not settled at the negotiation stage and proceedings have to be issued, they will be responsible for your

GEORGE MARTIN v EASYSHOP LTD

costs. If negotiations break down and proceedings have to be issued then unless you have reached this agreement with the insurers not only will you have wasted a great deal of time but you will also have incurred a great deal of costs for which the insurers may not be responsible.

3. Never unconditionally agree with the insurers to serve a writ and then not proceed with the action any further until the insurers have completed their investigations. The insurers will inevitably delay the matter for as long as possible.

STEP 8

Meg receives a reply from the Health and Safety Executive stating that according to their records the accident was not reported (copy letter not supplied). Meg writes to Ritson & Co. for a copy of the accident report book. She also writes to Smythes & Co., George's former employer, for details of any earnings lost as a result of the accident.

Commentary: Health and Safety Executive

The Reporting of Injuries, Diseases and Dangerous Occurrences Regulations (SIs 1985 No. 2023 and 1989 No. 1457) require the reporting of accidents at work to the local environmental officer. In the case of an employee all injuries which cause him/her to be absent from work for more than three days are notifiable. Major injuries are also notifiable. Failure to make such a report is a criminal offence. It may be that the Health and Safety Executive will investigate the accident; however, we have not pursued this line in the case study.

Document 18

Watkins & O'Dwyer
Solicitors

17 Sycamore Avenue
Oldcastle OL10 1BR
Tel. 011-111-1111
Fax 011-111-1111
DX Oldcastle 1000

Partners: J. Watkins
A. O'Dwyer

25 April 1997

Ritson & Co.
27 Lonsdale Terrace
Oldcastle OL7 7PP

Your ref: NP/BB/OK/133.1
Our ref: MD/JR/144.346

Dear Sirs

Re George Martin v Easyshop Ltd

Thank you for your letter dated 21 April. Please could you send us a copy of your client's accident report book and any other report of the incident.

If we do not hear from you within the next seven days we will apply for pre-action discovery pursuant to the Supreme Court Act 1981, s. 33(2).

Yours faithfully

Watkins & O'Dwyer

Commentary: Pre-action Discovery

1.   Where a claim may be made for damages for personal injuries or death, but has not yet begun (i.e., the writ has not yet been issued), then the court will permit the intended plaintiff to inspect documents in the intended defendant's possession and relevant to the issue of liability. The prospective applicant is first required to write to the other side to state his claim to the documents; this has become known as a Shaw letter after the case *Shaw* v *Vauxhall Motors Ltd* [1974] 1 WLR 1035. If the other side are not forthcoming an application can be made to the court under the Supreme Court Act 1981, s. 33(2). The application is made by originating summons supported by affidavit.

The applicant for disclosure need only show a 'reasonable prospect' that an action may commence, but the court will have regard to any defences the defendant may have, e.g., limitation.

The applicant must specify the document requested and show that it is relevant to the issue arising and that the person is likely to have them.

2.   Note that an order will not be made in the following circumstances:

(a)   against persons not likely to be a defendant to a future action;

(b)   to discover evidence relevant to the quantum of damages alone;

(c)   to discover the identity of the suspected party at fault;

(d)   where the claim is not related to personal injury.

3.   The down side of this application is that the applicant will normally have to bear the costs of the application. The person against whom an order is sought under this rule is entitled to his costs of the application and of complying with any order made unless the court orders otherwise (RSC Ord. 62, r. 6(1) and (9)).

Where the person against whom the order is sought is at fault, e.g., where he has been dilatory in replying to a proper request to disclose documents, the court may deny him his costs, or in exceptional cases order him to pay the applicant's costs of the application (see *Hall* v *Wandsworth H.A.* (1985) 129 SJ 188).

Note that costs in the cause is an inappropriate order on the application under this rule, because there is no certainty that an order for disclosure will lead to a cause or claim against the respondent.

4.   For the equivalent county court jurisdiction see the County Court Act 1984, s. 52(2); CCR Ord. 13, r. 7(1)(g).

5.   Legal aid is available for pre-action discovery and pre-action inspection. The solicitor should write to the Legal Aid Board stating why legal aid should be granted. It is likely that a limited certificate will be issued.

GEORGE MARTIN v EASYSHOP LTD

Document 19

Watkins & O'Dwyer
Solicitors

17 Sycamore Avenue
Oldcastle OL10 1BR
Tel. 011-111-1111
Fax 011-111-1111
DX Oldcastle 1000

Partners: J. Watkins
A. O'Dwyer

28 April 1997

Smythes & Co.
44 Highway
Oldcastle
OL4 3TY

Our ref: MD/JR/144.346

Dear Sirs

<u>Re George Martin, 33 Cherry Street, Oldcastle OL3 4LL</u>

We act for Mr Martin, a previous employee of yours, in connection with a claim against a third party for personal injuries arising out of an accident on 2 February 1996.

So that we can calculate our client's losses arising out of the accident we should be grateful if you would forward to us:

(a) details of our client's net and gross earnings for the 26 weeks prior to the accident indicating overtime pay (if any);

(b) details of our client's net and gross earnings since returning to work (18 March 1996) until the date he left (17 May 1996) again indicating overtime pay (if any);

(c) the amount of statutory sick pay received;

(d) details of any other sick pay you have paid to our client which is refundable to you in the event that our client's claim is successful;

(e) any other employment losses, e.g., bonus or promotion arising out of the accident. Was our client due for any increment? What were his future earnings likely to be?

(f) a copy of our client's contract of employment.

We would appreciate an early reply to the above if possible and thank you in anticipation of your assistance.

Yours faithfully

Watkins & O'Dwyer

Commentary: Letter to Employer

1.   Although we already have some of the information from the client we must obtain accurate wage details from the employer (unless the employer is the defendant whereby we would contact their solicitors). Things to look out for once you receive this information are:

(a)   were the client's earnings as per usual during the period before the accident, e.g., did he usually work overtime?

(b)   have there been any wage increases since the date the plaintiff left employment?

(c)   what 'perks' has the plaintiff lost, e.g., company cars, promotion, bonuses?

(d)   whether in addition to statutory sick pay the plaintiff received any payment under a sickness payment scheme and whether there is an obligation to refund this payment if the plaintiff's claim is successful. The plaintiff may state that he suffered no wage losses. However, his wage loss is exactly the same as a plaintiff who had not been paid under such a scheme as the plaintiff is under an obligation to refund it. Therefore, the special damages calculation should be set out as per normal stating the plaintiff's notional loss of earnings for that period.

2.   When full wage details cannot be obtained from the employer because the client has changed jobs, you may have to write to the tax office for copies of the client's tax returns.

3.   With a self-employed plaintiff you will probably have to contact the client's accountant. Consider also in this instance perhaps obtaining comparable earnings from different employers in the same field.

For the relevance of benefits see page 35, note 5.

STEP 9

Meg writes to George informing him of her progress to date and requesting his consent to the release of his hospital notes and GP notes for the purposes of instructing a medical expert.

GEORGE MARTIN v EASYSHOP LTD

Document 20

Watkins & O'Dwyer
Solicitors

17 Sycamore Avenue
Oldcastle OL10 1BR
Tel. 011-111-1111
Fax 011-111-1111
DX Oldcastle 1000

Partners: J. Watkins
A. O'Dwyer

30 April 1997

G Martin, esq
33 Cherry Street
Oldcastle
OL3 4LL

Our ref: MD/JR/144.346

Dear George

<u>Re your claim against Easyshop</u>

The insurers have now instructed solicitors and I have requested a copy of the accident report book.

I have also written to your previous employer for details of your earnings whilst in their employment.

The next step in the proceedings is to instruct a medical expert to prepare a report of your injuries. The expert I suggest is Mr Henry Fielding, an eminent orthopaedic surgeon. However, before I can instruct him, I require all of your GP notes and hospital notes so that he can prepare a full report. Therefore, I enclose two consent forms for the release of your records which you should sign and return to me in the pre-paid envelope provided. Without these records Mr Fielding will be unable to prepare a report and I will be unable to progress your case.

Mr Fielding will need to examine you before he prepares his report. He will contact you direct to arrange a convenient date for the examination. Please let me have a note of your losses and expenses in attending so that they can be included in your claim.

If you have any queries on the matters discussed in this letter or anything at all, please do not hesitate to contact me.

Yours sincerely

Meg Davis

GEORGE MARTIN v EASYSHOP LTD

Document 21

> I George Martin of 33 Cherry Street, Oldcastle, OL3 4LL hereby request you to release all my medical records, notes and x-rays etc. to my solicitors Messrs Watkins & O'Dwyer of 17 Sycamore Avenue, Oldcastle, OL10 1BR.
>
> Signed................. Dated..............

Commentary: Medical Release

1.   As a general rule only instruct a medical expert when it is clear that the client's case is not hopeless, i.e., there is a case to answer on liability.

2.   The timing of the report will often depend on the client's injuries. If the client is still in plaster there is little point in sending him to be examined. Similarly, if the client has just undergone surgery you should wait until the client has recovered and perhaps is back at work.

3.   As Meg intends to instruct an independent consultant then she must send with the letter of instruction the client's GP notes and hospital records, hence the consent forms. It will be necessary to explain to the client at a later date that the defendant will want to see the records to prepare their report (see page 79). Note also that the client has the right (subject to certain specified exceptions) to see his medical records post November 1991, pursuant to the Access to the Health Records Act 1990.

4.   It is of vital importance that the records are disclosed to Meg and not just the expert. Why? Because it may be that your expert produces an unfavourable report and you wish to instruct another expert. However, if the release forms only authorise the records to be disclosed to a named expert then the whole procedure will have to be repeated. In addition, at some stage you will want to instruct counsel who will want to see the records and have them explained by the expert. Finally, where possible you should try and familiarise yourself with the records and have them explained to you by your expert. For a detailed medical explanation consult a medical dictionary (see further page 59).

STEP 10

Meg receives the completed release forms from George. She writes to his GP and to the consultant at Oldcastle General Hospital.

She also receives a letter from Ritson & Co. and a copy of Easyshop's accident report book.

GEORGE MARTIN v EASYSHOP LTD

Document 22

Watkins & O'Dwyer
Solicitors

17 Sycamore Avenue
Oldcastle OL10 1BR
Tel. 011-111-1111
Fax 011-111-1111
DX Oldcastle 1000

Partners: J. Watkins
A. O'Dwyer

5 May 1997

Dr A. Shipley
Merrywell Medical Centre
21 Barnett Grove
Oldcastle
OL12 4QL

Our ref: MD/JR/144.346

Dear Dr Shipley

<u>Re George Martin d.o.b. 30.7.51.</u>
<u>33 Cherry Street, Oldcastle OL3 4LL</u>

We act on behalf of Mr Martin, a patient of yours, in connection with injuries received in an accident on 2 February 1996.

We should be grateful if you would forward to us Mr Martin's medical records. We enclose a signed authority from Mr Martin.

Yours sincerely

Meg Davis

50

GEORGE MARTIN v EASYSHOP LTD

Document 23

Watkins & O'Dwyer
Solicitors

17 Sycamore Avenue
Oldcastle OL10 1BR
Tel. 011-111-1111
Fax 011-111-1111
DX Oldcastle 1000

Partners: J. Watkins
A. O'Dwyer

5 May 1997

Records Department
Oldcastle General Hospital
Barrow Road
Oldcastle
OL4 7QL

Our ref: MD/JR/144.346

Dear Sirs

Re George Martin d.o.b. 30.7.51.
33 Cherry Street, Oldcastle OL3 4LL
patient number 2221XC

We act for Mr Martin in connection with injuries received in an accident on 2 February 1996 and for which our client received treatment at your hospital under the care of Mr Astley and later at the outpatient clinic under the care of Mr Goode.

We should be grateful if you could forward to us Mr Martin's medical records for the purposes of preparing a medical report. We enclose a signed authority from Mr Martin.

Yours faithfully

Watkins & O'Dwyer

Commentary: Letters to Hospital and GP

See commentary at page 49. With regard to the letters above, ensure that the client is easily identifiable. Remember that both the GP and the hospital may have more than one patient named Martin and will have hundreds of medical records. The easier you make their job, the sooner they will come back to you.

GEORGE MARTIN v EASYSHOP LTD

Document 24

Ritson & Co.

27 Lonsdale Terrace
Oldcastle
OL7 7PP

5 May 1997

Watkins & O'Dwyer
17 Sycamore Avenue
Oldcastle
OL10 1BR

Your ref: MD/JR/144.346
Our ref: NP/BB/OK/133.1

Dear Sirs

<u>George Martin v Easyshop Ltd</u>

Thank you for your letter of 25 April.

We enclose a photocopy of the relevant section of the accident report book and confirm that we have no other documentation relating to the incident. As you will see the report provides little information other than that the accident was reported.

Finally, are you yet in a position to let us have a copy of the medical report?

Yours faithfully

Ritson & Co.

Commentary: Accident Report Book

1.   In this instance the other side have supplied the accident report book without Meg having to go to court. They have probably agreed without too much of a struggle because the report reveals very little although it does give the name of the shopper who spoke to George just after the accident, Gina Wright. However, always be prepared to go to court if necessary (see commentary on pre-action discovery at page 45).

STEP 11

From the accident report book Meg contacts and interviews Gina Wright, the shopper who reported the accident.

GEORGE MARTIN v EASYSHOP LTD

Document 25

PROOF OF EVIDENCE

I Gina Wright of 22 Greengables Avenue, Oldcastle, OL15 1ER will say as follows:

1. On 2 February 1996 I was shopping at Easyshop at the shopping precinct. It was about 6.45 p.m. I had with me my 3-year-old daughter, Ruby. Normally, Ruby sits on top of the trolley but that night she insisted on walking beside me.

2. Ruby is rather inquisitive and I remember that I had to repeatedly restrain her from touching the goods on the shelves.

3. When we reached the third aisle I had let go of Ruby's hand for a moment to reach for a bottle of vinegar on the top shelf. Ruby thought that she would help me and she tried to grab a bottle of olive oil on the shelf below. Unfortunately, she missed and knocked three bottles from the shelf to the floor. The bottles were plastic and one split, spilling oil over the floor. I picked up the bottles and put them to the side.

4. I then took Ruby and went in search of a shop assistant. It took me a couple of minutes but I eventually found not a shop assistant but in fact a man who informed me he was the shop manager.

5. I told him what had happened and he said he would send someone to clean up the oil. I said he should do this as quickly as possible as anyone could slip on it and I said that I would pay for the damage. He told me not to bother, this was always happening and he would deal with it. His attitude was a little patronising and offended me — it was just the way he spoke to me as though I was stupid!

6. Although a little put out I continued with my shopping. I again went down the aisle where the oil had been spilt and was surprised that it had not been cleared up. This must have been about 10 minutes after I had reported it to the manager. There was a young female shop assistant in the aisle and I drew her attention to the oil. She said she would have it cleared up.

7. I continued with my shopping and was about two aisles away from the aisle where the oil had been spilt when I suddenly heard a shout. I immediately guessed what had happened and I went with Ruby to the third aisle. This was about five minutes after I had last been there.

8. Lying on the floor where the oil had been spilt was a man of about 40 years of age. He was moaning and obviously in great pain. The area where he had fallen was still covered in oil and there were no warning barriers. I went up to him and asked him if he was OK and told him that he had slipped on olive oil. I think I also told him how I had asked the shop assistants to clean up the oil or at least put up a warning barrier.

9. There were several shop assistants surrounding the man in addition to the manager who had instructed someone to call for an ambulance. I was so angry and upset that I went up to the manager and shook him by the arm. I think I called him a 'Stupid sod' and told him that he was irresponsible for not cleaning the spillage up when I had reported it and that the accident was all his fault. He merely said that the injured man was being attended to and that I should go home. However, he did take my name and address and said that this would be reported in the accident book.

10. As there was nothing I could do I left the shop with Ruby. I was so upset. I felt that it was partly my fault even though I had done everything I could do.

GEORGE MARTIN v EASYSHOP LTD

11. I don't know whether Easyshop have improved their standards as I have not been back to the shop. I'm afraid I was too upset by the incident to forget how badly I was treated.

Signed   Gina Wright   Dated   23 May 1997

Commentary: Proof of Evidence

Gina will have to give evidence at trial (if the matter goes to trial), therefore, it is wise to take a statement from her as soon as possible given that a considerable amount of time has elapsed since the incident and it will also be some time before the matter comes to trial. From the proof of evidence Meg will eventually prepare a witness statement, ready for exchange (see page 115).

If the witness refuses to co-operate there is very little Meg can do. It is possible to serve a subpoena/ witness summons (see page 126) to ensure that the witness attends trial, but this may not be worth doing. How will Meg know what the witness will say? Is it worth the risk?

STEP 12

Meg receives the GP notes and hospital records. She calls Mr Henry Fielding to inquire whether he will accept the case and to agree a fee.

She goes through the records before sending a letter of instruction to Mr Fielding.

Document 26

Watkins & O'Dwyer

Attendance Note

Your name   Meg Davis   Date   6 June 1997

Client's name   George Martin

Person attended   Mr Henry Fielding

Time start   10.35 a.m.   Time finished   10.45 a.m.

Phoning Mr Henry Fielding to request a medical report on George Martin. I discussed the case briefly with him and he indicated that he would be willing to prepare a report; however, he would not be able to see George until 1 July. I said really we wanted to move the case along as quickly as possible and after some discussion Mr Fielding said he would contact George tomorrow with a view to seeing him early next week. I said that I would send him a letter of instruction today but in the meantime gave him George's personal details so he could proceed to contact him.

We then discussed when the report would be completed and Mr Fielding agreed that it would be ready no later than three weeks from seeing George.

Finally, we agreed a fee of £300 subject to legal aid taxation. This would obviously be reviewed should it become necessary for Mr Fielding to appear as an expert witness.

GEORGE MARTIN v EASYSHOP LTD

Commentary: Attendance Note

See commentary at page 56, paragraph 6.

Document 27

Watkins & O'Dwyer
Solicitors

17 Sycamore Avenue
Oldcastle OL10 1BR
Tel. 011-111-1111
Fax 011-111-1111
DX Oldcastle 1000

Partners: J. Watkins
A. O'Dwyer

9 June 1997

Mr Henry Fielding
1 Avon Court
Oldcastle
OL22 7SY

Our ref: MD/JR/144.346

Dear Sir

Re George Martin d.o.b. 30.7.51
33 Cherry Street, Oldcastle OL3 4LL
Tel. no. 231 1366

Further to our recent telephone conversation we act for the above named in connection with a personal injury claim. Mr Martin was injured in an accident at the Easyshop supermarket when he slipped on some olive oil and fell on his back on 2 February 1996. He appears to have suffered serious back injuries.

We should be grateful if you would prepare a report for the purposes of a personal injury claim on the injury, the treatment given, present condition and future prognosis. There is a suggestion that our client was suffering from a degenerative condition which meant that his back was already in a weak condition before the accident.

Our client has received treatment from Mr Astley and Mr Goode at Oldcastle General Hospital. Our client's GP is Dr Shipley. We enclose the relevant hospital records and GP notes. We also enclose a copy of our client's statement to assist you.

The appointment should be made direct with our client. We confirm that we shall be responsible for your fee as agreed.

Yours faithfully

Watkins & O'Dwyer

GEORGE MARTIN v EASYSHOP LTD

Commentary: Letter of Instruction

1.   In this instance Meg has instructed an independent orthopaedic surgeon. As a general rule, only for very minor injuries would you think about instructing a General Practitioner. A GP is unlikely to have any significant experience of writing medico-legal reports. An initial report from a GP may be useful if there is a suggestion that the client is known for time wasting or for repeated visits to the doctor. Meg may also consider obtaining a psychiatric report as George states he has been suffering from depression since the accident.

2.   It is possible to instruct the consultant who treated the client in the hospital but only if the case is reasonably straightforward. If the consultant has had care of the client for several years then it would be extremely unlikely that the court would find that the consultant had been wrong and had been treating the client incorrectly.

However, in this case, where there is potentially an argument as to whether the client's condition is due totally to his accident or a degenerative condition, it is advisable to obtain an independent report. The consultant at the hospital may be a little biased towards the treatment he gave to the client, e.g., he may be slightly too enthusiastic about the client's prognosis.

3.   In addition to sending the client's medical records it is probably a good idea to send the client's statement, though at the same time stressing to the expert that the report should not deal with causation. If there have been any previous reports these also should be sent.

4.   A solicitor will build up his own choice of experts and it is of vital importance that the right expert is chosen. The expert's report could be determinative of whether you have a case and whether your legal aid is extended. However, as a starting point try the *Solicitors Journal Expert Witness Supplement*, November 1996 and/or *Gazette Guide to Expert Witnesses*, 1997 Edition, looking at case reports and seeing who acted as expert or asking counsel. Also consider APIL — the Association of Personal Injury Lawyers — which has its own database and the Law Society's Helpline which will undertake searches to find an appropriate expert.

5.   In the letter itself it is worthwhile setting out the client's injuries so the expert can see at a glance what the problem is and therefore indicate at an early stage if he feels the instructions are not within his area of expertise. In addition, Meg has here indicated that there may be a problem with prognosis given the client's previous medical history.

6.   Note that Meg has indicated that she will be responsible for the fee. You will see from the attendance note at page 54 that before instructing the expert she has checked that he is prepared to undertake the case, the period he requires to provide a report and his likely fee. Time limits are particularly important; experts are notoriously busy and it may be several weeks before he is able to see the client. Note that if the expert is particularly expensive it may be prudent to contact the Legal Aid Board for prior approval.

7.   The expert is asked to consult the client direct to arrange an appointment. If the expert has not done this within a reasonable time you should send a reminder to the expert. Often experts are extremely busy and need to be constantly monitored.

STEP 13

Meg proceeds to draft the writ and statement of claim and schedule of special damages (see pages 69 *et seq.* for the statement of claim and special damages calculation).

She receives the medical report which indicates that the prognosis for George is not good. She writes to George telling him of her progress to date.

She then proceeds to research the quantum of the claim.

GEORGE MARTIN v EASYSHOP LTD

Document 28

MEDICAL REPORT

1. CLIENT

NAME: George Martin

ADDRESS: 33 Cherry Street, Oldcastle, OL3 4LL

TELEPHONE: 091-231 1366

DATE OF BIRTH: 30.7.51

AGE: 45

OCCUPATION: Chartered Accountant

STATUS: Married, two children

2. REQUEST

NAME: Watkins & O'Dwyer

ADDRESS: 17 Sycamore Avenue, Oldcastle, OL10 1BR

REFERENCE: MD/JR/144.346

TELEPHONE: 011-111-1111

DATE OF REQUEST: 9 June 1997

3. EXAMINATION

DATE: 16 June 1997

PLACE: 1 Avon Court, Oldcastle, OL22 7SY

DURATION: 60 Minutes

RECORDS USED: Oldcastle General Hospital
Records of Dr Shipley,
General Practitioner

INVESTIGATIONS: Spinal x-rays, magnetic resonance imaging scan.

OTHERS PRESENT: None

4. REPORT

DATE: 1 July 1997

NUMBER: First

GEORGE MARTIN v EASYSHOP LTD

HISTORY

Mr Martin tells me that on 2 February 1996 he slipped and fell over in a supermarket injuring his back.

He was immediately transferred to the casualty department of Oldcastle General Hospital (as confirmed by the clinical records). He remained in hospital for two days under the care of Mr Astley. Mr Martin was found to have a trapped nerve in the lower part of his spine.

On 5 February 1996 he was discharged and his treatment was undertaken as an outpatient and he was immediately discharged to the care of his General Practitioner, Dr Shipley.

Mr Martin underwent intensive physiotherapy from 12 February to 18 March 1996 under the care of Mr Goode. He has continued to have physiotherapy since the accident. Mr Martin confirms that after a course of treatment there is some temporary improvement to his back, but he still suffers continual pain.

Relevant Past Medical History

Until the date of the accident Mr Martin had enjoyed good health and was extremely fit for a man of his age.

Restriction of Activities

Mr Martin has been forced to give up his employment as a chartered accountant, as he can no longer sit at his desk for long periods of time.

In his day to day activities he is severely limited. In particular, he can no longer play football, squash, badminton, golf or cricket. Mr Martin was extremely active before the accident. His lifestyle appears to have changed drastically. He can no longer drive or play with his children and is no longer intimate with his wife.

Present Symptoms

Mr Martin complains of persistent pain in the lower part of his back. Any movement, in particular bending forward, causes him great pain in the lower part of his back. He can sit only for an hour at a time and can only walk short distances. He is regularly prescribed analgesics by his General Practitioner.

Because his lifestyle is now severely restricted, as described in the previous section, Mr Martin is extremely depressed. He has gained approximately three stones in weight as a result of being unable to take any form of exercise and this has resulted in high blood pressure.

Examination

General

Mr Martin is 5ft 11in tall and weighs 17½ stones. He co-operated fully with the examination.

His back movements were severely limited by pain in the lumbar region. He had a lateral flexion of only 30 degrees on either side. Straight leg raising was only 20 degrees on both sides. Forward flexion until his fingertips reached just above his knees, no further. His reflexes were normal but the use of his legs is severely curtailed.

The lower spine was extremely sensitive and Mr Martin was clearly in great pain when I examined his third lumbar vertebrae. He had severe sciatic like pain and there was evidence of some muscle weakness in the surrounding area. Mr Martin indicated that on occasions he had a feeling of numbness in the area.

Opinion

I accept that Mr Martin suffered an entrapped nerve between his 2nd and 3rd lumbar vertebrae in a fall which took place on 2 February 1996. He received prompt and standard treatment for his injury.

I accept the history which Mr Martin has given as to the suffering which his injury has caused and the restriction of the activities he describes. From my examination of the x-rays there is a suggestion that Mr Martin was suffering from spondylolisthesis, although in my opinion this is far from certain. Even if Mr Martin was suffering from this condition it is far from certain that the condition would have progressed. Given Mr Martin's symptoms, in particular the sciatic pain and the muscle weakness, I am satisfied that his present condition has been caused by an entrapped nerve.

Progress

This man will continue to suffer intractable back pain for the remainder of his life. His mobility is severely restricted and is unlikely to improve. He is unlikely to be able to ever resume any sporting activities and at best can only hope for an increase in the time he can sit down and the distance he is able to walk. I am not optimistic, however, that this will occur. It may be possible to operate to release the nerve; however in this man's case this carries a high risk of increased pain and possibly increased disability.

Signed Mr H. Fielding   Dated 1 July 1997

Commentary: Medical Report

Listed below are a number of points Meg should consider on receiving the medical report:

1.   She should go through the report carefully with a good medical dictionary. If there are any technical terms that she does not understand then she should go back to the expert. Similarly, if there is anything negative or ambiguous in the report then she should take up these points with the expert to see whether the expert will review his opinion.

2.   She may consider showing the report to George. He may comment on anything that might reduce the damages, or he may comment that he thinks the injuries are more serious, e.g., that the accident has exacerbated a pre-existing but latent condition.

There is a view that the report should not be shown to the client if there is something in the report which is controversial or something which would upset the client. However, bear in mind that all information belongs to the client, therefore he/she has a right to see it.

3.   If the report is favourable to the client Meg should consider whether she needs to apply to the Legal Aid Board to remove any limitation on the certificate.

4.   Does the report indicate that Meg will need another report, say in six months' time? If so this date should be put in the diary.

GEORGE MARTIN v EASYSHOP LTD

5.   Does Meg need an additional report, e.g., from a psychiatrist? If in doubt she should seek the authority of the Legal Aid Board and the legally aided client or the privately paying client. If she needs to instruct another expert in the same field then she should ensure she tells the first expert. If she doesn't and the expert was to find this out inadvertently then he may be under the impression that his report was inadequate. Also, Meg must instruct an expert more senior to him. There is little point in instructing an expert of a comparable level to the first expert as it is likely that his opinion will be the same as his peer. Additionally, for the report to carry some weight the expert should be the most senior the Legal Aid Board or Meg's client can afford.

6.   In a difficult case Meg may consider arranging a conference with counsel attended by the expert and the client. She will check that the authority of the Legal Aid Board is not needed.

GEORGE MARTIN v EASYSHOP LTD

Document 29

(ROYAL ARMS)[5]

IN THE HIGH COURT OF JUSTICE
QUEEN'S BENCH DIVISION[1]
OLDCASTLE DISTRICT REGISTRY[2]

1997-M-No. 7321[3]

BETWEEN[4]

GEORGE MARTIN[6]   Plaintiff

and

EASYSHOP LIMITED[6]   Defendant

To the Defendant Easyshop Limited whose registered office is at Unit 7, Beech Court, Oldcastle, OL8 3MN.[7]

This Writ of Summons has been issued against you by the above named Plaintiff in respect of the claim set out on the back.

Within 14 days after the service of this Writ on you, counting the day of service, you must either satisfy the claim or return to the Court Office mentioned below the accompanying Acknowledgment of Service stating therein whether you intend to contest these proceedings.

If you fail to satisfy the claim or to return the Acknowledgment within the time stated, or if you return the Acknowledgment without stating therein an intention to contest the proceedings, the Plaintiff may proceed with the action and judgment may be entered against you forthwith without further notice.

Issued from the Oldcastle District Registry of the High Court this 3rd day of July 1997.

Note: This Writ may not be served later than 4 calendar months beginning with that date unless renewed by Order of the Court.

IMPORTANT

Directions for Acknowledgment of Service are given with the accompanying form.

GEORGE MARTIN v EASYSHOP LTD

The Plaintiff's claim is for:[8]

Damages for personal injuries and loss arising from an accident at the Defendant's supermarket on 2nd February 1996 when the Defendant negligently and/or in breach of statutory duty allowed oil to lie on the shop floor causing the Plaintiff to slip and fall.[9]

This action is not one which by virtue of Article 5 of the High Court and County Courts Jurisdiction Order 1991 must be commenced in a County Court.[10]

The cause of action in respect of which the Plaintiff claims relief in this action arose wholly or in part at Oldcastle in the district of the Registry named overleaf.[11]

This Writ was issued by Watkins & O'Dwyer of 17 Sycamore Avenue, Oldcastle, OL10 1BR.[12]

Solicitor for the said Plaintiff whose address is:

33 Cherry Street
Oldcastle
OL3 4LL

Solicitor's reference: MD.JR.144.346

Telephone number: 011–111–1111

NOTES: WRIT

In a contract or tort action in the High Court you will commence the action by writ. A writ is a form of originating process and by issuing a writ you have brought the matter before the Queen's courts and they have assumed jurisdiction to try the issue. For further details see RSC Ord. 5, r. 2.

There are two types of writ for this purpose: a writ claiming unliquidated damages (used in this case), and a writ claiming a liquidated sum, e.g., a debt. Listed below is a commentary on the format of a writ.

(1)   The action is proceeding in the Queen's Bench Division. Generally all contract and tort actions should be brought in this division (but see s. 61 and sch. 1 of the Supreme Court Act 1981 and *The White Book*, vol. 2, pt. 17, paras 5260 and 5347).

(2)   For convenience the writ has been issued out of Oldcastle District Registry as this is where the plaintiff resides. However, the writ could be issued out of any district registry or the Central Office (see further point (11)).

(3)   In the top right corner the court will give the case an action number. This number consists of the year of issue, the initial letter of the plaintiff's name and then a number which is the number of writs issued in that particular year.

(4)   On the left-hand side the court's seal is stamped. The date of the seal is very important for the time allowed for service of the writ and to establish that the action was begun within the limitation period.

(5)   If you are not using a pre-printed form which has the Royal Arms printed on top, ensure that the court staff emboss the Royal Arms at the top.

(6)   The writ then states the parties to the action. It is vitally important that the parties are correctly stated. There are a few points that you should consider:

62

GEORGE MARTIN v EASYSHOP LTD

(a) If the plaintiff is an individual then his full name should be set out. Plaintiffs under a disability must act by their 'next friend' whose certificate of consent and fitness must be filed on issue of the writ.

(b) If one of the parties is a firm then they should be described as such by the words 'a firm'.

(c) Do not abbreviate, e.g., write 'trading as' not 't/a', 'limited' not 'ltd'.

(d) In this case the defendant is a company. Before issuing the writ Meg should have done a company search to ascertain the correct title of the company and the address of their registered office. The company search will also indicate the financial position of the company which is particularly important for enforcement purposes. This should be viewed with caution, however, as a company which is in a dubious financial position may not have kept up to date with its accounting records.

(7) The writ is then self explanatory. The name and address of the defendant should be inserted (if a company the registered office address should be given) and the writ then goes on to inform the defendant that service must be acknowledged within 14 days inclusive of the day of service, and the consequences of not doing so, i.e., that judgment may be entered.

As indicated above, the writ may be issued out of any district registry and the writ should be completed as appropriate along with the date of issue.

(8) On the second page is the indorsement of claim, pursuant to RSC Ord. 6, r. 2. Put simply, this means that before the writ can be issued it must have the statement of claim stated (indorsed) on the writ or a concise statement of the nature of the action.

In this case, the writ is merely indorsed with a concise statement of the claim. The statement should state the relief and the remedy claimed. This is known as the general indorsement and will be used in a personal injury case when Meg serves a separate statement of claim which will set out the case in full. The general indorsement just gives the defendant an idea of the nature of the claim. The words 'statement of claim' should therefore be deleted on the back of pre-printed forms.

It is possible to put the entire statement of claim on the writ, which is known as a specially indorsed writ. In such a case you would obviously not have to serve a separate statement of claim. This is usually done in a debt action.

(9) Consider whether you need to plead interest on the writ. If interest is not included in the writ it is not fatal provided it is included in the statement of claim (see page 71). If the statement of claim was indorsed on the writ then interest would have to be pleaded and claimed in the prayer. See notes (9) and (10) on the statement of claim at page 73.

(10) As this is a personal injury case the writ must be indorsed to show that art. 5 of the High Court and County Courts Jurisdiction Order 1991 does not apply, i.e., the action is over £50,000 (see RSC Ord. 6, r. 2(1)(f), *The White Book*, 6/2/23, and *Practice Direction* [1991] 3 All ER 352). If the writ is not so indorsed, the court will assume that it could be heard by the county court and will proceed to transfer the action. The indorsement as shown must be signed by a solicitor. Meg has therefore researched quantum before issuing the writ.

See further on this point *Restick v Crickmore* [1994] 1 WLR 420, which held that if proceedings are incorrectly issued in the High Court then the plaintiff risks being struck out on the defendant's application. This penalty is not mandatory. The court will take into account the degree of misconduct and may transfer the case to the county court as appropriate.

Meg must also have an idea of quantum in order to decide what is the appropriate fee (see further page 67).

GEORGE MARTIN v EASYSHOP LTD

(11) As the action occurred in Oldcastle and the writ has been issued out of Oldcastle District Registry, the place of action indorsement should be completed. If an action arose wholly or partly in the district registry from which you are issuing, then by completing this indorsement it stops the defendant from applying to transfer the proceedings on the acknowledgment of service.

If the indorsement is not completed, the defendant can apply to have the proceedings transferred when completing the acknowledgment of service (see page 78, note 4). The plaintiff then has eight days to object.

(12) The writ must state the name and address of the plaintiff's solicitor. Note that the address for service will either be the business address of that solicitor or the address of the solicitor acting as agent. See point (5) in the notes for the acknowledgment of service at page 78 for how this differs from the acknowledgment of service.

Commentary: Damages

Damages are divided into two sections, namely general damages and special damages. General damages are not capable of precise calculation. They will be assessed by the trial judge, who will refer to earlier cases. General damages for pain and suffering do not have to be pleaded (see the statement of claim at page 72, note 7), but the particulars of injury must be given. The solicitor must however estimate the plaintiff's future loss of earnings. This is why the pleading refers to the medical report.

1. General damages:

(a) Future loss of earnings

To calculate the plaintiff's future loss of earnings, the court uses two figures known as the multiplier and multiplicand. The multiplicand is the plaintiff's net annual loss. This may not be fair to the plaintiff if his income was to rise dramatically, therefore the court will take this into account. The multiplier represents the number of years for which the plaintiff is to be compensated, i.e., the period for which he will be unable to work. However, if the plaintiff had, for example, 40 years left to work this could result in over compensation so the court will fix a much smaller multiplier. The multiplier takes into account the risk of further injury or death and the general vicissitudes of life. In practice, the court is unlikely to fix a multiplier greater than 16/17. Note, however, that with regard to the choice of multiplier the Civil Evidence Act 1995, s. 10 makes the Ogden Tables (the actuarial tables and explanatory notes which are issued by the Government's Actuary's Department for use in personal injury and fatal accident cases) admissible for assessing damages for future pecuniary loss in personal injury actions to include actions brought under the Fatal Accidents Act 1976 and the Law Reform (Miscellaneous Provisions) Act 1934. At the time of writing, however, this section of the Act is yet to come into force and no date has been given for its implementation.

The Ogden Tables can be used to a plaintiff's advantage in the assessment of his/her future losses. Currently the lump sum awarded to the plaintiff is discounted by approximately 4.5 per cent to take into account that if a plaintiff invested the sum prudently he would receive a 4–5 per cent return on the capital each year. The Ogden Tables, however, recommend that a smaller discount rate should be applied in accordance with index-linked government securities discount rate. In *Page* v *Sheerness Metal Co. plc*, *Wells* v *Wells* and *Thomas* v *Brighton H.A.* [1996] PIQR 261, at first instance the Ogden Tables were successfully relied on (the judge adopted a multiplier of 19 for future loss of earnings and a multiplier of 24 for future care), but on appeal the Court of Appeal held that the conventional guidelines were still applicable and the court should continue to apply a 4.5 per cent discount rate (see (1996) *The Times*, 23 October). Although plaintiffs may still seek to adduce the Odgen Tables without the assistance of s. 10 of the Act, until it comes into force the courts are unlikely to give their unequivocal approval to their use.

GEORGE MARTIN v EASYSHOP LTD

If George had been able to return to work he could have had an additional claim for loss of earning capacity, i.e., because of his injuries he was more prone to redundancy (see *Smith v Manchester Corporation* (1974) 17 KIR 1, which established this type of award).

The other losses covered under this head relate to non-pecuniary items.

(b) Pain and suffering

The award will take into account not only the pain and suffering at the time of the accident but also as a consequence of the accident. Damages also include compensation for any mental anguish and embarrassment. The plaintiff may also be awarded a sum to compensate for any stress caused by the fact that his life expectancy is reduced.

(c) Loss of amenity

This compensates for loss of quality of life, i.e., in George's case to compensate for the fact that he can no longer play sport, can no longer walk great distances and generally his quality of life has been considerably reduced.

There are other heads of damages, e.g., disappointment and discomfort.

In most cases you will instruct counsel to advise on the quantum of the claim (see page 82). As an estimate, however, consult *Kemp & Kemp, Halsbury's Monthly Review* and *Current Law* for comparable examples.

2. The Special Damages Schedule

Special damages represent the amount of the plaintiff's financial loss to date. They do have to be pleaded and Meg will also have to prepare a special damages calculation to be annexed to the statement of claim (see RSC Ord. 18, r. 12(1A); CCR Ord. 6, r. 1(5)). This is why she requested the client to complete a questionnaire (see page 3), and to keep receipts of all medical expenses. This schedule is to be deemed a pleading which cannot be departed from at the trial unless prior leave to amend is obtained (see RSC Ord. 25, r. 8(1A); CCR Ord. 17, r. 11(7)). The service of each further medical report should be accompanied by an updated special damages schedule.

The form of the schedule itself is outlined at 18/12/22 in *The White Book* and should include:

(a) loss of earnings already suffered;

(b) estimates of future loss of earnings;

(c) expenses already incurred, including medical or other expenses relating to or including the cost of care, attention, accommodation or appliances;

(d) estimate of future expenses;

(e) loss of pension rights.

With regard to (b) and (d) they can be at best only a rough estimate.

You will see that the claim for damages is presented gross, i.e., before deduction of benefits. Remember that in the case of a plaintiff who is still employed and in receipt of statutory sick pay this should be deducted from the plaintiff's actual earnings when comparing it with what the plaintiff should have earned.

GEORGE MARTIN v EASYSHOP LTD

With regard to interest on special damages, there is a question as to whether benefits should be included in calculating the amount of interest accruing on pre-trial special damages. It would appear that the relevant benefits should be deducted before the interest calculation. Why should the plaintiff be allowed to claim profit on something which he has already received?

For a further discussion on benefits see pages 35 *et seq*. See also page 73, note 9, for interest on damages.

STEP 14

Meg instructs a trainee solicitor to issue proceedings in Oldcastle District Registry. She hands him the relevant documentation together with a covering letter to the court. He attends at court, issues the proceedings and returns with the original writ and a sealed copy for service.

Document 30

Watkins & O'Dwyer
Solicitors

17 Sycamore Avenue
Oldcastle OL10 1BR
Tel. 011-111-1111
Fax 011-111-1111
DX Oldcastle 1000

Partners: J. Watkins
A. O'Dwyer

3 July 1997

Chief Clerk
Oldcastle District Registry
Quay Place
Oldcastle
OL6 7PP

Dear Sirs

<u>Martin v Easyshop Ltd</u>

We enclose:

(i)   original writ and two copies, indorsed with a certificate of value;

(ii)   legal aid certificate for filing;

Kindly note no fee is payable as the plaintiff is in receipt of income support.[1]

Please issue the writ and return the original to us together with the copy for service.

Yours faithfully

Watkins & O'Dwyer

NOTES: COURT FEES

(1)   See commentary immediately below.

Commentary: Issuing Proceedings

When you issue proceedings in the High Court you will require not only the writ but enough copies to provide a copy for the court and for each defendant. In addition, do not forget the court fee and that you must file the original Legal Aid Certificate at court (see Civil Legal Aid (General Regulations) 1989, reg. 50). From 15 January 1997 there is a sliding scale for High Court fees which is dependent on the size of the claim. This scale ranges from a fee of £120 for a claim of £10,000 or less (the old High Court fee) to a fee of £500 for a claim of £100,000 or more or one which is unlimited (see the Supreme Court Fees (Amendment) Order 1996 (SI 1996 No. 3189). See also the latest increases to the county court fees discussed at page 153.

GEORGE MARTIN v EASYSHOP LTD

Previously those who were in receipt of income support or suffering extreme hardship were exempt from the payment of court fees in both the High Court and the county courts, but this was abolished under the new Order. However, these fee exemptions have been reintroduced following the judgment in *R v Lord Chancellor ex parte Witham* (1997) NLJ 14 March which held that art. 3 of the Order was ultra vires s. 130 of the Supreme Court Act 1981 and therefore the abolition of fee waivers was unconstitutional. Consequently the Lord Chancellor has now reintroduced them.

STEP 15

The writ duly issued is returned together with a further sealed copy for service (the writ to be retained by Meg will be stamped 'original' by the court). Meg serves the proceedings on the other side. She also writes to Mr Fielding enclosing payment of his fee note, having obtained payment on account from the Legal Aid Board.

Document 31

Watkins & O'Dwyer
Solicitors

17 Sycamore Avenue
Oldcastle OL10 1BR
Tel. 011-111-1111
Fax 011-111-1111
DX Oldcastle 1000

Partners: J. Watkins
A. O'Dwyer

3 July 1997

Ritson & Co.
27 Lonsdale Terrace
Oldcastle
OL7 7PP

Your ref: NP/BB/OK/133.1
Our ref: MD/JR/144.346

Dear Sirs

Martin v Easyshop Ltd

We enclose the following by way of service:

   (i)   sealed copy writ;
   (ii)   original writ;[1]
  (iii)   acknowledgment of service;
  (iv)   statement of claim;
   (v)   medical report of Mr Henry Fielding;[2]
  (vi)   schedule of special damages;
 (vii)   notice of issue of legal aid.

Kindly acknowledge safe receipt by returning to us the original writ duly indorsed.

Yours faithfully

Watkins & O'Dwyer

GEORGE MARTIN v EASYSHOP LTD

NOTES: SERVICE OF PROCEEDINGS

(1)   The defendant's solicitor will accept service, therefore you should serve the original writ together with a copy of the writ and the acknowledgment of service. The defendant's solicitor will indorse on the original writ that he/she accepts service and return it to you (RSC Ord. 10, r. 1(4)). The date of service will be when the indorsement was made. The defendant's solicitors then have 14 days (inclusive of the day of service) to file the acknowledgment of service at court.

It is of course possible to serve the writ either personally by leaving it at the company's registered office, when service takes effect immediately, or by post, where service is deemed to have taken place, if first class post was used, the second working day after posting and if second class, the fourth working day after posting. See RSC Ord. 65, r. 2 and RSC Ord. 10, r. 1(2) respectively.

(2)   Along with the writ, the plaintiff's solicitor must serve the medical report and schedule of special damages and statement of claim (see RSC Ord. 18, r. 12(1)(A); or in the county court, CCR Ord. 6, r. 1). In addition, the plaintiff must serve a notice of issue of legal aid. Not only must the court be informed of the fact that the plaintiff is legally aided, but every other party in the action must be informed also. The reasons for this are obvious. An unassisted defendant is at risk as to costs against a legally aided plaintiff (see the notes on the legal aid letter at pages 15 *et seq.*).

Document 32

IN THE HIGH COURT OF JUSTICE   1997-M-No. 7321
QUEEN'S BENCH DIVISION
OLDCASTLE DISTRICT REGISTRY

(Writ issued 3rd July 1997)

BETWEEN

GEORGE MARTIN   <u>Plaintiff</u>

and

EASYSHOP LIMITED   <u>Defendant</u>

STATEMENT OF CLAIM[1]

1.   The Defendant[2] is and was at all material times the owner and occupier of premises known as Easyshop Limited of Unit 7, Beech Court, Oldcastle, a supermarket premises ('the shop').[3]

2.   On 2nd February 1996 the Plaintiff entered the shop as a lawful visitor under the Occupiers' Liability Act 1957 and as such was owed a duty of care pursuant to the said Act.

3.   The Plaintiff was walking down the third aisle of the shop, when he slipped on a quantity of olive oil lying on the floor, lost his balance and fell heavily to the floor, landing on his back.[4, 5]

4.   The said accident was caused by the negligence and/or breach of statutory duty under section 2 of the Occupiers' Liability Act 1957 of the Defendant, its servants or agents.[6]

PARTICULARS OF NEGLIGENCE AND/OR
BREACH OF STATUTORY DUTY

(a)   Failing to take any or adequate precautions for the safety of the Plaintiff.

GEORGE MARTIN v EASYSHOP LTD

(b) Exposing the Plaintiff to a risk of damage/injury of which they knew (or ought to have known).

(c) Allowing the Plaintiff to walk over a floor surface which was in a dangerous condition.

(d) Failing to give any proper warning to visitors of the danger posed by the presence of the oil.

(e) Allowing the floor to remain in a dangerous condition.

(f) Failing to pay any or sufficient heed to a report about the condition of the floor made by another customer, Ms Gina Wright, and as a result failing to prevent the Plaintiff slipping on the olive oil.

(g) Failing to take any or any reasonable care to ensure that the Plaintiff was reasonably safe in using the shop as a visitor.

5. By reason of the matters aforesaid the Plaintiff, who was born 30.7.51, sustained injuries, loss and damage[7].

PARTICULARS OF INJURY

The Plaintiff suffered serious back injuries, notably an entrapped nerve between the second and third lumbar vertebrae. He remained in hospital for two days and thereafter has undergone intensive physiotherapy to try and alleviate his constant pain. His employment as a Chartered Accountant was terminated on 17th May 1996 because of his ill health. He can no longer keep up his hobbies of squash, badminton, football, golf and cricket. The Plaintiff can no longer drive his car and can only walk short distances. The Plaintiff will further rely on the medical report of Mr H. Fielding dated 1 July 1997 annexed hereto.

PARTICULARS OF LOSS AND DAMAGE

(a)	Loss of earnings 18th March 1996 – 17th May 1996 8 half days for physiotherapy	£281.84
(b)	Value of clothing 1 suit	£275.00
(c)	Travelling expenses 49 sessions physiotherapy 12th February 1996 – to date @ £3.00 per journey	£147.00
	Visits to GP 12th February 1996 – to date @ £2.00 per journey	£86.00
	Visit to solicitor 7th March 1997 @ £5.50 per journey	£5.50
(d)	Prescription charges	£475.00
	Total	£1,270.34

[The Plaintiff will rely on the schedule of special damages dated 3rd July 1997 annexed hereto.][8]

6. Further, the Plaintiff claims interest pursuant to section 35A of the Supreme Court Act 1981 on the amount found to be due to the Plaintiff at such a rate and for such a period as the court shall think fit.[9]

AND the Plaintiff claims[10]

(1) Damages.

(2) Interest as aforesaid.

(SIGNED) Watkins & O'Dwyer

Served this 3rd day of July 1997 by Messrs Watkins & O'Dwyer of 17 Sycamore Avenue, Oldcastle, OL10 1BR Ref No MD/JR/144.346 Solicitors to the Plaintiff.

NOTES: STATEMENT OF CLAIM

(1) The first point to note is that this is a High Court action and as such the pleading is headed Statement of Claim.

(2) It really does not matter whether you refer to a company in the singular or the plural — what is important is that you are consistent throughout the pleading (see also contract case study at page 155, note 1).

(3) Usually paragraph 1 will be a definitive paragraph setting out who the parties are. For the purposes of the Occupiers' Liability Act 1957 the defendant must be an occupier — hence paragraph 1 of the statement of claim. For the use of 'all material times' see contract case study at page 155, note 2.

You will note also that the plaintiff is described as a visitor. Visitors are those persons who at common law would be treated as invitees or licensees (see Occupiers' Liability Act 1957, s. 1(2)). The common duty of care is specifically restricted to the purposes for which the visitor is invited or permitted by the occupier to be there (see s. 2(2)). If the visitor abuses the permission he will become a trespasser.

(4) Paragraphs (2) and (3) merely set out what happened — the narrative. Only specify exact details if you have them.

(5) Note that there should be a paragraph summing up what happened, i.e., that the plaintiff fell. It would not be fatal if this was omitted but for the sake of completeness this should be included.

(6) In this action it is alleged that not only was the defendant negligent but also it was in breach of s. 2(2) of the Occupiers' Liability Act 1957 and the common law duty of care. In all actions, before you draft the relevant pleadings always consider the possible causes of action. In this instance George has possible causes of action in negligence and breach of statutory duty. With regard to negligence, Meg must prove that the actual negligence caused the injury. As for the breach of statutory duty, Meg must deal specifically with the elements of the particular statutory duty. Under the Occupiers' Liability Act 1957, whether or not the defendant was in breach is determined in much the same way as an action for negligence, hence at paragraph 4 Meg has dealt with the particulars of negligence/statutory duty together, because they cover common ground. If the action was for breach of duty under the Factories Act 1961 then that should be pleaded separately because the requirements for breach of that statute are different from an action for negligence. However, the allegations of negligence can still be relied on as evidence of the breach of statutory duty.

Paragraph 4 sums up the situation and alleges how the defendant was at fault, i.e., breach of statutory duty and/or negligence. However, Meg cannot simply leave it like this. If she did, all that would happen

GEORGE MARTIN v EASYSHOP LTD

is that the defendant would come back and ask for further particulars of how they were at fault (see the request for further and better particulars in the contract case study at page 204). RSC Ord. 18 requires facts to be pleaded in sufficient detail.

The particulars themselves are simply listed in point form. Essentially Meg is alleging that the defendant was negligent/in breach of statutory duty because it failed to clean up the oil, left the floor in a dangerous state and as such failed to take reasonable care for the plaintiff's safety.

When actually phrasing the particulars of negligence think about what you are trying to say. You will note that at paragraph 4(a) and 4(b) Meg has pleaded in the alternative, e.g., and/or. Each allegation could be pleaded separately, although this is not strictly necessary in this case. Why does she do this? Well, if, for example, at paragraph 4(f) Meg simply pleaded 'the defendant failed to pay heed to Gina Wright', the defendant could then come back and say that it did listen to Gina Wright. However, by pleading in the alternative Meg states that even if the defendant did listen, it did not listen carefully enough, therefore pre-empting the defence. Similarly, stating that the defendant failed to take any or any reasonable care (see paragraph 4(g)) again pre-empts the defence of 'it did take some care.'

(7)   The next paragraph first states the plaintiff's date of birth (see *The White Book* at 18/7/5 and *Practice Direction (Personal Injuries or Death: Pleading)* [1974] 3 All ER 976) and effectively sums up what has happened as a result of the defendant's negligence. This is logical. Meg has said who the parties are, that the defendant was negligent and as a result the plaintiff has suffered the following pain and loss and damage. Now, in much the same way as Meg 'particularised' the negligence she particularises the loss and damage. The damages can be divided into two distinct sections — general and special damages (see page 64 for further details). It would be perfectly acceptable to simply head it particulars of special/general damages, although it is perhaps better to say 'particulars of injury', 'particulars of loss and damage' as these seem more meaningful.

With regard to the general damages, it would be quite correct to refer to the medical report and leave it at that. However, in our opinion it is better to give a brief synopsis of the plaintiff's injuries, not, however, to repeat the medical report verbatim. This is so that the defendant and the court can see at a glance from the pleading what the plaintiff's injuries are and the heads of damage pleaded without having to sift through the medical report in detail. There should be sufficient detail here to show the injuries, the period spent in hospital, the consequences of the injuries, e.g., that the plaintiff lost employment, hobbies etc. (loss of amenity claim), then to rely on the medical report for fuller detail.

Note: Remember there is no need to plead the specific amount of general damages you are claiming in respect of pain and suffering as these will be assessed by the court.

If you do not intend to rely on further medical evidence then this will be the only report you serve in the action.

With regard to special damages, these are simply listed, or referred to in a separate special damages calculation if they are particularly complicated. Note that the special damages calculation may have to be updated if you serve another medical report.

Ensure that you include all quantifiable losses, e.g., medical expenses, damage to vehicle, clothing etc.

(8)   The special damages schedule is far from complete. Here we have just listed George's quantifiable losses to date. In fact a separate document will be needed which must meet the requirements as set out at 18/12/22 in *The White Book* (see also page 65 commentary on special damages). So in George's case the schedule would set out his net wage multiplied by the appropriate multiplier. George is 45 years of age and anticipated working until he was 60. Thus for the remaining 15 years of his life a multiplier of perhaps 7–9 is appropriate. If George had lost any pension rights the schedule would then go on to detail these along with an estimate of future medical expenses. Finally if George had been able to work, perhaps on a part-time basis, the schedule would list his estimated future earnings and these would be deducted from George's estimated future losses. Note the section in square brackets would only be appropriate if a separate schedule was prepared.

(9) Finally, Meg must claim interest. Different rates apply, e.g., on general damages interest is normally assessed at 2 per cent until trial and there is no interest on future losses. Special damages carry interest at half the appropriate rate from the date of the accident to the trial (the appropriate rate coming from the average rate from the short term investment account for the relevant period). Rather than try and plead them all separately, it is usually dealt with in one all-embracing paragraph.

(10) The prayer is simply summing up the remedies you are claiming, i.e., damages and interest. Costs are always at the discretion of the court and should not be pleaded (unless you have a contractual right to recover costs in which case this should be pleaded).

Commentary: Pleadings

1. Meg has commenced a personal injury action in the High Court. The writ, therefore, must be indorsed with a statement that the action is not one which by art. 5 of the High Court and Civil Jurisdiction Order 1991 must be commenced in the county court. Effectively, what this means is that the claim must be for at least £50,000 to be commenced in the High Court. See pages 62 and 63 (note 10) for the appropriate indorsement of the writ. Whilst it may be possible to commence a contract action of a few thousand pounds in the High Court (see page 152 of the contract case study) a solicitor must commence a personal injury action in the county court if it is less than £50,000, otherwise the solicitor will find him/herself penalised in costs.

2. For the formal requirements of a pleading see the writ and RSC Ord. 18. As a reminder remember:

(a) The paragraphs should be numbered consecutively;

(b) One issue per paragraph if possible;

(c) Numbers, dates etc. should be expressed in figures not words;

(d) Anything lengthy, e.g., a damages calculation, should be referred to in a separate document.

3. Finally, no discussion on pleadings is complete without a note on evidence. RSC Ord. 18, r. 7(1) provides that every pleading must contain, and contain only, a statement in a summary form of the material facts on which the party pleading relies for his claim or defence, as the case may be, but not the evidence by which those facts are to be proved, and the statement must be as brief as the nature of the case admits. This rule is further indorsed by *Practice Direction (Civil Litigation: Case Management)* [1995] 1 WLR 262 which reiterates that facts, not evidence, should be pleaded.

There is, however, an exception to this rule provided by the Civil Evidence Act 1968, s. 11, by which a criminal conviction may be pleaded in a civil action as evidence of the offence committed. To be able to rely on this section the party must include particulars of:

(a) the conviction and the date;

(b) the court which made the conviction;

(c) the issue in the proceedings to which the conviction relates.

In fact there is very little the opponent will be able to do with a conviction. In reply, the other side can either:

(a) admit the conviction and its relevance;

(b) deny the conviction;

(c) allege it is erroneous;

(d) allege it is not relevant.

GEORGE MARTIN v EASYSHOP LTD

Document 33

Watkins & O'Dwyer
Solicitors

17 Sycamore Avenue
Oldcastle OL10 1BR
Tel. 011-111-1111
Fax 011-111-1111
DX Oldcastle 1000

Partners: J. Watkins
A. O'Dwyer

3 July 1997

Mr Henry Fielding
1 Avon Court
Oldcastle
OL22 7SY

Our ref: MD/JR/144.346

Dear Mr Fielding

<u>Re: Our Client George Martin d.o.b. 30.7.51.</u>
<u>33 Cherry Street, Oldcastle OL3 4LL</u>

Thank you for your medical report on the above named. We are now commencing proceedings on Mr Martin's behalf, and may contact you further in the future.[1]

We enclose a cheque for £300 in respect of your fee. Please would you return the enclosed fee note indorsed with your receipt.[2, 3]

Yours sincerely

Meg Davis

NOTES: EXPERT'S LETTER

We have included this letter to illustrate three points:

(1)   To remind the expert he may be required to advise further on the case.

(2)   To remind you to deal with disbursements as quickly as possible. If you pay promptly you will ensure that should you require the expert again, you will receive prompt advice.

(3)   Payments on account. You can claim a payment on account from the Legal Aid Board for any disbursement of £30 or over. You should ideally make the claim as soon as you know you are going to incur the disbursement (see further Civil Legal Aid (General) Regulations 1989, regs. 100 and 101).

STEP 16

The defendant's solicitors reply to Meg enclosing the original writ and requesting that George be medically examined by their expert. She writes to George explaining why he should agree to the examination. George agrees and Meg replies to Ritson & Co. informing them of this.

Document 34

Ritson & Co.

27 Lonsdale Terrace
Oldcastle
OL7 7PP

7 July 1997

Watkins & O'Dwyer
17 Sycamore Avenue
Oldcastle
OL10 1BR

Your ref: MD/JR/144.346
Our ref: NP/BB/OK/133.1

Dear Sirs

<u>Martin v Easyshop Ltd</u>

Thank you for your letter of 3 July. We have today forwarded the acknowledgment of service to the court stating an intention to defend and now return the original writ duly indorsed as having been received on 7 July 1997.

We would like the opportunity to have your client medically examined by our expert Mr Adams of 57 Briar Way, Oldcastle, OL3 3TT. Are you agreeable to this? Mr Adams will require access to your client's hospital notes and GP notes in order to prepare the report.

We look forward to hearing from you.

Yours faithfully

Ritson & Co.

GEORGE MARTIN v EASYSHOP LTD

Document 35

Acknowledgment of Service of Writ of Summons

In the High Court of Justice   1997-m-No. 7321

QUEEN'S BENCH **Division**

OLDCASTLE **District Registry**   Use black ink and capital letters

Plaintiff   GEORGE MARTIN

Defendant   EASYSHOP LIMITED   **SPECIMEN**

Part 1 (Your) (Defendant's) full name

> EASYSHOP LIMITED   (1)

Part 2 (Do you) (Does the Defendant) intend to contest: (2)

the whole of the Plaintiff's claim? ☑

part of the Plaintiff's claim? ☐

none of the Plaintiff's claim? ☐

Part 3 If you (the Defendant) have said that you do not intend to contest the whole, or part, of the Plaintiff's claim will you (the Defendant) be asking the court for a stay of execution? (3)   Yes ☐   No ☐

Part 4 (Do you) (Does the Defendant) wish to have the case transferred to: (4)

the Royal Courts of Justice? Yes ☐   No ☑

another District Registry? Yes ☐   No ☑

If to a District Registry, say which one

Part 5 I acknowledge that ~~I have~~ (the Defendant has) been served with a copy of the Writ of Summons (5)

Signed *Ritson & Co*   Date 7 JULY 1997

Defendant (Solicitor for the Defendant) (Authorised officer)

Address to which papers about this case should be sent:

> 27 LONSDALE TERRACE
> OLDCASTLE
> OL7 7PP

Solicitor's Ref.	Telephone No.	Fax No.
NP/BB/OK	011-123-1234	011-321-1234

Part 6 When completed this form should be returned to:

OLDCASTLE DISTRICT REGISTRY
QUAY PLACE
OLDCASTLE
OL6 7PP

GEORGE MARTIN v EASYSHOP LTD

Plaintiff's (Plaintiff's solicitor's) details

Address to which papers about this case should be sent:

> WATKINS & O'DWYER
> 17 SYCAMORE AVENUE
> OLDCASTLE
> OL10 1BR

Solicitor's Ref. MD/JR/144.346

Telephone No. 011-111-1111

Fax No. 011-111-1111

SPECIMEN

OYEZ The Solicitors' Law Stationery Society Ltd, Oyez House, 7 Spa Road, London SE16 3QQ

1997 Edition
2.97 F33279
5044217
★ ★ ★ ★

High Court E22

GEORGE MARTIN v EASYSHOP LTD

NOTES: ACKNOWLEDGMENT OF SERVICE

An acknowledgment of service is the equivalent of a reply to an invitation, the invitation being the writ. If the defendant wishes to contest the action the acknowledgment must be returned to the court within 14 days of service of the writ (inclusive of the day of service). See RSC Ord. 12, r. 5.

The form is self-explanatory. The defendant must complete the following:

(1)   Enter its full name (if a company state whether it is limited).

(2)   State whether it intends to contest the proceedings, either the whole of the plaintiff's claim or only part of the claim. If the answer is yes, it does intend to contest the matter, you may see it referred to as 'notice of intention to defend'. If the answer is no then the plaintiff can enter judgment in default pursuant to RSC Ord. 13. Note that the judgment will only be interlocutory if the amount claimed is unliquidated and there will have to be a further hearing for damages to be assessed under RSC Ord. 37.

(3)   Stay of execution. This is not relevant here. In a debt action, if the defendant does not give notice of intention to defend, the defendant can instead apply for a stay of execution. Essentially, the effect of this is that instead of the judgment being payable forthwith, the defendant has a respite of 14 days during which the judgment is automatically stayed, to allow a compromise to be made or to apply to the court for a further stay.

(4)   Transfer. If the writ was issued from a district registry and the indorsement as to the place or cause of action is not completed on the writ (see note 11 on the writ at page 64) then the defendant can apply for a transfer of proceedings to either another district registry or to the Central Registry. If the plaintiff fails to object to this request within eight days the proceedings will be transferred. If the plaintiff does object there will be a hearing to determine the most convenient place for the matter to proceed.

(5)   At the end of the form a space is left for the signature of the defendant or his solicitor and for the address for service.

(6)   The plaintiff's solicitor should indorse his/her address, reference and telephone number on the reverse side of the acknowledgment of service, as should the defendant's solicitor when returning it to the court.

Note: The defendant has returned the acknowledgment to the court indicating that it intends to defend the action. The date of the acknowledgment is the date the court receives it and not the date of posting (see RSC Ord. 12, r. 1(5)).

GEORGE MARTIN v EASYSHOP LTD

Document 36

Watkins & O'Dwyer
Solicitors

17 Sycamore Avenue
Oldcastle OL10 1BR
Tel. 011-111-1111
Fax 011-111-1111
DX Oldcastle 1000

Partners: J. Watkins
A. O'Dwyer

8 July 1997

George Martin, esq
33 Cherry Street
Oldcastle
OL3 4LL

Dear George

<u>Re your claim against Easyshop</u>

The defendant's solicitors have requested that you be examined by their medical expert, Mr Adams.

Although you may have some reservations about this, in all cases similar to yours the defendant has the right to produce their own report which of course they cannot do unless you agree to the examination. If you do not agree to the examination the proceedings will be stayed, which means that the court will order that your case cannot continue unless you agree to the examination.

In addition, the defendant's solicitors have requested that your hospital records and GP notes be made available. Whilst you may naturally be reluctant to agree to such a request, if the defendant's solicitors apply to the court it is likely that the court will order us to disclose the records, and this may include records prior to the accident. As there is likely to be a dispute on whether your present condition is due solely to the injuries you sustained in the accident then the court will probably grant the defendant's request. The decision on whether to disclose the documentation is naturally yours, but if you refuse to do so then the court will again probably stay the action.

Please confirm that you have no objection to your records being disclosed and that you are prepared to attend Mr Adams.

Mr Adams will then contact you direct to arrange a convenient appointment. He will wish to have details of your medical condition but you should not discuss the facts of the accident or liability for it; do not sign any documents without contacting me first.

Please let me have a note of your expenses in attending the examination as these will be refunded by the other side.

Yours sincerely

Meg Davis

GEORGE MARTIN v EASYSHOP LTD

Document 37

Watkins & O'Dwyer
Solicitors

17 Sycamore Avenue
Oldcastle OL10 1BR
Tel. 011-111-1111
Fax 011-111-1111
DX Oldcastle 1000

Partners: J. Watkins
A. O'Dwyer

14 July 1997

Ritson & Co.
27 Lonsdale Terrace
Oldcastle
OL7 7PP

Your ref: NP/BB/OK/133.1
Our ref: MD/JR/144.346

Dear Sirs

Martin v Easyshop Ltd

Thank you for your letter of 7 July.

We confirm that our client has agreed to be examined by your expert Mr Adams, subject to your undertaking to pay our client's expenses and that Mr Adams does not discuss matters of liability.

Please ask Mr Adams to contact Mr Martin direct to arrange a suitable appointment.

Yours faithfully

Watkins & O'Dwyer

Commentary: Conditions for Medical Examination

1. The courts have no power to order the plaintiff to undergo a medical examination. However, if the plaintiff refuses then the court will probably stay the action. Only if there is a real risk that the examination would cause further injury or severe discomfort to the plaintiff would a refusal probably be considered reasonable.

2. The plaintiff can insist on a number of conditions before agreeing to the examination, e.g., that the plaintiff's costs occasioned by the examination be met by the defendant, that only the plaintiff and the defendant's expert be present, that only the injuries are discussed and not liability. In addition, in the case of a minor it should be agreed that a parent/guardian also attend.

3. The plaintiff cannot insist that his own doctor be present at the examination nor that the defendant agree to give him a copy of the report. The latter is dealt with adequately by the rules of disclosure. With the exception of where the defendant wishes to instruct the plaintiff's own consultant or doctor, the plaintiff cannot object to the identity of the defendant's expert.

4. In addition to requesting the plaintiff be examined by their expert the defendant's solicitors have requested disclosure of the plaintiff's medical records. Obviously this does not favour the plaintiff. In this case it is inevitable that the records will refer to the plaintiff's pre-existing condition. It is also likely that the defendant will also require sight of the plaintiff's medical notes prior to the accident. At the moment Meg has simply ignored the request in the hope that the defendant's solicitors will forget about it. However, should they apply to the court then they are likely to be granted access certainly to the post-accident records and if the defendant's expert can demonstrate a need for seeing them, then access will also be granted to the pre-accident records. Now the onus is on the plaintiff to disclose all records. Where the plaintiff is claiming damages for loss of future earnings caused by personal injury he will have to disclose to the defendant's solicitors records covering all of his medical history (see *Dunn* v *British Coal Corporation* (1993) *The Times*, 5 March). As now the approach to litigation is 'cards on the table' it is unlikely that Meg would succeed in arguing that the records should not be disclosed until trial. So it is probably just as well she agrees to the request before the defendant applies to the court where they could be awarded the costs of the interlocutory application if the court is of the opinion that she has acted unreasonably.

Note: Meg eventually agrees to the defendant's solicitors' request and discloses the plaintiff's medical records to the defendant's solicitors.

STEP 17

Meg receives a call from the defendant's solicitors informing her that Mr Adams has contacted Mr Martin and the examination will take place on 25 July. They also confirm that they will agree to pay Mr Martin's expenses (attendance note not reproduced). George telephones.

Document 38

Watkins & O'Dwyer

Attendance Note

Your name   Meg Davis   Date 18 July 1997

Client's name   George Martin

Person attended   Client

Time start 2.35 p.m.   Time finished 2.45 p.m.

George Martin rang. He said that he was going to be examined on 25 July. I said that the defendant's solicitors had already told me this and reminded him to keep a note of his travelling costs.

I took the opportunity of explaining to George the latest developments in the case. I explained that I felt that Easyshop may be prepared to admit liability. However, in any event I felt that we had a strong case and if they did therefore file a defence I anticipated issuing a summons for summary judgment. I explained to George the effect of such a step. I also explained to George that I would also be making an application for an interim payment. I explained to George what this was and he indicated that this would help alleviate some of his financial problems as he was finding it very difficult to manage. I explained further to George that if he was to lose the action then he would have to pay the interim payment back to the defendant. George said I should still go ahead.

GEORGE MARTIN v EASYSHOP LTD

> I then explained to George that in any event I would need to instruct counsel to advise on quantum generally. When I received counsel's advice I would send a copy to George.

STEP 18

Meg instructs counsel to advise.

Document 39

IN THE HIGH COURT OF JUSTICE QUEEN'S BENCH DIVISION OLDCASTLE DISTRICT REGISTRY	1997-M-No. 7321

BETWEEN

GEORGE MARTIN   <u>Plaintiff</u>

and

EASYSHOP LIMITED   <u>Defendant</u>

INSTRUCTIONS TO COUNSEL TO ADVISE ON
QUANTUM[1]

Counsel is sent herewith the following copy documents:[2]

1. Proof of evidence of the Plaintiff, George Martin dated 8th April 1997.

2. Letter from the Defendant to the Plaintiff dated 23rd February 1996.

3. Defendant's accident report book.

4. Proof of evidence of Gina Wright dated 23rd May 1997.

5. Writ issued 3rd July 1997.

6. Statement of claim served 3rd July 1997.

7. Medical report of Mr Henry Fielding dated 1st July 1997.

8. Legal Aid Certificate dated 28th March 1997.

Instructing solicitors act for Mr George Martin, the Plaintiff in this action. Counsel will see from the Plaintiff's proof (doc 1) that on 2nd February 1996 the Plaintiff slipped on a quantity of olive oil lying on the floor of the Defendant's premises. Counsel will note that to date the Defendant's solicitors have failed to admit liability. Counsel is referred to the letter from the Defendant to the Plaintiff dated 23rd February 1996 (doc 2) which Instructing Solicitors would contend is an admission of liability. Counsel is also referred to the accident report book and the proof of evidence of Gina Wright (docs 3 and 4). Instructing Solicitors are of the opinion that both the Plaintiff and Ms Wright will be excellent witnesses should the case proceed to trial.[3]

GEORGE MARTIN v EASYSHOP LTD

Instructing Solicitors commenced proceedings in the High Court having regard to quantum which is easily in excess of £50,000 on full liability. The Defendant gave notice of intention to defend on 7th July 1997. The statement of claim was served on 3rd July 1997.

Counsel will note from Mr Fielding's report (doc 7) that the Plaintiff has sustained serious back injuries, notably an entrapped nerve. The Plaintiff was employed as an accountant but his employment was terminated on 17th May 1996 as he could no longer sit for lengthy periods. The Plaintiff has been unable to work since that date. The prognosis for the Plaintiff is not good, according to Mr Fielding's report. However, Counsel will note that there is a possibility that the Plaintiff was suffering from a degenerative condition, therefore there is a slight question over whether his present condition is solely the result of the accident. Instructing Solicitors have spoken to Mr Fielding who is firm in his opinion that the Plaintiff's condition is the result of the accident. The Plaintiff has also been forced to give up his hobbies of playing badminton, squash, football, golf and cricket. His family life has also been adversely affected and Counsel is referred to paragraphs 13 to 16 of the Plaintiff's proof.

As the Plaintiff is suffering severe financial hardship and has considerable medical expenses, Instructing Solicitors have made an application for an interim payment on the ground that the Defendant has admitted liability. Obviously, if the application for summary judgment is successful then the application could be made on the ground that liability has been established.

On the basis of the above, Counsel is asked to advise on liability and quantum with particular reference to the application for interim payment.[4]

Counsel is asked to contact Ms M. Davis of the Instructing Solicitors if he requires any further information.[5]

Dated 18th July 1997

NOTES: INSTRUCTIONS TO COUNSEL

(1)   Meg has decided to take counsel's advice on the quantum of damages. She is obtaining counsel's advice at this stage because it may be that the defendant's solicitors will make an offer in settlement or make a payment into court. In any event, Meg will want to know the quantum of the claim before the hearing of the application for interim payment, and when the claim is substantial then Meg will certainly want a second opinion.

The instructions are headed with what counsel is required to do, e.g., counsel is asked to advise on quantum.

(2)   The instructions themselves are constructed in a precise order. First, the solicitor lists all the documents that are relevant to the case, so, for example, here Meg has included the pleadings to date, the medical report and schedule of special damages (as counsel is being asked to advise on quantum these must be included) and the client's statement. By listing the documents in this way, not only is it easy for counsel to check that he has all the documentation, but it also encourages Meg to think what documentation she has and what is relevant. Usually, Meg would not send instructions without enclosing all the documents, but if the case is particularly urgent then she can send the additional documentation later.

(3)   The instructions begin with Meg identifying whom she is acting for and consequently on whose behalf counsel is instructed and then continue to give a narrative of the case. This will be the first time counsel has seen the case, therefore Meg must give him a complete history of the matter and what stage of the proceedings the case is at, together with an explanation of the documents enclosed. However, Meg

GEORGE MARTIN v EASYSHOP LTD

will not simply repeat anything which can easily be read in the documents, so in this case counsel is referred to the proofs of the plaintiff and Ms Wright.

(4) Then Meg explains exactly what advice is sought, in this instance advice on quantum. She should point out any particular difficulties — in this case there is a question mark over whether the plaintiff's condition is due solely to the accident. Where appropriate, she should give her viewpoint on the issue.

(5) The instructions then end with a closing paragraph stating what counsel is required to do and who to contact of the instructing solicitors. This information should also be stated in a covering letter along with any information on time limits and hearing dates.

Commentary: Instructions to Counsel

1. All instructions to counsel must have a backsheet (the backsheet has not been reproduced here). This is folded around the rest of the instructions or placed on top of them. On the backsheet is written:

(a) the full title of the case, e.g., court number of the case, names of the parties;

(b) the nature of the instructions, e.g., Instructions to Counsel to Advise on Liability;

(c) the name of the barrister and the address of chambers;

(d) the name and address of the instructing solicitors;

(e) a note, if the matter is legally aided, with the certificate number.

2. There is no real prescribed format for the instructions but as a checklist they should:

(a) be clear and easily understood;

(b) narrate the facts of the case where counsel is dealing with the matter for the first time;

(c) contain all relevant documentation, plus an explanation where necessary;

(d) specify what counsel is required to do;

(e) include the solicitor's opinion on the matter where appropriate.

3. As to when to instruct counsel there is as such no prescribed time but you should not instruct counsel until you have analysed the problem or if you are still waiting for some important further information. Finally you should ensure that you have the funds or will soon be put in funds to meet counsel's fee.

4. Finally, a quick word on who to instruct. This can be very difficult. Usually, a firm of solicitors will build up a working relationship with a set of chambers. However, if this is not the case or if the barrister you want is not available, then you could have a problem. The best recommendation is from other solicitors, though you could look at case reports to see which counsel acted in a case similar to yours if it is a specialised matter. Alternatively, there are various guides such as the *Legal 500* or *Chambers Directory* which list barristers and the work they do.

STEP 19

The defendant's solicitors serve their defence. On receipt of the defence, Meg writes to Ritson & Co. acknowledging receipt of their defence and indicating that she intends to issue a summons for summary judgment and interim payment. She then proceeds to issue the summons.

GEORGE MARTIN v EASYSHOP LTD

Document 40

IN THE HIGH COURT OF JUSTICE
QUEEN'S BENCH DIVISION
OLDCASTLE DISTRICT REGISTRY

1997-M-No. 7321

BETWEEN

GEORGE MARTIN Plaintiff

and

EASYSHOP LIMITED Defendant

DEFENCE[1]

1. Paragraph 1 of the Statement of Claim is admitted.[2]

2. Save that it is admitted the Plaintiff visited the shop on the date given, no admissions are made as to paragraphs 2 and 3.[3]

3. Paragraphs 4, 5 and 6 are denied.[4]

4. If, which is denied, the Plaintiff's injuries, loss and damage were caused by the Plaintiff's fall, as alleged in paragraph 3, it is alleged that the said fall was caused wholly or in part by the Plaintiff's negligence.[5]

PARTICULARS OF NEGLIGENCE

(a) Failing to look where he was walking.

(b) If, which is denied, there was olive oil on the floor, failing to take heed of or avoid the olive oil.

(c) Failing to take any other sufficient steps to avoid the oil and/or falling.

5. In the premises the Plaintiff is not entitled to the relief claimed or any relief for the reasons alleged or at all.[6]

Ritson & Co.

Served this 30th day of July 1997 by Messrs Ritson & Co. of 27 Lonsdale Terrace, Oldcastle, OL7 7PP Ref NP/BB/OK/133.1 Solicitors to the Defendant.

NOTES: DEFENCE

(1) The heading for the defence is as for the statement of claim, except that the document is obviously headed 'defence' and there is no requirement to state when the writ was issued.

(2) If you know something is true then you should not deny it. Ideally it should be admitted, but if the defendant would rather not do so then you should make no admission. Obviously, only admit

GEORGE MARTIN v EASYSHOP LTD

something if your client agrees that it is true. The first paragraph of the statement of claim is uncontroversial.

(3)   Easyshop has made no admissions on paragraphs 2 and 3 'save that' George's visit to the shop is admitted. By making 'no admission' Easyshop is effectively reserving its position and:

(a)   with regard to the alleged duty of care under the Occupiers' Liability Act 1957, the solicitors will probably want to research this in more detail.

(b)   with regard to the fall, Easyshop are saying that 'we didn't see what happened' and are therefore putting the onus of proving what happened on George.

By making no admission (as with a denial) you are putting the other side to proof. If they do prove what is being alleged then the cost of doing so may well fall to be paid by your client.

(4)   Paragraph 4 of the statement of claim says the fall was caused due to the default of Easyshop — this is denied. Paragraph 5 says that George has suffered injuries and loss and damage — this may well be true but it additionally says these are due to 'the matters aforesaid', i.e., to include Easyshop's alleged default — this is denied. As an alternative the defence will plead:

'3. Save that it is admitted the Plaintiff sustained injuries, no admissions are made as to the cause or extent of those injuries and the remainder of paragraphs 4, 5, and 6 are denied.'

In this alternative, whilst Easyshop admit the injury, they deny this is down to them and consequently deny all liability — they could have in mind that George's back simply seized up as he was carrying his shopping basket (possibly very heavy) around the shop, causing his complaint and him to fall over.

(5)   Here, Easyshop are raising the argument that George was contributorily negligent. If a defendant wants to set up a positive case against the plaintiff then the material facts should be pleaded (see RSC Ord. 18, r. 18).

(6)   The final paragraph is an all embracing paragraph used to sum up the defence. The words 'in the premises' means by reason of the matters set out in the defence. So in other words, by reason of the matters set out in the defence, the defendant denies that the plaintiff is entitled to any relief (which can encompass an injunction, damages, interest) claimed. This paragraph is included just in case the defence has missed something out!

Commentary: Defence

1.   The defence is the defendant's first pleading and must be served within 14 days of service of the statement of claim unless the statement of claim was indorsed on the writ, served with the writ, or served within 14 days of service of the writ, in which case 28 days after service of the writ. There are essentially two types of defence:

(a)   a defence which genuinely intends to defend the action until trial; and

(b)   a defence which is attempting to mitigate the effect of the statement of claim.

2.   Essentially the rules of pleading are as for the statement of claim, except the solicitor should consider the following points:

(a)   The solicitor should examine the statement of claim with the client in detail and ensure that it is understood. Then the solicitor should ask the client whether he/she admits any of it or does the client insist on denying it.

86

(b) If the defence does not specifically deny a fact, then the defendant is deemed to admit whatever is stated in the statement of claim. To contradict a fact is said to 'traverse it'. To admit a fact is to say that it 'is no longer in issue' (see RSC Ord. 18, r. 13).

(c) Can the defendant plead positively (see RSC Ord. 18, r. 8)? Examples of this are:

   (i) where you allege that the claim is not maintainable because it is statute barred;

   (ii) any matter the defendant wants to raise which changes the nature of the plaintiff's pleading, e.g., contributory negligence.

3. There are a number of specific defences which you should be familiar with. See RSC Ord. 18, r. 16 (CCR Ord. 9, r. 12) for the defence of tender before action and *The White Book*, 18/17/2 for a plea by way of set-off.

For an example and commentary on a counterclaim, see the contract case study at pages 186 *et seq.*

Document 41

Watkins & O'Dwyer
Solicitors

17 Sycamore Avenue
Oldcastle OL10 1BR
Tel. 011-111-1111
Fax 011-111-1111
DX Oldcastle 1000

Partners: J. Watkins
A. O'Dwyer

1 August 1997

Ritson & Co.
27 Lonsdale Terrace
Oldcastle
OL7 7PP

Your ref: NP/BB/OK/133.1
Our ref: MD/JR/144.346

Dear Sirs

Martin v Easyshop Ltd

Thank you for your letter of 30 July enclosing your defence. We will now be proceeding with a summons for summary judgment and interim payment which we will serve in due course.

Yours faithfully

Watkins & O'Dwyer

GEORGE MARTIN v EASYSHOP LTD

Document 42

IN THE HIGH COURT OF JUSTICE   1997-M-No. 7321
QUEEN'S BENCH DIVISION
OLDCASTLE DISTRICT REGISTRY

BETWEEN

GEORGE MARTIN   Plaintiff

and

EASYSHOP LIMITED   Defendant

LET ALL PARTIES concerned attend the District Judge in Chambers at Oldcastle District Registry, Quay Place, Oldcastle, OL6 7PP on Friday the 5th day of September 1997 at 10 o'clock in the forenoon on the hearing of an application by the Plaintiff:[1]

1. For interlocutory judgment in this action for damages to be assessed in respect of the Defendant's negligence referred to in the Statement of Claim, and interest as therein claimed, and the costs.

2. Further for an order pursuant to the Rules of the Supreme Court 1981 Order 29 Rule 10 that the Defendant do make an interim payment to the Plaintiff for the sum of £2,000 on the ground that if the claim proceeded to trial the Plaintiff will obtain judgment for substantial damages against the Defendant.

3. That the Defendant do pay the costs of this application.

TAKE NOTICE that a party intending to oppose this application or to apply for a stay of execution should send to the opposite party or his solicitor, to reach him no less than 3 days before the date above mentioned, a copy of an Affidavit intended to be used.[2]

DATED the 6th day of August 1997

This summons was taken out by Watkins & O'Dwyer, of 17 Sycamore Avenue, Oldcastle, OL10 1BR, Solicitors for the Plaintiff.[3]

To   Ritson & Co.
       27 Lonsdale Terrace
       Oldcastle
       OL7 7PP

       Solicitors for the Defendant

Time Estimate:[4]   2½ hours.

NOTES: SUMMONS

(1) Note the application is being heard at Oldcastle District Registry in front of a district judge and not a master as would be the case in the Principal Registry in London. The summons then goes on to detail the orders sought. An application for an interim payment may be included in a summons for summary judgment under RSC Ord. 14 (see RSC Ord. 29, r. 10(2)).

(2) The summons ends with (effectively) a reminder to the defendant to serve an affidavit in reply.

(3) It then states who the summons was taken out by and who it is to be served on.

(4)   Finally, the time estimate. The court when issuing a summons will ask for an approximate time estimate; the longer the time estimate the longer you will have to wait for a hearing date. How long will essentially come with experience, though always err on the generous side as even the most straightforward application may take 15 minutes, and where there are arguments to be presented or a complex affidavit to be gone through it will take considerably longer.

Note: Fee currently £30.

Commentary: Summons — Interim Payment

1.   This is perhaps a more unusual step to take in a personal injury action. An application for summary judgment, pursuant to RSC Ord. 14, is more often used in a debt action. In a personal injury matter there are more often than not disputed questions of fact which cannot be resolved on affidavit evidence alone. It will be only where the defendant submits no evidence in reply to the plaintiff's affidavit, or submits an affidavit which does not really identify a defence that the application will be granted, leaving quantum of damages to be assessed under the provisions of RSC Ord. 37.

2.   In this case it is apparent that the defendant has a poor defence to this action, taking into account the letter from the defendant to the plaintiff at page 9 which the plaintiff's solicitors will contend is an admission of liability. Therefore, Meg has issued the summons to put pressure on the insurers to accept liability. In addition, she has applied for an interim payment (RSC Ord. 29). An application for an interim payment asks the court to make an advance payment to the plaintiff on account of damages that he/she will eventually be awarded at trial. The plaintiff must establish that he/she has either (a) obtained a judgment on liability (hence the Order 14 application), or (b) obtained a formal admission of liability, or (c) that if the case went to trial he/she would recover substantial damages. In this case at present the application should be made on ground (c).

3.   The payment itself will not exceed a reasonable proportion of the damages which in the opinion of the court are likely to be recovered by the plaintiff after taking into account any contributory negligence, counterclaim or cross claim on which the defendant intends to rely. The court may also award interest on the amount of the interim payment at such rate and for such a period as it considers just (see *Independent Broadcasting Authority* v *EMI Electronics Ltd* (1980) 124 Build LR 1). In such a case the order should state the amount of interest awarded and how it is made up. The payment may be made in a lump sum or in instalments if the court considers this just. The payment does not include costs.

4.   Other factors the plaintiff must bear in mind are that the application will fail unless the defendant against whom it is sought is a public authority, or the defendant has the means to make the interim payment, or is insured, or now, pursuant to the Rules of the Supreme Court (Amendment) 1996 (SI 1996 No. 2892), is a person whose liability will be met under the MIB agreement. Clearly there is no problem here.

5.   One important point to consider when requesting an interim payment is the amount and the possible effect on legal aid and benefits. With regard to legal aid see the Civil Legal Aid (General) Regulations 1989, reg. 94. Interim payments are exempt from the statutory charge as long as the payment remains interim. Once the final award of damages is made the interim payment is included in the calculation for the statutory charge. The interim payment also does not have any effect on the plaintiff's current Legal Aid Certificate (see further Civil Legal Aid (Assessment of Resources) Regulations 1989, sch. 314B).

As for benefits, consider the amount the defendant will deduct to pass to the DSS when calculating how much to ask for. It may be that once the payments the plaintiff has received by way of benefits were deducted then the interim payment would be drastically reduced. It is advisable if possible to exhibit the CRU Certificate/Statement with the affidavit. If this is not possible at least have it at the hearing of your summons. Although the payment into court was £20,000 Meg has only made an application for an interim payment of £2,000. If George has capital of more than £8,000 he will cease to be eligible for income support, between £3,000–£8,000 there is a sliding scale. Meg clearly does not want to find that although she has obtained a substantial interim payment George subsequently loses his entitlement to income support. Therefore after taking into account any repayments to the Compensation Recovery Unit Meg is careful that George does not exceed the capital threshold.

GEORGE MARTIN v EASYSHOP LTD

6.   The summons is the method by which you make an interlocutory application in the High Court (the equivalent in the county court is a notice of application). This application is done on notice inter partes which means both sides are given the opportunity to attend (as opposed to ex parte where you don't give the other side notice — usually only in cases of urgency for an injunction). An interlocutory application essentially means a step on the way to trial.

7.   To issue the summons you take it (plus two copies) to court and ask them to fix a hearing date with a time estimate. As this is likely to be a lengthy application, Meg has issued the application now as it is unlikely to be listed for at least a month and more likely two months, given the time estimate of 2½ hours. In the intervening period Meg will instruct counsel and obtain his advice, and serve the affidavit, giving the other side plenty of notice. When you issue your summons, the court will seal it, give it a hearing date and keep one copy for the court file (outside London). You have now issued your summons and the date indorsed on the summons is called the return day. Then the summons is served on the other side (as opposed to notice of application in the county court where the court may serve it) along with the affidavit.

STEP 20

Ritson & Co. reply admitting liability. They make an offer of settlement which Meg feels to be ridiculously low. She telephones George, telling him of the offer. George accepts Meg's advice and Meg rejects the offer. (Attendance note re telephone calls to counsel and George are not reproduced.)

Document 43

Ritson & Co.

27 Lonsdale Terrace
Oldcastle
OL7 7PP

5 August 1997

Watkins & O'Dwyer
17 Sycamore Avenue
Oldcastle
OL10 1BR

Our ref: NP/BB/OK/133.1
Your ref: MD/JR/144.346

Dear Sirs

Re Martin v Easyshop Ltd

Thank you for your letter of 1 August.

For the purposes only of these proceedings our client is prepared to admit liability and consent to judgment for damages to be assessed. Kindly confirm that you therefore will not issue your Order 14 summons.

With regard to damages, our medical evidence indicates that your client was suffering from an existing back complaint and it is our view that it was only a matter of time before his condition would have been such as to affect his life in the manner for which he seeks compensation from our client.

Accordingly, we consider that whilst damages are appropriate for the pain and suffering arising out of the immediate incident, together with a relatively small amount for loss of earnings, we do not accept that your client is entitled to damages for matters which effectively arise out of his existing complaint.

GEORGE MARTIN v EASYSHOP LTD

In these circumstances we take the view that we should proceed quickly to an assessment hearing (at which time we confidently expect any award to be modest) and your proposed application for an interim payment is inappropriate and should be withdrawn.

We look forward to hearing from you.

Yours faithfully

Ritson & Co.

Document 44

Watkins & O'Dwyer
Solicitors

17 Sycamore Avenue
Oldcastle OL10 1BR
Tel. 011-111-1111
Fax 011-111-1111
DX Oldcastle 1000

Partners: J. Watkins
A. O'Dwyer

11 August 1997

Ritson & Co.
27 Lonsdale Terrace
Oldcastle
OL7 7PP

Your ref: NP/BB/OK/133.1
Our ref: MD/JR/144.346

Dear Sirs

<u>Martin v Easyshop Ltd</u>

Thank you for your letter of 5 August.

We are pleased to see your admission of liability.

We do not accept your contentions as to the limited extent of our client's damages claim and, accordingly, will be proceeding with the application for an interim payment. For this reason we suggest we do not withdraw our Order 14 summons (which we have now issued and will serve shortly) but simply request judgment by consent at the hearing and then proceed with the interim payment application on the basis of that judgment.

Yours faithfully

Watkins & O'Dwyer

GEORGE MARTIN v EASYSHOP LTD

Commentary: Correspondence between Plaintiff's and Defendant's Solicitors

1.   The defendant's solicitors have admitted liability. As the defence is weak, the insurers have probably taken the view that there is little to be gained by contesting an Order 14 application, and it is better to admit liability at this stage, thereby saving costs.

2.   The letter then continues with assertions that the plaintiff is unlikely to recover much in the way of damages. It is unlikely the defendant's solicitors will disclose their report before the hearing of the interim payment application. At this stage they are anxious to force the plaintiff into a compromise before the application for an interim payment and are hinting that their medical evidence indicates that the plaintiff's position is weak. Also, by suggesting that the parties should proceed quickly to the assessment hearing, they are attempting to put forward a strong front and perhaps force the plaintiff to capitulate. Additionally, if they subsequently make a payment into court (see page 94) they are preparing the ground in the hope that the plaintiff will feel so unsure of his case that he will accept the payment in. The defendant's solicitors are aware that Meg may copy all the correspondence she receives to her clients, so even if she is not convinced by their arguments, her client may be, and remember it is the client who is giving the instructions!

3.   Even where you are in a weak position (such as the defendant's solicitors) always consider writing a comprehensive letter knocking down the other side's case. If you can point out the flaws in their argument and, in addition, perhaps couple this with an interlocutory application, such as a request for further and better particulars (see page 204 of the contract case study), it will often unnerve the opposing solicitors and perhaps cause them to reconsider their position.

4.   Note that with regard to medical evidence, the defendant will usually disclose their medical evidence extremely late in the proceedings. There is very little the plaintiff can do about this. Only if the defendant is the plaintiff's employer can the plaintiff demand a copy of the report prior to it being sent to the defendant under the provisions of the Access to Medical Reports Act 1988. Usually, the defendant will disclose their medical evidence as late as possible. The only compensation for the plaintiff is that if there is disclosure by more than one party then it should be mutual exchange, medical for medical etc.

5.   When you receive the defendant's report this should be sent to your medical expert to see if any parts can be agreed or whether you require an amended or updated report (see page 113).

6.   In reply, Meg has little to say with regard to the appropriateness of the interim payment application. Clearly there is nothing to be gained by any protracted argument.

STEP 21

Meg receives counsel's advice (copy advice not reproduced). She also receives notice of payment into court from the defendant's solicitors. This is considerably lower than the amount indicated in counsel's advice.

Meg writes to George informing him of the payment in and sending him a copy of counsel's advice. George accepts Meg's advice and instructs her to reject the payment in. Meg proceeds to draft the affidavit in support of the interim payment application. She sends the affidavit to George, who returns it sworn.

Meg then serves the affidavit re the application for interim payment on Ritson & Co. and rejects the payment into court.

Commentary: Counsel's Advice

The advice should be studied (as with the medical report) and any ambiguities resolved. In this case, as there is a dispute about medical evidence, counsel has recommended that Meg obtains a further medical report (see page 113). As a warning, do not simply accept counsel's advice without question. If you are not satisfied go back to counsel and ask that he/she reconsider his/her opinion, or if necessary obtain a further advice from him/her. As a last resort go to a different counsel, but you will have to justify this, i.e., costs to the Legal Aid Board and/or the taxing officer on any taxation of your costs.

Document 45

Ritson & Co.

27 Lonsdale Terrace
Oldcastle
OL7 7PP

14 August 1997

Watkins & O'Dwyer
17 Sycamore Avenue
Oldcastle
OL10 1BR

Your ref: MD/JR/144.346
Our ref: NP/BB/OK/133.1

Dear Sirs

<u>Martin v Easyshop Ltd</u>

We enclose a notice of payment into court. This figure excludes the sum of £6,022.06 shown on the enclosed certificate of relevant benefits as the amount to be withheld by our client in accordance with the Social Security Administration Act 1992.

Kindly acknowledge safe receipt.

Yours faithfully

Ritson & Co.

GEORGE MARTIN v EASYSHOP LTD

Document 46

IN THE HIGH COURT OF JUSTICE
QUEEN'S BENCH DIVISION
OLDCASTLE DISTRICT REGISTRY

1997-M-No. 7321

BETWEEN

GEORGE MARTIN

Plaintiff

and

EASYSHOP LIMITED

Defendant

TAKE NOTICE that the Defendant EASYSHOP LIMITED has paid £20,000 into Court.

The said £20,000 is in satisfaction of all the causes of action in respect of which the Plaintiff claims

[The Defendant has withheld from this payment into Court the sum of £6,022.66 in accordance with section 93 of the Social Security Administration Act 1992]

DATED the 14 day of AUGUST 1997

....

To	WATKINS & O'DWYER	RITSON & CO
	17 SYCAMORE AVENUE	27 LONSDALE TERRACE
	OLDCASTLE OL10 1BR	OLDCASTLE OL7 7PP
	Ref MD/JR/144/346	Ref NP/BB/OK/133.1
	Plaintiff's Solicitor	Solicitor for the Defendant

GEORGE MARTIN v EASYSHOP LTD

1997–M–No. 7321

IN THE HIGH COURT OF JUSTICE

QUEEN'S BENCH DIVISION

OLDCASTLE DISTRICT REGISTRY

BETWEEN

GEORGE MARTIN   Plaintiff

and

EASYSHOP LIMITED   Defendant

NOTICE OF
PAYMENT INTO COURT

Ritson & Co
27 Lonsdale Terrace
Oldcastle
OL7 7PP

Solicitors for the Defendant

Reference
NP/BB/OK/133.1

GEORGE MARTIN v EASYSHOP LTD

Commentary: Payment into Court

1. The defendant has paid the money into court pursuant to RSC Ord. 22 in order to put pressure on the plaintiff to accept their offer. A payment into court is not an admission of liability but a powerful negotiating tactic. If the plaintiff refuses to accept the payment in, there are certain cost consequences (see further letter to George (below) and notes on page 98).

2. The plaintiff should acknowledge receipt of the notice within three days of receipt (although there is no specified sanction if he does not — see RSC Ord. 22, r. 1(2)). If the plaintiff is minded to accept the offer then he has 21 days to accept. Acceptance can be given later but only with the leave of the court.

3. The payment in is made net of social security benefits and the notice should be indorsed to show this. The payment includes interest but not costs. The plaintiff, if he accepts the payment in within the prescribed time limit, has the right to have his costs taxed up to the date of the acceptance and paid by the defendant.

4. Provided the notice of acceptance is given within 21 days, then the plaintiff is entitled as of right to seek recovery of costs from the defendant (see RSC Ord. 62, r. 5(4); CCR Ord. 11, r. 3(5)(a)). This is the case even if the defendant has stipulated that the monies paid into court are intended not only to be in satisfaction of the cause of action but, additionally, the plaintiff's costs. See further *Stafford Knight and Co. Ltd* v *Conway* [1970] 2 All ER 52 on this point.

5. Note that at the trial the judge will add the amount deducted in respect of social security benefits and deduct the amount of interest that had accrued at the time the payment in was made, in deciding whether the payment in has been beaten.

Document 47

Watkins & O'Dwyer
Solicitors

17 Sycamore Avenue
Oldcastle OL10 1BR
Tel. 011-111-1111
Fax 011-111-1111
DX Oldcastle 1000

Partners: J. Watkins
A. O'Dwyer

15 August 1997

G Martin, esq
33 Cherry Street
Oldcastle
OL3 4LL

Our ref: MD/JR/144.346

Dear George

Your claim against Easyshop

I have received today a notice of payment into court of £20,000 from the defendant's solicitors. The payment into court is an offer by the other side to you of payment to you of that money by way of damages.[1]

GEORGE MARTIN v EASYSHOP LTD

You have 21 days from today within which to accept this payment and if you do not do so, then the money will remain in Court and thereafter you will only be allowed to take the money out of Court in settlement of your claim with leave of the Court.

If you do not accept the payment in, then assuming the other side do not increase the payment in (in which case you would have a further 21 days to accept the new increased offer) or make an acceptable offer in settlement, then the matter will proceed to trial to decide the level of damages although the judge, at that trial, will not be aware of the payment in until after he has decided the level of damages which you should be awarded.

At trial there could be the following outcomes:

1. You are successful and recover from the defendant damages greater than the amount paid into court. In this situation the payment in will have no effect and the Court will order the monies in court to be released to you together with whatever additional sum the defendant is ordered to pay you. The defendant will also be ordered to pay most of your costs of the proceedings.

2. If you recover at trial damages and that award does not exceed the amount of the monies paid into Court, then although the Court will award you damages, the Court will only order the other side to pay your costs up to the date of the payment in and will then order you to pay the other side's costs incurred following the date of the payment into court. Note that these costs could be substantial as they will include the costs of the trial.[2]

3. If you are unsuccessful at trial you will fail to recover any damages, the monies in court will be paid out to the defendant and you will be responsible for the defendant's costs. However, as you are legally aided, the Court will only order that you pay an amount that is just and reasonable upon an enquiry into your means and, if you remain on income support, you would not pay any costs.[3]

You can therefore appreciate that a payment into court is effectively an offer to you to settle and if you do not accept that offer but fail to achieve a better settlement at trial, the Court will say that the costs following the offer made to you have been wasted because of your refusal and you should therefore have to bear those costs.

You may be under the impression that as you are legally aided, then you will not have to pay the other side's costs should you fail to beat the payment at the trial. However, I refer you back to my previous letter to you dated 7th March 1997 where I explained the effect of the statutory charge. Not only will you be responsible for the defendant's costs from the date of the payment in, but as you will have failed to recover all of your costs from the defendant, then the statutory charge will come into operation and the Legal Aid Board will deduct any outstanding amount they have paid out on your behalf from your damages. This could mean that you will be left with very little compensation, if any at all.

On the question of whether I consider you should accept the payment in, I have taken the advice of counsel (copy enclosed with this letter) on whether this offer should be accepted and he is of the opinion that the offer is considerably lower than what we would hope to achieve at trial and it should be rejected. I am of the same opinion. Considering your injuries and that the defendant has now admitted liability I think the offer is very low. However, I must remind you that the decision is yours to make and that it is impossible to predict exactly what award the Court will make.[4]

If you have any queries on the matters outlined above, please do not hesitate to contact me. Appreciating the 21 day period in which we have to accept the offer as of right, I would be extremely grateful if you could reply to this matter with some degree of urgency and let me hear from you without delay.

Yours sincerely

Meg Davis

GEORGE MARTIN v EASYSHOP LTD

NOTES: LETTER RE PAYMENT INTO COURT

See commentary at page 96.

Obviously we must inform the client of the offer made; however the letter to the client is extremely important when a payment into court is made. The following points should be noted:

(1) First, explain to the client what a payment into court means and how long he has to accept it. Then explain what will happen should he not accept it. Note the interesting recent Court of Appeal decision of *Hoppe & Hoppe v Titman* [1997] 1 WLR 841 which ruled that accepting a payment into court may not be the end of the litigation. The facts in brief are that Mr Titman (the defendant) had claimed the sum of £11,000 from the Hoppes (the plaintiffs) in respect of unpaid fees for architectural services. The Hoppes filed a defence alleging amongst other things that Mr Titman had not carried out his services with reasonable care and skill. Importantly, however, they did not plead a counterclaim. The Hoppes then went on to make a payment into court 'in full and final settlement' of Mr Titman's claim (including interest) which was duly accepted by him and the action was then stayed under the provisions of CCR Ord. 11, r. 3(3). Two months later the Hoppes acting as plaintiffs brought a claim against Mr Titman for breaches of contract (the claim essentially founded on the same facts as set out in their defence in the first action). Mr Titman made an application to strike out the proceedings under the principle of *res judicata* or alternatively as an abuse of process and argued that the Hoppes' present action should have been pleaded as a counterclaim in the first action. The Court of Appeal, however, held that the acceptance of a payment into court did not extinguish the Hoppes' right of action and therefore they could proceed with the second action.

(2) The cost consequences (see the notes in *The White Book* at 22/5/4). These must be explained very carefully to the client. If the plaintiff recovers more than the payment in at trial, then he will be awarded costs in the usual way and costs will be awarded against the defendant (costs follow the event). However, if the plaintiff equals or fails to beat the payment in, then the court will make a split costs order. The plaintiff will recover his costs up to the date of the payment in but will have to bear not only his own costs but also the defendant's costs thereafter. This could prove very costly for the plaintiff as it will include the defendant's trial costs.

This could in some cases mean that the plaintiff would recover no compensation at all. As the plaintiff is legally aided the statutory charge will apply, so not only will the defendant's costs be deducted from any award of damages, but the statutory charge will bite as the plaintiff will have failed to recover all of his costs from the defendant.

(3) In addition, the plaintiff must be reminded that he could lose the trial and could be liable to pay some of the defendant's costs pursuant to the Legal Aid Act 1988, ss. 12(1), 17(1) although any costs order against a legally aided party will not be enforced without leave.

(4) In this case Meg is recommending that the plaintiff reject the offer. If it were the converse situation, that is to say Meg is advising the plaintiff to accept the offer, she would have to remind the client of her duty to the Legal Aid Board. If the plaintiff refuses to accept a payment which his solicitor considers reasonable the position should be reported to the Legal Aid Board (see the Civil Legal Aid (General) Regulations 1989, reg. 70). It should be stressed to the plaintiff that this could mean the discharge of his certificate and that he would have to fund the action privately.

Document 48

Watkins & O'Dwyer
Solicitors

17 Sycamore Avenue
Oldcastle OL10 1BR
Tel. 011-111-1111
Fax 011-111-1111
DX Oldcastle 1000

Partners: J. Watkins
A. O'Dwyer

18 August 1997

Ritson & Co.
27 Lonsdale Terrace
Oldcastle OL7 7PP

Our ref: MD/JR/144.346
Your ref: NP/BB/OK/133.1

Dear Sirs

<u>Martin v Easyshop Ltd</u>

Thank you for your letter of 14 August enclosing notice of payment into court.

We have now taken our client's instructions and obtained counsel's advice which indicates that our client's claim is worth considerably more than your offer. Accordingly we write to inform you that we will not be accepting the payment in and to enclose by way of service our summons for summary judgment and interim payment together with affidavit in support of our application for an interim payment.

Finally, we wonder whether or not you are now prepared to let us have a copy of your medical report?

Yours faithfully

Watkins & O'Dwyer

Commentary: Letter from the Plaintiff's Solicitors re issue of Summons

1. Note that the summons for both applications must be served at least 10 clear days before the return day. Now pursuant to RSC (Amendment) 1994 (SI 1994 No. 1975 (L10)) a summons (other than a time summons) must be served within 14 days of issue accompanied by affidavit evidence. Always ensure however that both the summons and the affidavit are served as early as possible. If you serve the affidavit late then the defendant will simply argue at the hearing that it has not had enough time to prepare its arguments and the court will adjourn it. If you serve the affidavit early, this will prevent the defendant from arguing that it did not have enough time to prepare. However, note that Meg did not serve the

GEORGE MARTIN v EASYSHOP LTD

summons immediately, but waited until the defendant's solicitors had served the defence. If Meg had served the summons then the defendant's solicitors would not have had to serve a defence, as the service of such a summons extends the time for service of a defence. If the defendant is given leave to defend the action at the hearing of the Order 14 application, then time effectively begins to run from the date of the order and the defendant has a further 14 days to serve a defence. By waiting until the defence has been served before serving the summons, you keep the pressure on the defendant to serve a defence and then once the defence has been served keep the pressure on by serving a summons for summary judgment.

2. There is no specific time limit in the rules for the defendant to serve an affidavit in reply to the summary judgment application. However, the summons does indicate that if the defendant wishes to serve an affidavit, it must be served at least three days before the return day.

Document 49

Plaintiff: George Martin: 1st
Sworn 20th August 1997
Exhibits GM1

IN THE HIGH COURT OF JUSTICE
QUEEN'S BENCH DIVISION
OLDCASTLE DISTRICT REGISTRY

1997-M-No. 7321

BETWEEN

GEORGE MARTIN   Plaintiff

and

EASYSHOP LIMITED   Defendant

AFFIDAVIT IN SUPPORT OF APPLICATION
PURSUANT TO ORDER 29

I, George Martin of 33 Cherry Street, Oldcastle, OL3 4LL, chartered accountant MAKE OATH and say as follows:

1. I am the Plaintiff in this action and the matters to which I hereafter depose are within my own personal knowledge or otherwise come to me from the source stated. I make this Affidavit in support of my application for an order for an Interim Payment against the Defendant pursuant to Order 29 of the Rules of the Supreme Court.[1]

2. My solicitors inform me that the writ was issued on 3rd July 1997 and sent by way of service together with the statement of claim to the Defendant's solicitors under cover of a letter dated 3rd July 1997. The Defendant then gave notice of intention to defend on 7th July 1997, with a defence being served on 30th July 1997.[2]

3. On 1st August 1997 my solicitors wrote to the Defendant's solicitors informing them of the intention to proceed with an application for judgment. This then brought an admission of liability from the Defendant by its solicitor's letter dated 5th August 1997, a true copy of which is now produced and shown to me at page 1 to 'GM1' and accordingly I make this affidavit on the basis that by the time my application for an interim payment is heard I will have judgment for damages to be assessed.[3]

GEORGE MARTIN v EASYSHOP LTD

4. The details of the accident are set out in the statement of claim (at the time of the accident I was 44 years of age, my date of birth being 30th July 1951) and as a result I suffered personal injuries as set out in the report from Mr Henry Fielding as annexed to my statement of claim which also accurately recites the events immediately following the accident to include my losing consciousness due to the pain, my subsequent admission to hospital and my resultant hospitalisation for 2 days.[4]

5. After I left hospital on 5th February 1996, I returned home for convalescence until I returned to work on 18th March 1996, although during the period after leaving hospital to date I have been undergoing regular check-ups and intensive physiotherapy. Included at page 2 of GM1 is a schedule I have prepared listing all my visits to my local GP and the hospital together with the reason for the visits and the treatment received. The need for continuing care is highlighted in Mr Fielding's report in his prognosis.[5]

6. As a result of my continuing absences from work for ongoing treatment and due to pain together with my inability to sit at my desk for a continuous period of more than 1 hour at a time, my employers, Smythes & Co., asked me to leave their employment and I did so on 17th May 1996. The partners of the firm called me into a meeting and explained their reasons for terminating my employment and there is included at page 3 to GM1, a true copy letter from Smythes & Co. to me dated 20th May 1996 confirming my employment was terminated on 17th May 1996 due to my inability to properly perform my job due to the consequences of the injuries I had sustained in the accident.[6]

7. I had been employed by Smythes & Co. as a chartered accountant in the Audit Department with a salary of £40,000. I obtained a 2:2 honours degree in Accounting in 1972 and then qualified as a Chartered Accountant in 1977. I joined Smythes in 1985. Included at page 4 to GM1 is a true copy letter from Smythes & Co. to my solicitors providing details of my earnings for the 6 months prior to my departure and an indication of my likely pay increase.[7]

8. Since leaving Smythes & Co. I have been unable to obtain alternative employment and am presently registered unemployed. I have written for employment to all accounting firms in Oldcastle and surrounding areas (as listed in the Institute of Chartered Accountants index to firms), but have only managed to obtain three interviews. On each occasion I have been unsuccessful with the reason given due to my inability to work at a desk for any continuous period and my likely absences from work due to the consequences of my injuries. I include at pages 5 to 7 to GM1 true copies of my letters from the three firms with whom I had interviews confirming the reason they could not take me on being due to the reasons I mentioned.[8]

9. My social life has been severely curtailed by the accident. I used to play squash and badminton regularly and was a member of Marsh Sports and Leisure Club. However, I have not been able to play since the accident and realistically there is no prospect of being able to play again. I would additionally from time to time participate in other sports such as football, golf and cricket, but again these are no longer an option.[9]

10. My family life has also been adversely affected. I am married with two children, a boy aged 13 and a girl aged 9. I can no longer take part in the rough and tumble with my children or participate with them in any particular physical activity.

11. I am unable to drive for any great distance due to my inability to stay in a sitting position for any length of time. This has affected my family life to the extent that my wife does not drive and this therefore severely curtails the trips we used to have as a family, from day trips to family holidays driving to Scotland, Wales and Ireland — these will no longer be possible.

12. Due to my inability to carry out any particular physical exercise, my physical condition has deteriorated from what I previously would have said as very fit and active for my age to a condition now where it requires effort just to go for a walk and I have put on significant weight and am now

GEORGE MARTIN v EASYSHOP LTD

17½ stones (at 5ft 11ins tall) against 14½ stones prior to the accident. Unsurprisingly intimacy with my wife has been severely affected.

13.   I have incurred expenses which I consider are directly attributable to the accident of £1,269.84 as set out in the schedule included at page 8 to GM1. I will continue to incur expenses in respect of such things as taxi fares when the pain is such that it prevents me from driving.[10]

14.   At the date of the said accident the Defendant was insured with respect to my claim herein with Marlowe Insurance Group plc of Grays Court, Kings Street, Oldcastle, OL3 4JP.[11]

15.   On 14th August 1997, the Defendant paid into court the sum of £20,000 (GM1, page 9). On the advice of my solicitor I rejected the offer.[12]

16.   I believe that I have a good cause of action against the Defendant, and that my accident was caused by the negligence of the Defendant and that I would be awarded substantial damages at trial. However, the action is unlikely to come on for trial until early next year.

17.   In all the circumstances I would respectfully ask the court to make an Order for an Interim Payment.

SWORN by the above named deponent
at 14 White Street, Oldcastle
in the County of Oldshire
this 20 day of August 1997

George Martin
(signed)

Before me......................
Solicitor/Commissioner for Oaths

NOTES: AFFIDAVIT RE INTERIM PAYMENT

(1)   In accordance with the applicable rules for drafting affidavits (see below) the first paragraph sets out the identity of the deponent and states under which order the application is being made.

(2)   Paragraphs 2 and 3 set out the plaintiff's details and the other requirements as specified by paragraph RSC Ord. 29, r. 10(1)(e)(i) of the rules, i.e., the stage of the action you have reached and whether the defendant admits liability. Essentially, Meg is just giving a narrative of the case so far.

(3)   Paragraph 3 continues by specifying the ground under which the application is made. RSC Ord. 29, r. 11 specifies three grounds under which the application can be made. In this case Meg is making the application on the ground that the defendant has admitted liability and judgment is to be entered. The application could also be made on the ground that if the action proceeded to trial the plaintiff would win substantial damages.

(4)   As for the statement of claim, the plaintiff's age at the time of the accident is specified. The actual details of the accident are not repeated in the affidavit; the statement of claim is, however, exhibited. In accordance with RSC Ord. 29, r. 10(1)(e)(i) the pleadings must be available. Then in accordance with paragraph (f)(i) of the same rule the medical report of Mr Fielding is exhibited. Note, however, that the affidavit states at length the consequences of the accident, i.e., unconsciousness etc. This informs the court what the plaintiff suffered as a result of the accident without the district judge being required to plough through the medical report in meticulous detail.

(5)   The affidavit then continues in a similar vein at paragraph 5 by stating what treatment the plaintiff required as a result of the accident. The affidavit demonstrates that after the accident the plaintiff underwent a variety of treatments and did not make a speedy recovery.

(6) Pursuant to RSC Ord. 29, r. 10(1)(f)(v) the past and future loss of earnings should be set out in detail. In this instance the plaintiff has been forced to leave his employment because of his injuries. Note that the affidavit states that the plaintiff had no alternative but to leave and did not leave voluntarily.

(7) At paragraph 7 the affidavit sets out the plaintiff's educational and employment history. This may seem unnecessary, but it should be included as it demonstrates that the plaintiff was an educated professional man with a promising future which has now been cut short. The court will take this into consideration in assessing the plaintiff's future loss of earnings.

(8) Paragraph 8 is equally important. It shows that it is not only George's employers who believe he is now unemployable. Additionally, it also shows that George has tried to find work in an attempt to mitigate his damages.

(9) Paragraphs 9 to 12 relate to George's loss of amenity claim. Be wary of considering the plaintiff in isolation when considering this head of damages, i.e., don't just consider what effect the injury has had on the plaintiff alone, but consider the effect it has had on the plaintiff's family, e.g., George can no longer play with his children, there are no more family holidays, his relationship with his wife has deteriorated. Additionally, paragraph 9 states the usual things you associate with a loss of amenity claim, e.g., George is now unable to play sports. Remember that the affidavit must state everything the plaintiff can no longer do.

(10) Paragraph 13 emphasises that George's loss is a continuing one. RSC Ord. 29, r. 10(1)(f)(v) provides that the affidavit should say why the plaintiff requires an interim payment. Here George has considerable ongoing expenses. Note, however, the plaintiff does not have to show a particular need for the interim payment (see *Stringman* v *McArdle* [1994] PIQR 230) but if he does have a particular need then the writers can see no reason why the affidavit should not say so. See also the recent case of *Chiron Corporation* v *Murex Diagnostics Ltd (No. 11)* (1996) *The Times*, 15 March which said that as long as there is evidence establishing with reasonable certainty the minimum sum likely to be recoverable in damages, the court can make a substantial interim award despite there being difficult points of law or fact still to be decided.

(11) In accordance with RSC Ord. 29, r. 11(2) Meg verifies that the defendant has the means to pay the damages requested, i.e., they are insured. See further page 89, paragraph 4.

(12) The affidavit then specifies that the defendant has made a payment into court. Note that if liability had not been admitted and Meg was also applying for summary judgment, then there will have to be a separate affidavit in support of the summary judgment application, as the payment in cannot be disclosed until all matters of liability have been decided (see RSC Ord. 22, r. 7).

Commentary: Affidavits

1. Whereas a pleading should not contain any evidence (excepting that already discussed), the purpose of an affidavit is to state evidence. An affidavit is essentially used when it is deemed unnecessary for the witness to attend and the evidence can be easily and expediently dealt with in a written format.

2. The actual style of the affidavit is very much prescribed by the rules of court, in particular RSC Ord. 41 (or CCR Ord. 20, r. 20).

3. Before drafting any affidavit it is vital that you familiarise yourself with the requirements of the applicable order. For the actual presentation of the affidavit see *Practice Direction (Evidence: Documents)* [1983] 1 WLR 922 as amended by *Practice Direction (Evidence: Documents)* [1995] 1 WLR 510 which was implemented to standardise the presentation of all affidavits.

GEORGE MARTIN v EASYSHOP LTD

4. The affidavit should state the title to the case, i.e., the writ heading. However, also in the top right-hand corner, it should state the identity of the deponent (that is the person making the affidavit), the number of the affidavit in relation to that person, the party on whose behalf the affidavit is sworn, the number of exhibits, and the date the affidavit is sworn. In the county court it should additionally include the date the affidavit is filed.

Then between the 'tram lines' it is appropriate to put a heading, namely the affidavit of ... in support of whatever application. It is not wrong if there is no heading, but anything that makes a document clearer must be worthwhile.

5. In accordance with RSC Ord. 41 the affidavit must be expressed in the first person and then state the address and occupation of the deponent. If the deponent was representing a company then it should state his/her role in the company and the address at which the company carries on business.

6. As you can see, the affidavit is divided into numbered paragraphs, numbered consecutively, and each paragraph as far as possible deals with one issue. This is again in accordance with Ord. 41, r. 1.

7. The first paragraph of the affidavit is fairly standard. Before drafting the affidavit you must consider who is going to make it. In practice it is usually the client who will make the affidavit as most of the facts of the case will be within his/her personal knowledge: as an example the directors of a company will have an intimate knowledge of the dealings of the company, the solicitor will not. Only in the most straightforward cases will the solicitor swear the affidavit.

The first paragraph includes:

(a) The reasons why the affidavit is made — in this case the plaintiff is giving evidence in support of his application for an interim payment. Meg must ensure that the affidavit complies with the applicable rules of court, in this case Order 29 (interim payment).

(b) The statement as to the truth and the contents of the affidavit and that it is made from the deponent's personal knowledge. Affidavits are a medium to present evidence and as such must comply with the rules of evidence. However, there is one very important exception to this, for the purposes of interlocutory applications where first hand hearsay is admissible providing that it is declared as such, the source of the hearsay is identified and the deponent believes the hearsay to be true. (Note that the notice provisions contained in the Civil Evidence Act 1995 do not apply to affidavit evidence (see RSC Ord. 38, r. 21(4) and CCR Ord. 20, r. 15(5); and see further commentary at page 118).) This is a rather long way of saying that if the information is not within the knowledge of the deponent then you simply need to say so and say where it comes from. (Note that the deponent is also allowed to give an opinion where appropriate, another exception to the rules of evidence.)

Above all else remember that the affidavit is the sworn evidence of the deponent and as such it must be true and correct.

8. Finally there are two other requirements which you must consider.

First the jurat — this is the wordy section at the end of the affidavit which must be signed by the deponent in the presence of a solicitor or commissioner for oaths or authorised court officer. (Practising solicitors and barristers are now entitled to call themselves commissioners for oaths, but you will find most solicitors strike out 'Commissioners for oaths' as an option.)

The affidavit is usually sworn in front of a solicitor from a nearby firm or at court. The current fee for an affidavit is £5 and for each exhibit £2, an exhibit being any document that you wish to refer to in the body of the affidavit. The only rule that you must remember is that the affidavit should not be sworn in front of a member of your firm.

The second point to note is with regard to amended affidavits. If there is a mistake in the affidavit this can be simply remedied by manuscript amendment prior to being sworn. The deponent must initial the corrections as does the person taking the oath.

Note: When the affidavit is complete, do not forget to file at court.

It would not be unusual at this stage for the defendant's solicitors to propose a without prejudice meeting to discuss quantum, particularly when they are aware that Meg has now obtained counsel's opinion. However, we have assumed that Meg proceeds to the hearing.

STEP 22

Meg receives an affidavit from Ritson & Co. regarding the interim payment application (copy not supplied). She forwards a copy to counsel for his comments and prepares for the forthcoming hearing.

Document 50

Watkins & O'Dwyer

Note

Your name   Meg Davis   Date 4 September 1997

Client's name   George Martin

Time start 3.35 p.m.   Time finished 4.15 p.m.

Considering further advice of counsel, generally reviewing file of Martin v Easyshop in preparation for hearing of interim payment application tomorrow.

Commentary: Defendant's Affidavit

The defendant has served an affidavit exhibiting their medical report in reply to George's affidavit for an interim payment. It has done this so that they may rely on its medical evidence. For the purposes of this case study you should assume that the affidavit opposes the application for interim payment on the grounds that George's condition is due largely to the degenerative condition and not the accident and he is therefore unlikely to recover much by way of damages. In a hearing of this nature it would not be unusual to brief counsel to appear; however we have not done so in this case. If you do intend to instruct counsel as a matter of courtesy tell the other side.

STEP 23

The hearing takes place and Meg is successful in her application for interim payment. At the hearing the district judge gives directions to take the matter up to the assessment of damages.

GEORGE MARTIN v EASYSHOP LTD

Document 51

Watkins & O'Dwyer

Attendance Note

Your name   Meg Davis   Date 5 September 1997

Client's name   George Martin

Person attended   Hearing re applications for summary judgment and interim payment

Attending District Judge Barratt re Order 14 application and application for interim payment. I discussed the matter with Mr Barker of Ritson & Co. before the appointment. However we were unable to reach an agreement as to the quantum of the claim.

Entering before District Judge at 2.20 p.m. I informed District Judge Barratt that the defendant had now admitted liability and therefore the Order 14 application was not contested.

With regard to my application for an interim payment I took the District Judge through the affidavit of George Martin and pointed out that my client would be unable to manage financially if the application was not granted. I referred the court to the medical report which indicated that the plaintiff would be unlikely to work again as an accountant. I also referred the court to the defendant's payment into court.

In reply Mr Barker pointed out that his evidence indicated that the plaintiff's condition was caused by a degenerative condition and not the fall and it was uncertain as to whether or not he would return to work. He referred the court to the report of Mr Adams.

I replied that in the opinion of Mr Fielding the plaintiff's fall had brought about his present condition of an entrapped nerve, and it was far from certain that the plaintiff was suffering from any degenerative condition.

District Judge Barratt said it seemed clear that the plaintiff would obtain substantial damages for loss of earnings, though the amount was far from certain. However, given that the defendant had made a payment into court, he did not feel it unreasonable to order that the defendant pay £2,000 by way of an interim payment.

District Judge Barratt then went on to consider the directions for the future conduct of the action. It was agreed that the automatic directions were appropriate save that the time limits were varied.

I then asked for the costs of the application. Mr Barker said that as damages were still to be assessed, costs should be in the cause. District Judge Barratt said that as I had been successful then I should have my costs in any event.

Engaged in hearing 1hr 20mins

Travelling time   10mins

Waiting time   20mins

Commentary: The Hearing

1.   At the hearing George is given, on the defendant's admission, interlocutory judgment on his Order 14 application, i.e., final only as to liability. There will have to be a further hearing where damages are assessed pursuant to RSC Ord. 37. The subsequent hearing is likely to be in front of a district judge in open court. As damages are likely to be high it may be appropriate to refer the matter to a High Court judge. Meg has also obtained an interim payment which will be paid out of the monies in court. The interim payment must not be communicated to the court until all questions of liability and the amount of the damages has been decided.

Meg will now want to obtain further medical evidence and/or counsel's opinion.

2.   The court has then given directions for the future conduct of the action. Directions are simply a list of steps for the future conduct of the action. In a personal injury matter, in both the High Court and county court, what are called the automatic directions apply (see RSC Ord. 25, r. 8). Essentially the list is designed to get the parties ready for trial. The directions take effect 14 days after close of pleadings, which is 14 days after service of a defence or 28 days after service of a defence and counterclaim. However, in this case the situation is slightly different. Liability has been admitted, therefore the court considers which of the automatic directions must be complied with to get the case ready for the hearing on quantum.

3.   It is often the case that the parties will try and agree directions before the hearing if the automatic directions do not apply. The court will then consider these directions, decide whether they are appropriate, and make what further directions it considers necessary.

4.   Pursuant to RSC Ord. 37, r. 1 and the notes in *The White Book* at 37/1/1 where judgment has been given and damages are to be assessed there is no need to apply separately for directions (i.e., to take out a summons for directions). Hence the district judge will look at the case and the directions sought by the parties. He can make any directions as to the particulars of special damages, discovery, evidence or any other matters, (see the notes in *The White Book* at 37/2/2). He may also direct that the evidence may be given by affidavit if appropriate.

5.   Listed below is a commentary on each of the automatic directions.

   (a)   Discovery and inspection (see RSC Ord. 24, r. 2)

      Discovery is when the parties in the action reveal to each other details of all the relevant documents they hold. Generally the term 'discovery' is taken to mean the disclosure and subsequent inspection of the relevant documents. Discovery enables each party to evaluate the strength of the other side's case and hopefully promote a settlement. It must be carried out honestly and thoroughly. The parties must disclose all relevant documents (providing they are not privileged), even if they are harmful to their case. A document is classed as relevant if it concerns a point in issue, will advance a party's case or damage the case of one's opponent, or it will save costs. In addition the document must be 'in a party's possession, custody or power'.

      Privilege which excuses disclosure falls into four classes:

   (i)   Legal professional privilege

      Documents falling into this category include:

- Lawyer/client communications. Such documents will be privileged if they are written by or to the solicitor in his professional capacity and for the purposes of obtaining legal advice or assistance for the client.

GEORGE MARTIN v EASYSHOP LTD

- Communications between the solicitor and a third party. Such documents will be privileged if they come into existence after litigation is contemplated or commenced and they are made with a view to litigation, either to give or obtain advice or for the purposes of obtaining evidence.

- Communications between the party personally and a third party. These documents will only be privileged if the dominant purpose for which they were prepared was to obtain legal advice (see *Waugh* v *BRB* [1980] AC 521). If these documents were made prior to the proceedings, then it is unlikely that they will attract privilege. Legal professional privilege is curtailed fairly strictly to the client/lawyer relationship.

(ii) Documents which are without prejudice. The definition of 'without prejudice' is that nothing said without prejudice can be referred to at trial unless the parties consent. However, do not think that using these magic words in a letter will automatically mean that it is without prejudice; it will be the contents of the letter which will determine whether or not it is without prejudice. There must be a dispute between the parties and the letter must be an offer to settle.

(iii) Documents tending to incriminate the party who would produce them. An example of this is where the document would incriminate the party's spouse.

(iv) Documents privileged on the grounds of public policy/public interest.

As liability has been admitted discovery will be limited to those documents relating to special damages. This would also be the case in an action that arises out of a road traffic accident. The special damages are normally agreed with the other side. However if they are not, the plaintiff will have to prove every item by way of producing receipts and proving his loss of earnings.

Discovery is within 14 days of close of pleadings and inspection seven days thereafter.

Note that the litigant himself is under a duty to give complete and true discovery and that the obligation is a continuing one. In *Vernon* v *Bosley* (1996) *The Times*, 19 December the plaintiff had been awarded substantial damages in January 1995 for psychiatric injuries inflicted after seeing his two daughters drown in a car driven by the defendant. Liability was not in dispute. Some months after the judgment the defendant's solicitor received anonymously two judgments dated January 1995 relating to separate proceedings involving the defendant concerning contact with his remaining children. These judgments indicated that the defendant's psychiatric condition had improved considerably. These reports were not privileged as they related to proceedings under the Children Act 1989 and the court held that they should have been disclosed to the defendant before judgment was given in 1995. Any litigant was under a duty to the court and that continued until judgment was given notwithstanding the nature of his legal advice. The plaintiff knew when he was giving evidence that the position had altered and the evidence he was giving was no longer true, and he was under a duty not to mislead the court. His barrister was also under a duty; if the plaintiff had failed/refused to disclose the reports then the barrister should have withdrawn from the case. Accordingly, the plaintiff's damages were significantly reduced.

(b) Expert evidence to be disclosed within 14 weeks

This is the main direction the parties will have to agree upon. Essentially the parties have to disclose the substance of the expert evidence on which they intend to rely. If reports are not disclosed then usually they cannot be produced at trial unless the court makes an order to the contrary. The automatic directions provide for exchange of up to two medical reports, reports to be exchanged within 14 weeks of close of pleadings. This is appropriate in this case as Meg will be instructing a further expert in the light of the defendant's report. Obviously Meg has already disclosed one report when pleadings were served and could if she wished simply rely on this evidence.

GEORGE MARTIN v EASYSHOP LTD

Note that if the plaintiff has obtained an unfavourable report this does not have to be disclosed. Only that evidence which a party intends to rely on at trial need be disclosed to the other side.

There are no further experts that Meg wishes to rely on (the automatic directions make provision for one non-medical expert at trial).

(c) Exchange of witness statements

From 16 November 1992 pursuant to the automatic directions, within 14 weeks of close of pleadings, parties must serve written statements of the oral evidence they intend to rely on at trial. This provision was introduced in an attempt to speed up matters and facilitate settlements. As liability is no longer in issue the only witness statements Meg will wish to rely on will be those statements which establish that the client can no longer work and the effect the injury has had on his lifestyle. She will therefore serve the client's witness statement and additionally take a statement from his wife, children and perhaps even George's friends with whom he used to play sport.

If there is a potential problem with a witness statement it is perhaps advisable to ask for a longer period before exchange to enable counsel to settle the statements.

See page 115 for the actual witness statement.

STEP 24

Meg draws up the order (in the High Court the party whose application is heard has the obligation to draw up the order), has it sealed at court and serves a sealed copy on Ritson & Co. Meg obtains the payment out and forwards this to George (copy letter not supplied).

GEORGE MARTIN v EASYSHOP LTD

Document 52

IN THE HIGH COURT OF JUSTICE   1997-M-No. 7321
QUEEN'S BENCH DIVISION
OLDCASTLE DISTRICT REGISTRY

BETWEEN

GEORGE MARTIN   Plaintiff

and

EASYSHOP LIMITED   Defendant

The 5th day of September 1997

The Defendant having given notice of intention to defend herein and the Court having under Order 14, Rule 3, ordered that judgment as hereinafter provided be entered for the Plaintiff against the Defendant

IT IS THIS DAY ADJUDGED that the Defendant do pay the Plaintiff damages to be assessed and costs in the assessment.

1997–M–No. 7321

IN THE HIGH COURT OF JUSTICE

QUEEN'S BENCH DIVISION

OLDCASTLE DISTRICT REGISTRY

DATED 5th SEPTEMBER 1997

BETWEEN

GEORGE MARTIN   Plaintiff

AND

EASYSHOP LIMITED   Defendant

JUDGMENT
UNDER ORDER 14, RULE 3

Watkins & O'Dwyer
17 Sycamore Avenue
Oldcastle
OL10 1BR

Plaintiff's Solicitor

Solicitor's Reference
MD/JR/144.346

GEORGE MARTIN v EASYSHOP LTD

Document 53

IN THE HIGH COURT OF JUSTICE   1997-M-No. 7321
QUEEN'S BENCH DIVISION
OLDCASTLE DISTRICT REGISTRY

BEFORE DISTRICT JUDGE BARRATT IN CHAMBERS

BETWEEN

GEORGE MARTIN   <u>Plaintiff</u>

and

EASYSHOP LIMITED   <u>Defendant</u>

ORDER

UPON hearing Solicitors for both parties

And upon reading the Affidavits of George Martin and Nigel Peters

And upon judgment having been given for the Plaintiff with damages to be assessed

IT IS ORDERED THAT:

(1)   The sum of £2,000 be paid out of the monies paid into Court by the Defendant forthwith to the Plaintiff as a payment on account of any damages which the Defendant may subsequently be held liable to pay to the Plaintiff.

(2)   The Plaintiff within 28 days to serve on the Defendant their schedule of special damages, such schedule to be agreed if possible.

(3)   The Plaintiff and the Defendant to disclose their expert medical evidence upon which they intend to rely by 1st October 1997 and, in the absence of agreement, the Plaintiff and the Defendant be at liberty to call expert medical evidence limited to 2 witnesses for the Plaintiff and Defendant respectively.

(4)   The Plaintiff to serve on the Defendant witness statements as to facts on whom they intend to rely at the assessment hearing no later than 56 days prior to the hearing.

(5)   The matter to be listed for an assessment hearing before the District Judge for the first available date after the 2nd December 1997. Estimated length 2 days.

(6)   Costs to be the Plaintiff's in any event.[1]

Dated 5th September 1997.

NOTES: ORDER

(1)   The order merely reflects the automatic directions (see commentary at pages 107 *et seq.*). The only other point to add is that 'costs are the plaintiff's in any event' meaning that the costs of this application will be awarded to the plaintiff regardless of the outcome of the final hearing. This is because the plaintiff was successful on his application and the costs involved were accordingly incurred because the defendant failed to consent to a valid request from the plaintiff at the outset.

STEP 25

Meg sends a copy of the defendant's medical report, which they have now disclosed, to Mr Fielding for comment (this letter has not been reproduced) and proceeds to instruct a further expert in accordance with counsel's instructions.

Document 54

Watkins & O'Dwyer
Solicitors

17 Sycamore Avenue
Oldcastle OL10 1BR
Tel. 011-111-1111
Fax 011-111-1111
DX Oldcastle 1000

Partners: J. Watkins
A. O'Dwyer

9 September 1997

G Johnson, esq
193 Banbury Way
Oldcastle
OL6 37Y

Our ref: MD/JR/144.346

Dear Mr Johnson

Re Our Client George Martin, d.o.b. 30.7.51.
address 33 Cherry Street, Oldcastle, OL3 4LL

We act for the above named in connection with a personal injury claim. Mr Martin was injured in an accident at Easyshop Ltd. He suffered serious back injuries, notably an entrapped nerve.

We should be grateful if you would prepare a report for the purposes of a personal injury claim on the injury, the treatment given, present condition and future prognosis. You will note it is alleged that our client was already suffering from spondylolisthesis.

We have already obtained a report from Mr Fielding and we enclose this together with a copy of our client's statement, hospital records and relevant GP notes. We also enclose a copy of the defendant's medical report. You will note that it appears to contradict the report of Mr Fielding in that it concludes that our client's present condition is due solely to the spondylolisthesis.

The appointment should be made direct with our client who can be contacted on telephone number 231 1366. We confirm that we will be responsible for your fee.

Yours sincerely

Meg Davis

GEORGE MARTIN v EASYSHOP LTD

Commentary: Letter to Expert

See commentary at page 56. Here we can see why it is important to have the medical notes disclosed to the solicitor and not the expert. It may be prudent to check with the Legal Aid Board to ensure you have authority to instruct another expert. However where the defendant has admitted liability, this should not be a problem.

STEP 26

Meg receives a call from Mr Fielding. He has now reviewed the defendant's medical report.

Document 55

Watkins & O'Dwyer

Attendance Note

Your name   Meg Davis   Date 12 September 1997

Client's name   George Martin

Person attended   Mr Fielding

Time start 2.50 p.m.   Time finished 2.55 p.m.

Mr Fielding rang. He said he had reviewed the defendant's report, but he had really nothing to add to his original report. He felt that there was a possibility that Mr Martin's spine was not as strong as that of a spine of a healthy person, but this was certainly not the cause of his present disability. At the very most his previous condition only had a minor effect on his present condition. He said he would put his views in writing.

I queried whether there would be any times when he would not be able to attend the hearing to give evidence. Mr Fielding indicated that he would be on holiday from 6–13 October, but other than that he would be available until March next year. I said that counsel would probably wish to have a conference in the next month or so and that I would be serving him with a subpoena before the hearing as a matter of courtesy.

Commentary: Witnesses

Note that it is important to find out if your witnesses will be unavailable at any time before arranging a hearing date. Meg has also said that she will serve Mr Fielding with a subpoena. A subpoena is only strictly necessary to ensure that the witness will attend the trial, and is perhaps associated with the reluctant witness. However, frequently experts wish to be served with a subpoena, first to remind them of the hearing date, and second so that they can arrange their busy schedules accordingly. For the format of the subpoena see page 126.

Note that whilst this matter is not proceeding to trial but instead an assessment hearing, the attendance of witnesses may still be compelled by the issue of a writ of subpoena pursuant to RSC Ord. 37, r. 1(3).

STEP 27

Meg then prepares the draft witness statement. She arranges to see George and to go through the witness statement and special damages schedules. George agrees that these are correct.

GEORGE MARTIN v EASYSHOP LTD

Document 56

IN THE HIGH COURT OF JUSTICE
QUEEN'S BENCH DIVISION
OLDCASTLE DISTRICT REGISTRY

1997-M-No. 7321

BETWEEN

GEORGE MARTIN

Plaintiff

and

EASYSHOP LIMITED

Defendant

WITNESS STATEMENT OF GEORGE MARTIN

I George Martin of 33 Cherry Street, Oldcastle, OL3 4LL will say as follows:

1. I am 46 years old and my date of birth is 30.7.51. I am married and have 2 children, a son aged 13 and a daughter aged 9.

2. Up to 2nd February 1996 I worked for Smythes & Co., a firm of chartered accountants, as a chartered accountant in the audit department. I had joined them in 1985 after obtaining a degree in accountancy and qualified as a Chartered Accountant in 1977.

3. On 2nd February 1996, at approximately 6.45 p.m., I was shopping in the Defendant's supermarket at Unit 7, Beech Court, Oldcastle when I slipped on some olive oil which had been spilt on the floor, fell over and landed on my back very heavily.

4. I recall feeling tremendous pain at the base of my back. I tried to sit up but I could not move.

5. Within seconds there were people around me asking me if I was OK, could I move and I remember one lady saying something about having warned the manager about the oil 5 minutes ago and still nobody came to clear it up. I then lost consciousness and the next thing I remember is waking up in the Oldcastle General Hospital. This was at approximately 10 p.m. and I must therefore have been unconscious for about 3 hours.

6. I was being attended to by Mr Astley, a consultant orthopaedic surgeon. I was x-rayed and scanned and Mr Astley told me that I had a serious back injury and it was the type of injury that was difficult to treat and I would suffer recurring pain probably for the rest of my life.

7. I remained in hospital for 2 days, leaving on the morning of 5th February when I returned home for further convalescence.

8. I continued to receive treatment at the out patients' clinic from Mr Goode, undergoing physiotherapy twice a week (travelling to and from hospital by taxi as I could not, due to my injury, drive).

9. At the start of this physiotherapy treatment I was unable to sit at all and had to keep my back straight due to the pain. I could walk for very short distances using a stick, but certainly could not negotiate the stairs. I was therefore sleeping downstairs and having to be attended to constantly by my wife (who does not go out to work) which included bathing me in our downstairs bathroom and helping me to use the toilet, and sometimes having to use a bedpan which the hospital supplied.

115

GEORGE MARTIN v EASYSHOP LTD

10. The pain at that time was constant, varying in degrees from a background pain up to tremendous shooting pains when I moved. I was on a constant course of painkillers supplied by the hospital through the dispensary and these, coupled with the pain, made me continually tired and irritable.

11. After the end of the first 6 weeks of physiotherapy I could walk, slowly, for the greater distances and could negotiate the stairs with care. The pain had also subsided in both duration and frequency, but was still a major factor in my discomfort and would often be excruciating if I in any way jarred my back.

12. At that point I returned to work on 18th March and my employer had bought a special chair for me which could be set to various positions by using a control box which operated electric motors in the body of the chair. My office was also relocated on the ground floor of the office building and it was also obvious that everyone was going out of their way to help me, from fetching me cups of tea to arranging taxis to take me between home and work.

13. I continued to have ongoing treatment and I annex hereto at page 1 a schedule of visits to my local GP and the hospital, together with the reasons for the visits and the treatment received. It can be seen that, for the period 18th March to 17th May, I needed time off work frequently to attend for continuing treatment and, over and above this, I was unable to attend work on a number of occasions due to the pain being too great. Additionally, whilst at work I would often need to lie down for long periods due to the pain.

14. As a result of my continuous absences from work and lack of productivity whilst there, together with the lack of any optimism for improvement, the partners of the firm called me to a meeting on 17th May and told me they would have to let me go, explaining their reasons which were entirely due to the absences etc. I mentioned above.

15. I was not particularly surprised at this turn of events and I was grateful for their attempts to help me back into employment. I left that day and they paid me a lump sum in the amount of £10,000 as a gesture of thanks and goodwill.

16. Since leaving Smythes & Co. I have attempted to find full and part-time work with accountancy firms in Oldcastle, but to no avail. Of 26 letters sent to the various firms, I only obtained three interviews, but each of those three firms rejected me, quoting my inability to work at a desk for long periods and likely absences from work as the reason.

17. My social life has been severely curtailed by the accident. I used to play squash and badminton regularly and was a member of Marsh Sports and Leisure Club. However I have not been able to play since the accident and realistically there is no prospect of being able to play again. I would additionally, from time to time, participate in other sports such as football, golf and cricket but again these are no longer an option.

18. My family life has also been adversely affected. I am married with two children, a boy aged 13 and a girl aged 9. I can no longer take part in the rough and tumble with my children or participate with them in any particular physical activity.

19. I am unable to drive for any great distance due to my inability to stay in a sitting position for any length of time. This has affected my family life to the extent that my wife does not drive and this therefore severely curtails the trips we used to have as a family, from day trips to family holidays driving to Scotland, Wales and Ireland — these will no longer be possible.

20. Due to my inability to carry out any particular physical exercise, my physical condition has deteriorated from what I previously would have said as very fit and active for my age, to a condition now where it requires effort just to go for a walk and I have put on significant weight

GEORGE MARTIN v EASYSHOP LTD

and am now 17 ½ stones (at 5ft 11ins tall) against 14 ½ stones prior to the accident. Unsurprisingly, intimacy with my wife has been severely affected.

21.   With regard to my financial losses, when I left Smythes & Co. I was earning £40,000 gross per annum which worked out at £493.25 per week, paid monthly. I was paid by Smythes & Co. up to 17th May and then, as I say, received a lump sum payment of £10,000. I have not been able to earn since leaving Smythes and have been since 31st January registered unemployed. Annexed at page 2 is a schedule of benefits I have received since my accident.

22.   I have additionally incurred expenses for such items as prescription charges and taxi fares. Annexed at page 3 is a schedule of those expenses.

This Statement consisting of 3 pages is true to the best of my knowledge, information and belief and I make it knowing that if I say anything which I do not believe to be true I may be liable to be prosecuted.

Signed   George Martin   Dated 16th September 1997

Commentary: Witness Statement

1.   There is no prescribed form but you should refer to RSC Ord. 38, r. 2A and the *Practice Direction* of 1983 (*The White Book*, 41/11/1) on affidavits. The heading of the action should be at the top of the statement, all pages should be numbered (although it is not here), and whilst not strictly necessary, it should contain a statement that the statement is true to the best of the deponent's knowledge and belief.

2.   In this case Meg will have seen George on several occasions to update his original proof of evidence and obtain further information. It is from this additional information, the original proof of evidence and George's affidavit re his interim payment application, that she has prepared the witness statement.

3.   The statement should contain all of the evidence in chief the witness proposes to give at the hearing. For example, the statement meticulously sets out the effect the injuries had on George's lifestyle and the expenses he has incurred because of his injuries (note the schedules to be annexed to the statement have not been reproduced, but would largely follow the special damages calculation but contain additional information, e.g., why George incurred a particular expense). Remember, the witness will not be able to adduce any other evidence without the leave of the court.

4.   Although not really applicable in this case it is a question of tactics as to what to put in the witness statement, subject to the overriding principle that you must not mislead the court. You must consider whether a potentially damaging piece of evidence is likely to come out in cross-examination or try and mitigate its effect by adducing it as evidence-in-chief. Is it better to leave the evidence out or can you describe it in a less damaging way? Note for example in this witness statement, Meg has purposely left out the fact that George was told he had a weak back by Mr Astley in hospital.

5.   There may be a further statement prepared for counsel prior to trial for the purposes of re-examination and cross-examination.

If you are not ready to exchange, or are unwilling to do so, then you should apply to the court by way of an interlocutory application.

Finally, under RSC Ord. 38, r. 2A(6) where a party serving a statement under this rule does not call the witness, no other party may put the statement in evidence at the trial. Further, paragraph 11 provides that no person can make use of the statement other than in the proceedings in which it was served unless the party serving it gives consent, the court gives leave or it has been put in evidence.

Further Commentary: The Effect of the Civil Evidence Act 1995

The witness statement reflects the changes brought about by the Civil Evidence Act 1995. The rules of court implementing the Act came into force on 31 January 1997 (see Rules of the Supreme Court (Amendment No. 2) 1996 (SI 1996 No. 3218), rr. 8 and 9, and the County Court (Amendment No. 2) Rules 1996 (SI 1996 No. 3219), rr. 2 and 3). They do not apply to proceedings where:

(a) directions have been given, or orders have been made, as to evidence to be given at the trial or hearing, or

(b) where the trial or hearing has begun,

before 31 January 1997.

Now evidence shall not be rendered inadmissible on the grounds that it is hearsay, which is defined under s. 1(2) of the Act as 'a statement made otherwise than by a person while giving oral evidence in the proceedings which is tendered as evidence of the matters stated'. Whereas before the introduction of the Civil Evidence Act 1995 Meg would have edited out all of the hearsay evidence from the proof of evidence, now when drafting the witness statement this is no longer the case and such evidence is now admissible. So, for example, at paragraph 4 of George's witness statement it is perfectly permissible for him to say 'I remember one lady saying something about having warned the manager about the oil five minutes ago and still nobody came to clear it up'. Note, however, that the hearsay evidence must still be credible.

A party wishing to adduce hearsay evidence must normally give notice to the other side and give particulars of that evidence though the parties may agree to waive the notice procedure (ss. 2(1), (2), (3); RSC Ord. 38, r. 21; CCR Ord. 20, r. 15). If a party fails to comply with the notice procedure that in itself will not render the hearsay evidence inadmissible, though pursuant to s. 2(4) the court may take this into account in considering the weight to be attached to the hearsay evidence and furthermore the party may be penalised in costs.

RSC Ord. 38, r. 21; CCR Ord. 20, r. 15 stipulate that the hearsay notice should:

(a) state that it is such a notice;

(b) identify the hearsay statement;

(c) identify the maker of the hearsay statement;

(d) state why the maker will not give oral evidence (note that in this case as Gina Wright will be giving evidence this requirement is superfluous).

If, as in George's case, the hearsay evidence is contained in a witness statement the notice should identify that part of the statement which contains the hearsay evidence (RSC Ord. 38, r. 21; CCR Ord. 20, r. 15).

Where witness statements are served then the hearsay notice should be served at the same time on every other party. Where no witness statements are served:

(a) in the High Court where the cause or matter is required to be set down for trial or hearing or adjourned into court the hearsay notice should be served within 28 days after it is set down or adjourned or within such other period as the court may specify (RSC Ord. 38, r. 21); and

(b) in any other case the hearsay notice must be served within 28 days after the date on which an appointment for the first hearing is obtained or within such other period as the court may specify;

(c) in the county court at least 28 days before the day fixed for the trial or hearing the hearsay notice must be served and filed in court save that where no defence is filed or the defence is filed less than 28 days before the date fixed for trial this time limit shall not apply unless the court directs otherwise (CCR Ord. 15, r. 15).

Note that although compliance with time limits will not prove fatal to the admissibility of hearsay evidence, if that evidence is contained in a witness statement then the parties must adhere to the time limits for exchange (see further page 176, note 5(c)).

Under s. 2(1) of the Act the other party may request any additional details of the hearsay evidence which are 'reasonable and practicable'. For example, a party could request that the time and place the hearsay statement was made and to whom it was made is specified. Clearly the expense of providing this information will be a factor which will have to be considered under the 'reasonable and practicable' test. Note that neither the Act nor the rules specify a time limit for requesting this further information.

A further change introduced by s. 3 of the Act is that if a party adduces hearsay evidence but then decides not to call that person as a witness then his/her opponent may call that person as a witness for the purposes of cross-examining that witness as if the witness had been called and his statement were put in examination-in-chief (see RSC Ord. 38, r. 22; CCR Ord. 20, r. 16). Previously no other person could make use of the statement unless the party serving it gave consent or the court gave leave. Should a party wish to cross-examine the maker of the statement then he/she must apply to the court within 28 days of service of the hearsay notice. Further if the maker of the statement is not called by the party tendering the hearsay evidence then another party may adduce evidence to attack that witness's credibility providing he/she gives notice to the other party within 28 days of service of the hearsay notice.

As for the 1968 Act, under s. 4 the court will continue to assess the weight to be attached to the hearsay evidence and will consider:

(a) whether it would have been reasonable and practical to call the witness instead;

(b) whether the statement was made contemporaneously;

(c) whether the evidence is multiple hearsay;

(d) any motive of any persons involved to conceal or misrepresent matters;

(e) if the statement has been edited or made in collaboration with another or for a particular purpose;

(f) whether the statement has been purposely adduced as hearsay to prevent a proper evaluation of its weight.

It may be, therefore, where a party has a very weak reason for not calling the witness then the other party will not rely on s. 3 and call the witness, but instead leave the court to draw an adverse inference under s. 4.

Commentary on the remaining provisions is outside the scope of this work (for a detailed commentary on the Act see Northumbria Law Press Impact Series — Civil Evidence Act 1995) but note that pursuant to s. 11 the Act only applies to civil proceedings where the strict rules of evidence apply; consequently it does not apply to the small claims court and industrial tribunals. Further, both the High Court and county court rules do not apply to any interlocutory proceedings as they are not the final hearing of the matter, save that they will apply to any hearing concerning the assessment of damages.

Finally, note that the rule governing the admissibility of opinion evidence remains unchanged.

GEORGE MARTIN v EASYSHOP LTD

STEP 28

Meg receives the second medical report from Mr Johnson (copy not supplied). She serves Mr Fielding's report on Ritson & Co., together with an updated special damages schedule and her witness statement. Ritson & Co. write back suggesting a without prejudice (for the meaning of this see page 107) meeting of the experts to try and agree the medical evidence. This takes place, and the areas of dispute are produced in a joint statement.

Document 57

Ritson & Co.

27 Lonsdale Terrace
Oldcastle
OL7 7PP

29 September 1997

Watkins & O'Dwyer
17 Sycamore Avenue
Oldcastle
OL10 1BR

Your ref: MD/JR/144.346
Our ref: NP/BB/OK/133.1

Dear Sirs

Martin v Easyshop Ltd

Thank you for your report which we received today. We write to enquire whether you are agreeable to our mutual experts meeting on a without prejudice basis to try and narrow down the areas in dispute.

We await your reply.

Yours faithfully

Ritson & Co.

Commentary: Joint Meeting of Experts

1. The reply to this letter and subsequent telephone calls to experts have not been reproduced for the sake of brevity.

2. To hold a meeting of this kind is good practice; it saves time ultimately at the final hearing and it may be possible to even agree the medical evidence. The meeting is held on a without prejudice basis (for the meaning of this see page 107), therefore allowing free discussion. At the end of the meeting a joint statement will be produced indicating the areas that the experts are in agreement. This in line with paragraph 4 of the *Practice Direction (Civil Litigation: Case Management)* 1995 (*The White Book*, vol. 2, pt. 30, para. 973/1) which stresses that the parties should try as far as possible to narrow down the issues, in particular the expert issues in dispute.

3. If one side refuses to agree to the meeting, the other party can apply to the court. As the court can now order the parties to hold a meeting pursuant to RSC Ord. 38, r. 38(3), it is likely the application would succeed.

GEORGE MARTIN v EASYSHOP LTD

4. Note that as Meg has served a further medical report she must serve an updated special damages schedule (see RSC Ord. 25, r. 8(1A)).

STEP 29

The experts meet and a joint statement is produced. Meg writes to George (copy letter not reproduced) informing him of her progress to date.

Commentary: Statement from Experts

The joint statement has not been reproduced. The areas in dispute remain the actual cause of the plaintiff's condition, i.e., whether his present condition was due to the fall or a degenerative condition as alleged by the defendant.

STEP 30

Meg calls Mr Barker at Ritson & Co. He confirms that he is ready for the hearing. Meg checks that all the directions have been complied with and applies for a hearing date. She serves notice of this on Ritson & Co.

Commentary: The Assessment Hearing

The procedure for obtaining a further hearing is set out at RSC Ord. 37, r. 2(2). Meg will take a copy of the judgment (a photocopy indorsed with the court seal will suffice) to the listing section and obtain an appointment. Notice of appointment must be served on the party against whom the judgment was given at least seven days before the appointment.

STEP 31

Meg sends the second report of Mr Johnson and the experts' joint statement to counsel along with a brief.

Document 58

IN THE HIGH COURT OF JUSTICE
QUEEN'S BENCH DIVISION
OLDCASTLE DISTRICT REGISTRY

1997-M-No. 7321

BETWEEN

GEORGE MARTIN   Plaintiff

and

EASYSHOP LIMITED   Defendant

BRIEF TO COUNSEL TO ATTEND AT OLDCASTLE DISTRICT
REGISTRY ON 9TH DECEMBER 1997 TO REPRESENT THE PLAINTIFF ON AN
ASSESSMENT OF DAMAGES HEARING

Counsel is sent herewith:

1. Papers previously before Counsel.

2. Copy Witness Statements of:

GEORGE MARTIN v EASYSHOP LTD

    (a)   George Martin dated 16th September 1997.

    (b)   Laura Martin dated 16th September 1997.

3.   Copy Affidavit of G. Martin sworn 20th August 1997.

4.   Copy Affidavit of N. Peters sworn 2nd September 1997.

5.   Copy joint report of Mr H. Fielding, Mr R. Adams and Mr A. Johnson dated 30th September 1997.

6.   Copy Order 14 Judgment dated 5th September 1997.

7.   Copy Order for Interim Payment and Directions dated 5th September 1997.

8.   Copy attendance note of Counsel's advice dated 4th September 1997.

9.   Copy correspondence.

10.   Copy notice of assessment hearing.

Counsel will recall this matter in which he has previously advised Instructing Solicitors for Mr G. Martin on quantum and Counsel is referred to the papers previously before him, together with his Advice and the attendance note of his telephone advice following his consideration of the other side's medical report of Mr Adams.

Counsel will see that summary judgment for damages to be assessed was given on 5th September 1997 on the Defendant's admission and at the same hearing an Order for an interim payment was made equivalent to the amount paid into Court by the Defendant 4 weeks earlier as per the Notice of Payment In.

Counsel will see the directions set out in the Order (doc 7) and will see these have been complied with — the medical experts having had a joint meeting and produced the joint report included at doc 5 and witness statements of Mr Martin and his wife having been served on the other side on 23rd September 1997.

The assessment of damages hearing has now been listed for 9th December with a time estimate of 2 days. Counsel is therefore briefed to represent the Plaintiff at the hearing.

Should Counsel wish to see Mr Martin in conference prior to the hearing, or require any further information, or considers Instructing Solicitors should deal with any outstanding matters prior to the hearing, he should not hesitate to contact Ms Davis of Instructing Solicitors.

Dated 23rd October 1997

Commentary: Brief

1. The instructions to counsel to attend a hearing are called a 'brief', e.g., 'Brief to Counsel to attend Trial'. 'Instructions' are to prepare written work, a 'brief' concerns oral representation. Note, however, that the solicitor will be in attendance at the hearing to, at the very least, take a note of the evidence.

2. Essentially there is very little to add by way of commentary that has not already been said when we discussed instructions to counsel. Again, all documents should be sent, e.g., pleadings, medical reports etc. However, it should not include irrelevant summonses or previous instructions to counsel.

Do not send the original documents to counsel; they are frequently lost. The documents should be arranged in a sensible order in a ringbinder file divided as appropriate.

3. As you can see, in this instance Meg has only included the information in the brief which she considers relevant, i.e., that quantum is in dispute and referring counsel to the joint statement of the experts and the various witness statements. To summarise, the brief should bring counsel up to date with the progress of the litigation in particular whether there are any evidential difficulties, have there been any attempts to negotiate a settlement, is the client prepared to settle and is there a pre-hearing conference.

4. Remember that the matter is legally aided and that a copy of the certificate should be enclosed and the backsheet indorsed with the legal aid reference number. The Legal Aid Certificate may have had to have the limitation removed to allow counsel to be briefed, but this would have happened when the action was 'set down' for hearing.

5. With reference to the final paragraph of the brief, at the very least counsel will want to see Mr Martin in conference for an hour or so before the hearing, but it will probably be useful for this to take place a week or so before the hearing.

6. The Bar's 'Written Standards for the Conduct of Professional Work: General Standards' states that a barrister is not considered to accept the work until he has expressly accepted it. Therefore check with your counsel a day or so after delivering the brief.

7. Bear in mind also that the brief fee covers only the first day of a hearing and thereafter counsel is entitled to be paid a refresher for each subsequent day. Note that the brief fee is still payable even if the case subsequently settles, though the solicitor and counsel may come to some mutual agreement in the event that this should happen. In legal aid cases counsel can receive an interim payment from the Legal Aid Board of up to 75 per cent of his fees. As to the remainder of his fee, counsel is still reliant on the solicitor submitting his bill for taxation (see the Civil Legal Aid (General) Regulations 1989, reg. 112).

STEP 32

Meg writes to George and informs him of the hearing date (copy letter not supplied). She writes to counsel informing him of the same and also to the two medical experts, Mr Fielding and Mr Johnson. She issues two subpoenas for both experts respectively.

GEORGE MARTIN v EASYSHOP LTD

Document 59

Watkins & O'Dwyer
Solicitors

17 Sycamore Avenue
Oldcastle OL10 1BR
Tel. 011-111-1111
Fax 011-111-1111
DX Oldcastle 1000

Partners: J. Watkins
A. O'Dwyer

30 October 1997

Mr H. Fielding
1 Avon Court
Oldcastle
OLZ 7SY

Our ref: MD/JR/144.346

Dear Mr Fielding

<u>Re George Martin</u>

I refer to your report and the recent meeting with the defendant's expert, Mr Adams. As you are aware we have been unable to agree all of the medical evidence with the other side, and I now have a hearing date of 9 December 1997 at Oldcastle District Registry, Quay Place, Oldcastle at 10.00 a.m. It will of course be necessary for you to attend, and as a matter of courtesy I shall be serving you with a subpoena nearer the time.

I will be contacting you again presently to arrange a meeting on the date of the hearing. In the meantime, please let me know an estimate of your fee for attending the hearing.

Yours sincerely

Meg Davis

Commentary: Letter to Expert Advising of Forthcoming Hearing

As soon as Meg has a hearing date she must notify her client and experts as soon as possible, so if there is a problem it can be resolved quickly. You will have seen previously that Meg checked with the experts that they would be available in the next few months before listing the matter ready for hearing. Meg also indicated that she would be serving the experts with a subpoena (for commentary on this see page 128).

Note: We have not reproduced the equivalent letter to Mr Johnson as this is largely the same as the letter to Mr Fielding. Meg will of course also be serving him with a subpoena.

GEORGE MARTIN v EASYSHOP LTD

STEP 33

Meg instructs a process server to serve the subpoenas on the two experts.

Document 60

Watkins & O'Dwyer
Solicitors

17 Sycamore Avenue
Oldcastle OL10 1BR
Tel. 011-111-1111
Fax 011-111-1111
DX Oldcastle 1000

Partners: J. Watkins
A. O'Dwyer

4 November 1997

Mr P. Boone
109 Bracken Way
Oldcastle
OL1 E22

Our ref: MD/JR/144.346

Dear Mr Boone

<u>Mr Henry Fielding and Mr Barney Johnson</u>

I enclose an original and copy subpoenas for service on Mr Henry Fielding of 1 Avon Court, Oldcastle, OLZ 7SY, telephone number 243 1122 and Mr Barney Johnson of 193 Banbury Way, Oldcastle, OL6 37Y, telephone number 277 9900. Both gentleman are medical experts and if they are not found at their home addresses they will probably be found at Oldcastle General Hospital or Newtown Infirmary. Please contact them both to arrange a suitable appointment.

Please effect service and I additionally enclose a cheque for each of them by way of conduct money which should accompany the documents.

I should be grateful if you would inform me as soon as possible when service has taken place, and let me have a note of your fees.

Yours sincerely

Meg Davis

GEORGE MARTIN v EASYSHOP LTD

Document 61

Subpoena ad test.
(General Form)
(O. 38, r. 14)

IN THE HIGH COURT OF JUSTICE   1997.—m.—No. 7321

QUEEN'S BENCH **Division**

OLDCASTLE DISTRICT REGISTRY

Between

GEORGE MARTIN   Plaintiff

AND

EASYSHOP LIMITED

Defendant

Elizabeth the Second, by the Grace of God, of the United Kingdom of Great Britain and Northern Ireland and of Our other realms and territories Queen, Head of the Commonwealth, Defender of the Faith,

(1) Names of witnesses.

To (¹) HENRY FIELDING

SPECIMEN

WE COMMAND YOU

to attend at the sittings of the QUEEN'S BENCH   Division of Our High Court of Justice at (²) OLDCASTLE DISTRICT REGISTRY QUAY WALLS, OLDCASTLE

(2) "the Royal Courts of Justice, Strand, London" or name of town and address of court outside the Royal Courts of Justice.

(3) "Plaintiff" *or* "Defendant".

on the day fixed for the trial of the above named cause, notice of which will be given to you, and from day to day thereafter until the end of the trial, to give evidence on behalf of the (³) PLAINTIFF

Witness, LORD IRVINE OF LAIRG

Lord High Chancellor of Great Britain,

the 3rd   day of NOVEMBER 1997.

126

GEORGE MARTIN v EASYSHOP LTD

Issued on the 3 day of NOVEMBER , 19 97

by WATKINS & O'DWYER
17 SYCAMORE AVENUE
OLDCASTLE OL10 1BR
[Agent for

]

Solicitor for the PLAINTIFF

Note: If the writ is to be served in Scotland or Northern Ireland in pursuance of an order of the Court insert after "We command you" the words "wherever you shall be within the United Kingdom" and add at the foot of the writ the following: — Take notice that this writ is issued by the special order of the High Court of Justice in England dated the   day of   19   , pursuant to section 36 of the Supreme Court Act 1981.

SPECIMEN

OYEZ The Solicitors' Law Stationery Society Ltd., Oyez House, 7 Spa Road, London SE16 3QQ   10.92 F23341
5052010
* * * * *

High Court G1

GEORGE MARTIN v EASYSHOP LTD

Commentary: Process Server

1.   Meg has instructed a process server because a subpoena must be served personally (a witness summons in the county court may be served by post). A process server is experienced in this area and will no doubt be quicker (and perhaps cheaper) than a fellow member of her firm.

2.   Conduct money is a sum of money to cover the witness's travelling expenses and the witness is also entitled to be paid later for his loss of income (see where Meg checked with the witness as to his estimated fee). Note also that Meg told the process server to contact the witnesses to arrange a suitable appointment. As these are our witnesses then they should be told when service is to be effected and not suddenly accosted at home or at work.

3.   To issue a subpoena a completed form of *praecipe* must be taken to court along with the appropriate fee. The subpoena must be served within 12 weeks of issue and usually not less than four days before the hearing.

4.   There are two types of subpoena; the subpoena *ad testficandum* where the witness is required to give evidence (used in this scenario) and a subpoena *duces tecum* where the witness is required to produce documents at trial.

STEP 34

The hearing takes place and George is awarded a substantial amount of damages.

Document 62

Watkins & O'Dwyer

Attendance Note

Your name   Meg Davis   Date 9 December 1997

Client's name   George Martin

Person attended   Hearing re-assessment of damages

Time start 10.00 a.m.   Time finished 4.10 p.m., 10 Dec 1997

Attending District Judge Cooke re hearing assessment of damages. In attendance Mr Pierce, counsel, Mr Fielding, Mr Johnson and George Martin for the plaintiff. The defendant was represented by Mr Cooper (counsel), Mr Barker of Ritson & Co., and Mr Johnson (their medical expert).

The facts of the case were briefly reiterated. Counsel for the plaintiff said there had been some agreement between the medical experts and referred the court to the joint statement. However, he said the cause of the plaintiff's condition was still disputed.

Counsel indicated that special damages had been agreed.

The plaintiff then gave evidence as per his witness statement. Mr Cooper cross-examined him on the duration and severity of the pain he suffers and whether he had suffered back problems previously.

Mr Fielding and Mr Johnson then gave their evidence stating that the prognosis for the plaintiff was not good and in their opinion his condition was due largely to the fall. Mr Adams the defendant's expert said that in his opinion the plaintiff's condition was the result of the spondylolisthesis.

District Judge Cooke said that on the evidence before him it seemed clear that whilst there was a dispute about the plaintiff's previous condition, it was apparent that the plaintiff's spine was not that of a healthy person. However, he was satisfied that the plaintiff had sustained an entrapped nerve by falling in the supermarket. Whether his present condition was totally due to the fall was uncertain. However the fall had certainly left him unable to work or live a normal lifestyle and therefore he was prepared to find in favour of the plaintiff. He assessed the damages in total at £198,103.

Commentary: Hearing

1.   After the assessment hearing the district judge records his decision on the order, plus the order re costs. The judgment is then filed at court.

In assessing damages the court will take into account the interim payment made to the defendant. Also deducted from the damages will be the amount as stated on the certificate of total benefit pursuant to the Social Security Administration Act 1992, now replaced by the Social Security (Recovery of Benefits) Act 1997 (see pages 35 *et seq.*). This will be then forwarded by the defendant's solicitors to the DSS. If there is any money outstanding in court this will also be paid out on account of the award of damages.

2.   Under the Supreme Court Act 1981, s. 35A interest may be awarded on damages until the date of judgment, whilst under the Judgments Act 1838, s. 17 interest runs from the time of entering judgment. In the case of an interlocutory judgment there has been confusion as to the relevant date for the purposes of these acts. It has now been decided that interest pursuant to s. 17 of the 1838 Act runs from the date damages are assessed or agreed, that is in this case the date of final judgment and not after the summary judgment hearing, as this is an interlocutory judgment only. Therefore up to the date of the final hearing interest may be awarded under s. 35A of the 1981 Act (see RSC Ord. 37, r. 2(3)).

STEP 35 — ALTERNATIVE A

Meg is unable to agree costs with the defendant's solicitors. She therefore proceeds to draw up the bill of costs and proceed to taxation.

GEORGE MARTIN v EASYSHOP LTD

Document 63

VAT REG. NO. 264 9561 99

IN THE HIGH COURT OF JUSTICE   1997-M-No. 7321

QUEEN'S BENCH DIVISION

OLDCASTLE DISTRICT REGISTRY

BETWEEN

GEORGE MARTIN   Plaintiff

and

EASYSHOP LIMITED   Defendant

TAXED OFF				PLAINTIFF'S BILL OF COSTS	LEGAL AID FUND			INTER PARTES		
L/A		L/P			VAT	Disbs.	Charges	VAT	Disbs.	Charges
				PLAINTIFF'S BILL OF COSTS to be taxed on the Standard Basis and paid by the Defendant, and in accordance with Regulation 107 of the Civil Legal Aid (General) Regulations 1989, pursuant to the Judgment herein dated 10th December 1997.						
				LEGAL AID CERTIFICATE NO. 08/01/97/ 0001/W issued to the Plaintiff on 28th March 1997, to prosecute an action for damages for personal injuries against Easyshop Limited, as a result of an accident suffered by the Plaintiff on 2nd February 1996 (Certificate limited to all steps up to but excluding setting down).						
				RESUME						
				The Plaintiff claimed damages for personal injuries and loss suffered as a result of an accident on 2nd February 1996, when he fell over in the Defendant's supermarket at Oldcastle, as a result of slipping on some oil that had been spilt on the floor.						
				The proceedings were defended by the Defendant. It was asserted by the Defendant, through its insurers, that the Plaintiff was a contributory negligent. Full instructions were taken from the Plaintiff throughout. The Plaintiff sustained entrapped nerve in his back.						

GEORGE MARTIN v EASYSHOP LTD

TAXED OFF			LEGAL AID FUND			INTER PARTES		
L/A	L/P		VAT	Disbs.	Charges	VAT	Disbs.	Charges

– 2 –

Medical evidence was obtained from Consultant Orthopaedic Surgeon. Schedule of Special Damages was prepared in relation to the Plaintiff's losses which included significant loss of earnings. The Defendant, following the issue and service of proceedings, filed Acknowledgment of Service recording an intention to defend. The Plaintiff's solicitor instructed Counsel to advise on quantum. The Defence was served denying the liability. The Plaintiff's solicitor issued Summons for Summary Judgment and Interim Payment. The Defendant's solicitors admitted liability. The Defendant made payment into Court which was rejected. Affidavit evidence in support of Summons for Interim Payment was filed on behalf of the Plaintiff. The Defendant served Affidavit in opposition. After contested hearing on 5th September 1997, Judgment was formally entered for damages to be assessed and Order was made for Interim Payment to the Plaintiff of £2,000.00. The matter then proceeded to assessment of damages. The Plaintiff obtained further medical evidence from Mr. Johnson. Both Orthopaedic Surgeons were called to give evidence for the Plaintiff at hearing. Counsel was briefed on behalf of the Plaintiff. At hearing on 9th December 1997, Judgment was entered for the Plaintiff for the sum of £198,103.00 with costs to be taxed on the Standard Basis.

The matter was, throughout, conducted by an Assistant Solicitor.

GEORGE MARTIN v EASYSHOP LTD

TAXED OFF				LEGAL AID FUND			INTER PARTES		
L/A	L/P		VAT	Disbs.	Charges	VAT	Disbs.	Charges	

– 3 –

PART 1 — PRE-CERTIFICATE COSTS TO DATE OF ISSUE OF LEGAL AID CERTIFICATE

A charging rate of £56.00 per hour has been applied herein, with letters and telephone calls charged at 6 minute units of the hourly rate.

4. Preparation

PART A — WORK DONE

1. The Client (i)

Attendances and correspondence with the Plaintiff.

Attendances

7th March 1997. Attendance upon the Plaintiff to take comprehensive instructions as to the accident and injuries suffered. Obtaining instructions for his statement. 1 hour.

Engaged 1 hour upon attendance	£56.00
3 letters written	16.80
2 telephone calls	11.20
	84.00
TOTAL PART A	£84.00

PART B

General care and conduct of proceedings at 50%

TOTAL PART B	£42.00
TOTAL PARTS A & B	£126.00

Inter Partes Charges: 126 00

Total Charges: 126 00

GEORGE MARTIN v EASYSHOP LTD

TAXED OFF				LEGAL AID FUND			INTER PARTES		
L/A	L/P			VAT	Disbs.	Charges	VAT	Disbs.	Charges
			– 4 –						
			PART 2 — COSTS FROM ISSUE OF LEGAL AID CERTIFICATE ON 28TH MARCH 1997						
			Inter Partes						
			The charging rates applied herein are as follows:						
			Hourly rate 60.00						
			Letters and telephone calls at 6 minute units of hourly rate						
			3rd July 1997						
			(1) Writ issued.						
			3rd July 1997						
			Writ, Statement of Claim, Medical Report and Schedule of Special Damages served.						
			7th July 1997						
			Acknowledgment of Service filed by Defendant recording intention to defend.						
			18th July 1997						
			Instructions to Counsel to Advise on Quantum.						
			30th July 1997						
			Defence received.						
			6th August 1997						
			(2) Summons for summary Judgment and Interim Payment issued.						
			Paid fee on issue.					30	00	
			14th August 1997						
			Notice of Payment into Court received.						
								30	00	

GEORGE MARTIN v EASYSHOP LTD

TAXED OFF				LEGAL AID FUND			INTER PARTES			
L/A	L/P			VAT	Disbs.	Charges	VAT		Disbs.		Charges

– 5 –

20th August 1997

(3) Affidavit of the Plaintiff in support of Summons for Interim Payment with one exhibit.

Oath fee — Inter Partes Disbs. 7 | 00

18th August 1997

Summons served.

5th September 1997

(4) 1. Attending hearing of Summons when Judgment was formally entered for damages to be assessed and Order for Interim Payment of £2,000 made. (Costs in cause.)

(a)(i) Hearing 1 hour 20 minutes.	80.00
(ii) Care and conduct at 50% to reflect contested hearing.	40.00
(b) Travelling to and from Court and waiting time 30 minutes.	30.00
	150.00

— Inter Partes Charges 150 | 00

23rd October 1997

Brief delivered to Counsel.

10th December 1997

(5) 1. Attending hearing with Counsel when Judgment was entered for Plaintiff for the sum of £30,000 — Defendant was ordered to pay the Plaintiff's costs, to be taxed on the Standard Basis.

(a)(i) Hearing 10 hours	600.00
(ii) Care and conduct at 35%	165.00
(b) Travelling to and from Court 30 minutes	30.00
	795.00

— Inter Partes Charges 795 | 00

(6) Counsel's fee for Brief and Conference — Inter Partes VAT 87 | 50, Disbs. 500 | 00

Totals: Inter Partes VAT 87 | 50, Disbs. 507 | 00, Charges 945 | 00

134

GEORGE MARTIN v EASYSHOP LTD

– 6 –

(7) 4. Preparation

PART A — WORK DONE

1. The Client (i)

Attendances upon and correspondence with the Plaintiff.

7th April 1997. Consideration of Plaintiff's instructions. Preparing Proof of Evidence of Plaintiff (5 A4 pages). 30 minutes.

Engaged 30 minutes	28.00

Attendances

18th August 1997. Attendance to take instructions on medical evidence obtained. Obtaining instructions for Affidavit in support of Summons for Interim Payment. Taking instructions on Payment into Court. 1 hour.

Engaged 1 hour upon attendance	60.00
10 letters written	60.00
5 telephone attendances	30.00
	150.00

2. Witnesses (ii)

Attendance upon Miss Wright. Obtaining approval of her Proof of Evidence.

Attendances

23rd May 1997. Attendance for instructions for statement. 30 minutes.

Engaged 30 minutes upon attendance	30.00
1 letter written	6.00
	36.00

3. Expert Evidence (iii)

Correspondence with Consultant Orthopaedic Surgeon, Mr. Fielding, to obtain report.

2 letters written	12.00

135

GEORGE MARTIN v EASYSHOP LTD

TAXED OFF			LEGAL AID FUND			INTER PARTES		
L/A	L/P		VAT	Disbs.	Charges	VAT	Disbs.	Charges

– 7 –

(8)   Paid fee for medical report of Mr. Fielding. — Inter Partes Disbs. **300 00**

4.   Other Parties (vii)

Telephone attendance upon and correspondence with the Defendant, its insurers and solicitors.

15 letters written	90.00
5 telephone calls	30.00
	120.00

5.   Others

a.   The Court

Correspondence with the court as to the listing of matter for assessment of damages.

2 letters written.	12.00

b.   Counsel

Attendances upon Counsel and Counsel's Clerk as to listing of matter for hearing and Counsel's availability.

2 letters written.	12.00

6.   Special Damages (vi)

Obtaining from employer, particulars of pre-accident earnings and payments made after accident. Preparing Schedule of Special Damages and future loss.

2 letters written.	12.00
Engaged 2 hours collating documents, making calculations and preparing schedule.	120.00
	132.00

7.   Documents (ix)

17th June 1997. Preparing Writ of Summons. Drafting and settling Statement of Claim. (3 pages) 1 hour.

2nd August 1997. Preparing Summons for Summary Judgment and Interim Payment. 15 minutes.

Total carried forward — Inter Partes Disbs. **300 00**

TAXED OFF			LEGAL AID FUND			INTER PARTES		
L/A	L/P		VAT	Disbs.	Charges	VAT	Disbs.	Charges

– 8 –

2nd August 1997. Consideration of half a page. 5 minutes.

12th August 1997. Preparing Affidavit of the Plaintiff (3 pages). Collating documents for exhibiting (15 pages) 30 minutes.

15th August 1997. Consideration of Notice of Payment into Court. Re-reading medical evidence to assess quantum. 15 minutes.

5th September 1997. Preparing for fully contested hearing of Summons for Judgment and Interim Payment. Extracting Authorities for use at hearing. 30 minutes.

21st October 1997. Collating documents and preparing Brief to Counsel (10 pages). 1 hour.

Engaged 3 hours 35 minutes.   215.00

8. Notices

Preparing Notice of Issue of Legal Aid Certificate.

Engaged 6 minutes on 31st March 1997.   6.00

TOTAL PART A   £723.00

PART B

General care and conduct of proceedings at 50%

TOTAL PART B   £361.50

TOTAL PARTS A & B   £1084.50   [Inter Partes: Disbs. 1,084 | Charges 50]

Legal Aid Costs

Correspondence with Legal Aid Board

1 letter written at prescribed Legal Aid rate   7.40   [Legal Aid Fund: Charges 7 | 40]

Totals carried: Legal Aid Fund Charges 7 | 40 — Inter Partes Disbs. 1,084 | Charges 50

GEORGE MARTIN v EASYSHOP LTD

TAXED OFF				LEGAL AID FUND			INTER PARTES		
L/A	L/P			VAT	Disbs.	Charges	VAT	Disbs.	Charges
		– 9 – (9) 5a. Taxation of costs (attendance required) (i) Preparing for and attending taxation Engaged 1 hour 60.00 (ii) Care and conduct of proceedings at 35% 21.00 (iii) Travelling to and from Court and waiting time at Court 30 minutes. 30.00 111.00					111	00
								111	00

GEORGE MARTIN v EASYSHOP LTD

TAXED OFF				LEGAL AID FUND			INTER PARTES		
L/A	L/P		VAT	Disbs.	Charges	VAT	Disbs.	Charges	
		– 10 –							
		SUMMARY							
		Part 1							
		PAGE 1							
		PAGE 2							
		PAGE 3							126	00
								126	00
		LESS TAXED OFF						–	–
								126	00
		ADD VAT ON PROFIT COSTS						22	05
		ADD DISBURSEMENTS						–	–
								148	05
		ADD VAT ON DISBURSEMENTS						–	–
		TOTAL PART 1						148	05

GEORGE MARTIN v EASYSHOP LTD

– 11 –

TAXED OFF				LEGAL AID FUND			INTER PARTES			
L/A	L/P		VAT	Disbs.	Charges		VAT	Disbs.		Charges
		Part 2								
		PAGE 4						30	00	
		PAGE 5					87	50	507	00	945	00
		PAGE 6								
		PAGE 7						300	00	
		PAGE 8			7	40				1,084	50
		PAGE 9							111	00
		LESS TAXED OFF			7 –	40 –	87	50	837	00	2,140 –	50 –
		ADD VAT ON PROFIT			7 1	40 30	87	50	837	00	2,140 374	50 59
		ADD DISBURSEMENTS			8 –	70 –				2,515 837	09 00
		ADD VAT ON DISBURSEMENTS			–	–				3,352 87	09 50
		ADD PART 1			8 –	70 –				3,439 148	59 05
					8	70				3,587	64
		TAXING FEE			0	45				269	07
		TOTAL			9	15				3,856	71

140

GEORGE MARTIN v EASYSHOP LTD

– 12 –

TAXED OFF				LEGAL AID FUND			INTER PARTES		
L/A	L/P			VAT	Disbs.	Charges	VAT	Disbs.	Charges
		SCHEDULE OF INTER PARTES COSTS FROM ISSUE OF LEGAL AID CERTIFICATE AT LEGAL AID RATES							
		The rates applicable under the Legal Aid in Civil Procedings (Remuneration) Regulations 1994 are as follows:							
		Advocacy and preparation	74.00						
		Attending hearings and conferences with Counsel	36.40						
		Travelling and waiting	32.70						
		Letter written	7.40						
		Telephone calls	4.10						
		(1) Issue of Writ							
		(2) Summons for Summary Judgment and Interim Payment							30 00	
		(3) Affidavit of the Plaintiff in support of Summons for Interim Payment							7 00	
		(4) Attendance at hearing of Summons for Summary Judgment and Interim Payment without Counsel:								
		Hearing: 1 hour 20 minutes Travel and waiting 30 minutes								98 67 16 35
		(5) Attending hearing of assessment of damages with Counsel:								
		Hearing: 2 hours Travelling and waiting 30 minutes								72 80 16 35
		(6) Counsel's fee for Brief						87 50	500 00	
		(7) Preparation								
		Attendances 1 hour 30 minutes 34 letters written 10 telephone calls								111 00 251 60 41 10
		Special Damages Documents/Notices								
		4 hours 41 minutes								420 57
		(8) Fee for medical report							300 00	
		(9) Taxation of costs								111 00
							87 50	837 00	1,139 44

Note: We have shown the bill taxed as drawn. In practice this would be exceptional!

GEORGE MARTIN v EASYSHOP LTD

Legal Aid Taxation certificate

Legal Aid Taxation Certificate

Plaintiff/~~Petitioner~~

GEORGE MARTIN

Defendant/~~Respondent~~

EASYSHOP LIMITED

In the	HIGH COURT OF JUSTICE QUEEN'S BENCH DIVISION OLDCASTLE ~~County Court~~/District Registry
Case No.	1997-M-7321
Legal Aid Certificate No.	08/01/97/27344/G
Solicitors Ref.	MEG DAVIS

The costs in this matter have been taxed as set out in boxes A, B and C below and are claimed from the Legal Aid Fund. *(please tick)*

The costs are those of the [X] Plaintiff   [ ] Petitioner
                            [X] Defendant [ ] Respondent [ ] Other

They were taxed in the [X] High Court [ ] County Court

Total pre-certificate costs, which are not being claimed, were (Include disbursements, profit costs and VAT)   £ 148.05

SPECIMEN

Dated 6 JUNE 1998   Signed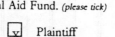
                                       (Solicitor)

A. Legal aid inter partes costs
(Do not include any pre-certificate costs inter partes costs or the costs of taxation.)

Profit costs	1028.44
VAT	179.98
Counsel's Fees	500.00
VAT	87.50
Disbursements	337.00
VAT (where appropriate)	
Total	£ 2132.92

B. Legal aid only costs
(Do not include the costs of taxation.)

Profit costs	7.40
VAT	1.30
Counsel's Fees	—
VAT	—
Disbursements	—
VAT (where appropriate)	—
Total	£ 8.70

C. Costs of taxation
(Allowed in respect of A and B above)

Part A Taxation costs	111.00
VAT	19.42
Taxing fee (where appropriate)	269.07
Part B Taxation costs	
VAT	0.45
Taxing fee (where appropriate)	
Total	£ 399.94

D. Total Claimed
(Add totals A, B and C)

Total part A	2132.92
Total Part B	8.70
Total part C	399.94
Total	£ 2541.56

Sealed by the court on _____

Commentary: Taxation *Inter Partes*

1. Meg will need to prepare a very detailed bill itemising all the work carried out for the action together with the costs claimed for each particular item. This bill is almost invariably drawn up by a law costs draftsman. We have reproduced the bill of costs. Before instructing a law costs draftsman, see the *Gazette*, 27 March 1996, page 40 which gives advice on how to 'get the best' from your law costs draftsman. We do not reiterate the advice in full here but two points seem to be of particular importance:

   (i)   all correspondence should be filed in chronological order; and

   (ii) the solicitor should ensure that there are sufficient attendance notes to justify the time spent (see on this point commentary at page 160).

Another useful source is the 'Supreme Court Taxing Office Guide' published by HMSO, a guide produced by the Masters of the Supreme Court Taxing Office.

2. Easyshop has been ordered to pay George's costs. The taxation of these costs is known as *inter partes* taxation. Easyshop will be required to pay 'a reasonable amount in respect of all costs reasonably incurred and any doubts which the taxing officer may have as to whether the costs were reasonably incurred or reasonable in amount shall be resolved in favour of the paying party' (see RSC Ord. 62, r. 12). This is known as the standard basis of taxation.

Note: Contrast this with the taxation of costs which may take place between a solicitor and client under which the client will be required to pay 'all costs ... except in so far as they are of an unreasonable amount or have been unreasonably incurred and any doubts which the taxing officer may have as to whether the costs were reasonably incurred or were reasonable in amount shall be resolved in favour of the receiving party'. This is known as the indemnity basis of taxation and demonstrates why the successful party should not expect to recover all of the costs from the losing party (see client care letter in the contract case study, page 163).

3. At the same time as preparing the bill for *inter partes* taxation, Meg will also prepare the bill for taxation of the costs she will recover from the Legal Aid Fund. As George is legally aided, Meg cannot look to him personally for payment of her costs — she can only obtain payment from the Legal Aid Fund (unless she is prepared to accept costs recovered from the other side in full settlement). In practice, the bill to be prepared by the law costs draftsman will incorporate both the *inter partes* costs and the costs which Meg will seek to recover from the Legal Aid Fund known as legal aid taxation.

Note: In a legal aid case, where there is no order for costs *inter partes* and proceedings have been issued, the costs to be recovered from the Legal Aid Fund must be taxed by the court unless the total costs, including disbursements, do not exceed £1,000, in which case the costs may be assessed by the Legal Aid Board. If proceedings have not been issued and there is no recovery of costs *inter partes*, the costs may only be assessed.

In taxing or assessing the costs, regard will be had to the prescribed rates introduced by the Civil Legal Aid (General) (Amendment) Regulations (No. 2) 1994 and the Civil Legal Aid (Remuneration) Regulations 1994. See also *Practice Direction (No. 1) of 1994 (Legal Aid Taxation)*.

The bill of costs assumes that Meg is entitled to recover the costs for the work carried out prior to the issue of the Legal Aid Certificate.

Note: Against the Legal Aid Fund, there are prescribed rates for solicitor's costs for preparation, advocacy, attending hearings and conferences with counsel, preparation, attendance, routine letters written, routine telephone calls and travelling and waiting. The prescribed rates differ in the county court and High Court and there are different rules applicable depending on whether or not the firm is a franchise. The prescribed rates for preparation and attendances are higher where the solicitor's office is situated within Legal Aid area 1. Against the paying party there are no prescribed rates for solicitor's

GEORGE MARTIN v EASYSHOP LTD

costs. The rates are in the discretion of the court. Against the paying party the rates allowed are generally higher than the prescribed rates. The prescribed rates include, where appropriate, allowance for care and conduct. In appropriate cases the taxing officer may allow the prescribed rates to be enhanced (see the Legal Aid in Civil Proceedings (Remuneration) Regulations 1994, reg. 5(1)).

4. Once the bill is prepared, Meg will lodge it with the court, together with a copy of the judgment and her papers. This would probably be the whole file, including all disbursements and vouchers. For a full list see RSC Ord. 62, r. 29(7).

Note: It is the practice of some courts not to require the lodgment of file of papers. Practitioners should check with the court in question as to the court's practice.

Meg must also, within the next seven days, serve a copy of the bill on the defendant's solicitors and inform the court that she has done so.

Meg must apply for a taxation appointment within three months of the order for taxation or she will need the leave of the court to tax out of time. The taxing officer will then conduct a provisional taxation and give notice to both parties. If either party is unhappy, then an objection must be lodged within 21 days. If an objection is made, the court will fix a hearing date when both parties will attend. At the hearing the taxing officer will tax the bill by adjudicating upon the representations made by each party.

5. In allowing costs, the taxing officer in the High Court will refer to the criteria found in RSC Ord. 62, Appendix 2, Part 1, para. 2. This means that he will consider:

(a) the complexity of the item or of the cause or matter in which it arises and the difficulty or novelty of the questions involved;

(b) the skill, specialised knowledge and responsibility required of, and the time and labour expended by, the solicitor or counsel;

(c) the number and the importance of the documents (however brief) prepared or perused;

(d) the place and circumstances in which the business involved is transacted;

(e) the importance of the cause or matter to the client;

(f) where money or property is involved, its amount or value;

(g) any other fees and allowances payable to the solicitor or counsel in respect of other items in the same cause or matter, but only where work done in relation to those items has reduced the work which would otherwise have been necessary in relation to the item in question.

The taxing officer will look at each item and consider:

(a) First, whether to allow the hourly rate charged by the solicitor. Remember that costs are made up of the solicitor's fee and profit costs. If too senior a fee earner was used or too high an hourly rate charged, then the hourly rate may be reduced.

(b) Second, the taxing officer will consider the profit claimed, often referred to as 'mark-up' or 'care and conduct'. The mark-up includes an allowance for supervising junior staff. Normally the mark-up will be 50 per cent, except for routine hearings or hearings attended with counsel. There will be no mark-up on travelling and waiting time. Sometimes the taxing officer will allow a greater mark-up if the matter was particularly difficult.

(c) Third, the taxing officer will consider the amount of time claimed. If the taxing officer considers that the amount of time claimed was unreasonable, the taxing officer may reduce the time. This is why on attendance notes you should always record how much time was spent for each item of work. The taxing officer may also disallow items where he/she does not consider it reasonable for the paying party to pay for such item, although the item would be reasonably charged to the Legal Aid Fund.

(d) Fourth, the taxing officer will consider the disbursements claimed in the bill of costs to decide whether these are reasonable in amount.

(e) Fifth, the taxing officer will assess a reasonable sum for the costs of the taxation, that is the time spent preparing for the taxation and attendances and time spent travelling and waiting.

(f) Finally, the taxing officer will tax the legal aid costs.

Note: It will be seen in the bill of costs that there are items with a number in brackets, i.e., page 5 — '4 September 1997 (4) Attending hearing of Summons'. This is to facilitate the taxation of the Legal Aid Schedule (see page 12 of the bill).

6. The costs of the taxation will generally be paid by the paying party, subject to the court's discretion (see RSC Ord. 62, r. 27). In a legal aid case, unless the costs of taxation were unreasonably incurred through misconduct or neglect, they will be payable by the paying party. In the specimen bill of costs they have been taxed and assessed at the amount claimed.

As you can see the bill is indorsed with the firm's name and business address and must be signed by that solicitor or a partner in the firm (RSC Ord. 62, r. 29). In addition the solicitor should ensure that:

(a) all legal aid certificates (if any) listed on the bill of costs and any amendments are enclosed if they have not already been filed with the court;

(b) vouchers for all disbursements are enclosed and are in the order that they appear in the bill;

(c) a further copy of the bill is enclosed;

(d) the VAT registration number is indorsed on the top of the bill if the solicitor is VAT registered and VAT is recoverable on costs.

The bill is also indorsed with a notice that the solicitor has complied with the Civil Legal Aid (General Regulations) 1989, reg. 105A. Where an assisted person has a financial interest in the proceedings, e.g., statutory charge or a contribution to the Legal Aid Certificate, the solicitor must serve him with a copy of the bill and inform him as to the extent of his right to make written representations.

7. Finally two other points we wish to consider:

(a) Witness fees. In the High Court and on Scale 2 in the county court, there is no maximum specified. The court will take into account the time spent travelling by the witness and his/her loss of earnings and any other expenses reasonably incurred.

(b) VAT. As George is not registered for VAT and the legal services were not in connection with his business, then an amount equal to the VAT should be added to the bill to be paid by the unsuccessful party. This is because George will have to pay VAT on his solicitor and client costs.

GEORGE MARTIN v EASYSHOP LTD

STEP 35 — ALTERNATIVE B

Meg agrees costs with the defendant's solicitors.

Commentary: Agreed Costs

The other alternative is that costs are agreed. In most cases costs will be agreed *inter partes* — why?

(a) There is possibly a three month wait for taxation. The insurers will have to pay interest on costs which will accumulate on the costs pursuant to the Judgments Act 1838, s. 17 in favour of the client and the Legal Aid Fund. Therefore they will want the matter resolved as quickly as possible. Note: Interest is at present only recoverable in the county court where the cumulative amount of the judgment and costs exceed £5,000.

(b) The insurers will not wish to pay the costs of the taxation and the taxing fee, from 15 January 1997 calculated at 7.5 per cent of the taxed bill inclusive of VAT).

Even where costs are agreed in prescribed rate cases, the solicitor may still make a claim for costs that could not be recovered *inter partes*. Such costs can be assessed by the Legal Aid Board if the amount does not exceed the assessment limit (currently £1,000). If they do exceed the assessment limit, they must be taxed by the court. This situation may occur where:

(a) there are items in respect of which there is no *inter partes* costs order;

(b) there is an *inter partes* costs order but the paying party is not responsible for the extent of the costs (see the Civil Legal Aid (General) Regulations 1989, reg. 106A; *Legal Aid Handbook 1996/97*, paragraph 14–12; and *Practice Direction*, No. 3, 1994, paras 22–26).

Conclusion

Finally we explain what happens at the end of proceedings. All monies, interest and costs are paid to the solicitor for the assisted party who must pay them to the Legal Aid Board. Part of the damages may be released to the paying client on the condition that the solicitor retains sufficient monies to safeguard the fund and undertakes that the claim on the fund does not exceed that amount.

The interim payment is now taken into account as part of the damages and could be used to meet the statutory charge if applicable. Remember also that it will be taken into account in the assessment of damages.

Any outstanding disbursements should be cleared, e.g., expert fees etc. The file is then closed.

CONTRACT ACTION:
RENT-A-TENT LTD v *HAWTHORN LTD*

Introduction

This case study follows a contract action. The solicitor, Tom Wood, is consulted by Anne Francis, the managing director of Hawthorn Ltd, the defendant in the action. The plaintiff is alleging a breach of contract.

As with the personal injury case study, what follows does not represent the entire file on this matter. It is intended to give an idea of how a commercial litigation case may be run. Additionally, it illustrates that the role of the defendant's solicitor is of equal importance to that of the plaintiff's solicitor in terms of tactics and in deciding what is the overall aim of the litigation. Finally, the case demonstrates that the matter does not end with judgment. At all times the solicitor must be aware of how to enforce the judgment and the practical problems that it may entail.

RENT-A-TENT LTD v HAWTHORN LTD

STEP 1

Tom Wood is a solicitor in the civil litigation department of Watkins & O'Dwyer, of Oldcastle. On 5 June 1997 he meets with Anne Francis, the managing director of Hawthorn Ltd, a joinery firm specialising in shopfitting and other specialist projects.

Anne hands Tom the following documents:

(a) Letter Before Action (see below).

(b) Summons and Particulars of Claim (see pages 150 *et seq.*).

(b) Form N9 (Defence, Admission, Counterclaim) (see page 169).

(c) File of papers consisting principally of correspondence between Hawthorn Ltd and the plaintiff Rent-A-Tent Ltd (see pages 171 *et seq.*).

Set out below is the Letter Before Action, the Summons and Particulars of Claim which you should read together with the notes and commentary.

Document 1

Nixons

16 High Street
Oldcastle
OL1 2XL

13 May 1997

Our ref: PT/4/101

Ms Anne Francis
Hawthorn Limited
4 Willow Vale
Oldcastle
OL9 2WN

Dear Madam

<u>Re Rent-A-Tent Ltd</u>

We act for Rent-a-Tent Ltd and have been consulted by them in connection with the defective manufacture and supply by you of 300 portable dancefloor tiles.

We understand that on or about 13 January 1997[1] you agreed to manufacture 1,000 of the tiles on our client's behalf at a fully inclusive cost per tile of £35 + VAT, the tiles to be manufactured by reference in all material respects to a specimen tile supplied to you by our clients. Further, you were aware that our clients required these tiles both for use with their principal business as marquee hirers and additionally to market for sale to third parties. You were aware that our client had an order for the sale of 300 tiles to Oldcastle University and for this reason it was agreed by you as a condition of the contract that 300 tiles would be delivered to our client by no later than 28 February.[2]

148

In breach of your obligations you failed to deliver the 300 tiles by 28 February and these tiles were not delivered until 21 March. Further, the tiles are defective in terms of manufacture and quality of finish to the extent that they are unacceptable to our client and you should therefore take this letter as notice of rejection.[3] The tiles were certainly not manufactured in accordance with the sample tiles delivered to you and Oldcastle University have refused to take delivery of any tiles as a result of the delay and defects complained of.

Accordingly we are instructed to inform you that our client has no intention of settling your invoice dated 15 April, and further we have advised our client to look to you for payment of damages arising out of our client's inability to market the dancefloor for sale, or otherwise use the same in the course of their business.

We look forward to hearing from you within the next seven days with confirmation that you withdraw your invoice and an admission of liability whereupon we will discuss the appropriate level of damages. In default of hearing from you we have instructions to commence proceedings without further notice or delay.

Yours faithfully

Nixons

Partners: J. D. Nixon, P. T. Turner, H. A. Tubby

NOTES: LETTER BEFORE ACTION

For notes on a letter before action see the personal injury case study at page 35. The salient points to note from this letter are:

(1) The date of the alleged agreement is quoted, along with the number and price of the tiles to be manufactured. As Rent-A-Tent allege that Hawthorn is in breach of the agreement, the agreement should be identified.

(2) The terms of the contract which Hawthorn allegedly breached are set out in full followed by details of the alleged breach so Hawthorn can understand Rent-A-Tent's complaint.

(3) Additionally, this letter acts as an unequivocal notice of rejection. If the plaintiff failed to give notice of rejection, the defendant could argue that by not rejecting the goods the plaintiff had implicitly accepted them, alleged defects and all.

RENT-A-TENT LTD v HAWTHORN LTD

Document 2

County Court Summons (1)

| Case Number *Always quote this.* | OL794762 (2) |

In the OLDCASTLE **County Court**

The court office is open from 10am to 4pm Monday to Friday

THE COURTHOUSE
PRIORY STREET
OLDCASTLE
OL2 4TP

Telephone: 01261 453724

Seal

This summons is only valid if sealed by the court.
If it is not sealed it should be reported to the court.

Keep this summons. You may need to refer to it.

(1) Plaintiff's full name address

RENT-A-TENT LIMITED
76 FETTER LANE
OLDCASTLE   OL16 2SU
(REGISTERED OFFICE)

(2) Address for sending documents and payments *(if not as above)* **Ref./Tel. No.**

NIXONS
16 HIGH STREET
OLDCASTLE   OL1 2XL
REF: PT/4/101 TEL: 01261277454

(3) Defendant's full name *(eg Mr, Mrs or Miss where known)* **and address Company no.** *(where known)*

HAWTHORN LIMITED
4 WILLOW VALE
OLDCASTLE   OL9 2WN
(REGISTERED OFFICE)

What the Plaintiff claims from you

Brief description of type of claim

BREACH OF CONTRACT   (3)

Particulars of the Plaintiff's claim against you   (4)

SEE ATTACHED PARTICULARS
OF CLAIM

SPECIMEN

My claim is worth   £5,000 or less ☐   over £5,000 ☑ (5)

Total claim over £3,000 and/or damages for personal injury claims over £1,000

I would like my case decided by   trial ☑   arbitration ☐

Signed
Plaintiff or Plaintiff's solicitor
(or see enclosed "Particulars of claim")

Amount claimed see particulars   (6)
Court fee   150.00
Solicitor's costs   TO BE TAXED
Total Amount

Summons issued on   29 MAY 1997

What to do about this summons

You have 21 days from the date of the postmark to reply to this summons
(A limited company served at its registered office has 16 days to reply)
If this summons was delivered by hand, you have 14 days from the date it was delivered to reply

You can
- dispute the claim
- make a claim against the Plaintiff
- admit the claim and costs in full and offer to pay
- admit only part of the claim
- pay the total amount shown above

You must read the information on the back of this form. It will tell you more about what to do.

N2 Default summons (amount not fixed) (Order 3, rule 3(2)(b))

RENT-A-TENT LTD v HAWTHORN LTD

Please read this page: it will help you deal with the summons

If you dispute all or part of the claim

You may be entitled to help with your legal costs. Ask about the legal aid scheme at any county court office, citizens' advice bureau, legal advice centre or firm of solicitors displaying the legal aid sign.

● Say how much you dispute on the enclosed form for defending the claim and return it to the court office within the time allowed. It is not enough to contact the plaintiff by letter or telephone. The court will arrange a hearing and/or will tell you what to do next.

● If you dispute only part of the claim, you should also fill in the part of the form for admitting the claim and either pay the amount admitted to the court or make an offer of payment.

● If the court named on the summons is not your local county court, and/or the court for the area where the reason for the claim arose, you may write to the court named asking for the case to be transferred to the county court of your choice. You must explain your reasons for wanting the transfer. However, if the case is transferred and you later lose the case, you may have to pay more in costs.

How the claim will be dealt with if defended

If the total the plaintiff is claiming is £3,000 or less and/or the claim for damages for personal injury is worth £1,000 or less, it will be dealt with by arbitration (small claims procedure) unless the court decides the case is too difficult to be dealt with in this informal way. Costs and the grounds for setting aside an arbitration award are strictly limited. If the claim is not dealt with by arbitration, costs, including the costs of help from a legal representative, may be allowed.

If the total the plaintiff is claiming is more than £3,000 and/or he or she is claiming more than £1,000 for damages for personal injury, it can still be dealt with by arbitration if you or the Plaintiff asks for it and the court approves. If your claim is dealt with by arbitration in these circumstances, costs may be allowed.

If you want to make a claim against the Plaintiff

This is called a counterclaim

Fill in the part of the enclosed form headed 'Counterclaim'. If your claim is for more than the Plaintiff's claim you may have to pay a fee – the court will let you know. Unless the Plaintiff admits your counterclaim there will usually be a hearing. The court will tell you what to do next.

If you admit owing all the claim

● If the claim is for more than £3,000 and/or includes a claim for damages for personal injury for more than £1,000, you may make a payment into court to compensate the Plaintiff (see **Payments into Court** box). The figure of £3,000 includes interest claimed under contract but **excludes** costs and interest claimed under section 69 of the County Courts Act 1984. Send a notice or letter with your payment, saying that it is in satisfaction of the claim. If the Plaintiff accepts the amount paid, he is also entitled to payment of his costs.

● **If you need time to pay,** complete the enclosed form of admission and give details of how you propose to pay the Plaintiff. You must reply within the time allowed. If your offer is accepted, the court will send an order telling you how to pay. If it is not accepted, the court will fix a rate of payment based on the details given in your form of admission and the Plaintiff's comments. Judgment will be entered and you will be sent an order telling you how and when to pay.

● **If the Plaintiff does not accept the amount paid or offered,** the court will fix a hearing to decide how much you must pay to compensate the Plaintiff. The court will tell you when the hearing, which you should attend, will take place.

If you do nothing

Judgment may be entered against you. This will make it difficult for you to get credit.

General information

Court staff cannot give you advice on points of law, but you can get help to complete the reply forms and information about court procedures at **any** county court office or Citizens Advice Bureau. The address and telephone number of your local court is listed under 'Courts' in the phone book. When corresponding with the court, please address forms or letters to the Chief Clerk. Always quote the whole of the case number which appears at the top right corner on the front of this form; the court is unable to trace your case without it.

Costs

In addition to the solicitor's costs for issuing the summons, you may have more costs to pay if the court enters judgment against you.

Registration of judgments

If the summons results in a judgment against you, your name and address may be entered in the Register of County Court Judgments. **This will make it difficult for you to get credit.** A leaflet giving further information can be obtained from the court.

Interest on judgments

If judgment is entered against you and is for £5,000 or more the Plaintiff may be entitled to interest on the full amount.

Payments into Court

You can pay the court by calling at the court office which is open 10 am to 4 pm Monday to Friday.

You may only pay by:
- ● cash,
- ● banker's or giro draft,
- ● cheque supported by a cheque card,
- ● cheque (unsupported cheques may be accepted, subject to clearance, if the Chief Clerk agrees).

Cheques and drafts must be made payable to HM Paymaster General and crossed.

Please bring this form with you.

By post

You may only pay by:
- ● postal order,
- ● banker's or giro draft,
- ● cheque (unsupported cheques may be accepted, subject to clearance, if the Chief Clerk agrees).

The payment must be made out to HM Paymaster General and crossed.

This method of payment is at your own risk and you must:
- ● pay the postage,
- ● enclose this form,
- ● enclose a self addressed envelope so that the court can return this form with a receipt.

*The court **cannot** accept stamps or payments by bank and giro credit transfers.*

Note: You should carefully check any future forms from the court to see if payments should be made directly to the Plaintiff.

To be completed on the court copy only

Served on:

By posting on: **SPECIMEN**

Officer:

Not served on (reasons):

OYEZ The Solicitors' Law Stationery Society Ltd, Oyez House, 7 Spa Road, London SE16 3QQ

1996 Edition 1.96 F31129

5039650

County Court N2

RENT-A-TENT LTD v HAWTHORN LTD

NOTES: SUMMONS

Although in this scenario Tom is acting for the defendant company, we have, where appropriate, included commentary on the plaintiff's documents.

(1)   For contract and tort actions the county court has unlimited jurisdiction (see the County Courts Act 1984, s. 15 and the High Court and County Courts Jurisdiction Order 1991). (In a personal injury claim where the claim is under £50,000, then the action must be commenced in a county court.) However, even if the claim is limited to a few thousand pounds, you may prefer to issue in the High Court to give you more control over service and frankly it is more expedient to do so to get the claim quickly off the ground and when considering default judgment and effectiveness of enforcement. (Also remember interest is payable on all judgments in the High Court, but only on £5,000 or more in the county court.)

The summons is equivalent to the High Court writ. There are two types of summons — a default summons which covers all actions for debt or damages; and a fixed date summons used in cases where the plaintiff is seeking the recovery of land or goods or an equitable remedy, e.g., an injunction. There are however several different forms; for example there are two forms for a default summons: N1 — for a fixed amount, i.e., a debt and fixed costs and an N2 (used in this case), for an unliquidated amount, i.e., damages.

(2)   In the top right-hand corner the court will give the action a case number. The initial two letters stand for the prefix letters used by that particular county court in all cases originating from there, in this case OL. In the index to the County Court Practice (in *The Green Book*), there is a list of all the prefixes used by each county court.

(3)   The plaintiff need only give a brief description of the type of claim, for example in a personal injury case it could be 'damages for personal injury and consequential losses'.

(4)   Particulars of claim. If your particulars are short (e.g., in a simple debt collection claim) they can be set out here. However, usually a separate particulars of claim is prepared in which case the words 'see attached particulars' are indorsed here.

(5)   Where the plaintiff has an unliquidated claim then you must state that the amount involved is likely to exceed £5,000, otherwise the court will deem it to be less than that amount and the matter may be allocated to either a circuit or district judge for determination. Additionally, the plaintiff must indicate whether the matter is to be dealt with via arbitration. Where the claim does not exceed £3,000 (or £1,000 for a personal injury case) there is no discretion: it must be dealt with by arbitration and is commonly referred to as a small claim. The increase in the small claims limit for non-personal injury cases (the limit was previously £1,000) came into effect for proceedings issued on or after 8 January 1996 by the County Court (Amendment No. 3) Rules 1995 (SI 1995 No. 2838). Note that in valuing the claim no account is taken of statutory interest or of any counterclaim (see further CCR Ord. 19, r. 3(1)). This change in the County Court Rules has caused one particular dilemma concerning a personal injury claim. If the plaintiff has a claim for personal injuries which also includes a claim for non-personal injury damages then it appears that the latter must be ignored in calculating the personal injury value of the claim. In such a case only where the personal injury element alone exceeds £1,000 or the total value of the claim exceeds £3,000 would the claim not be automatically referred to arbitration. Note also that the increase in the limit has effectively removed many cases from the legal aid scheme — legal aid is not available for cases automatically referred to arbitration. This together with the fact that normally, in arbitration cases, there will be no costs order except where one of the parties has behaved unreasonably, will undoubtedly dissuade many would-be litigants. However, see the case of *Azfal v Ford Motor Company* [1994] PIQR 418, where the court said that in some cases the normal costs rules of arbitration are not appropriate, namely where the case involved a difficult point of law or the facts were exceptionally complex. Additionally, the court held that the provisions of CCR Ord. 19 (in the reference to the arbitration scheme) relating to costs take precedence over the provisions of CCR Ord. 11 which usually gives rise to an automatic right

to taxed costs on a payment into court (for a discussion of payment into court see the personal injury case study at page 98).

(6)   With regard to solicitors' costs these initially depend on the amount claimed and are similar to the 14 day costs on a writ. However, in an unliquidated claim the words 'to be taxed' are inserted as shown (see CCR Ord. 38, r. 18). Court fees are prescribed by the County Court Fees (Amendment) Order 1996 (SI 1996 No. 3190) and depend on the amount claimed. For example, they range from a £10 fee for a £100 claim to a maximum fee of £500 for a claim which is over £100,000 or unlimited. We have limited the claim to £50,000 and the fee is therefore £150. For details on fee exemptions see page 68.

Commentary: Summons

On receipt of the summons and particulars of claim from the plaintiff, the court will attach the blank form of admission, defence and counterclaim (N9). The court will seal the summons and enter the action number in the top right-hand side (see note 2). The summons must then be served within four months of issue (the same time limit as for service of the writ). In personal injury cases pursuant to CCR Ord. 7, r. 18A the solicitor can use postal service. However, in all other cases the court will usually effect service but the solicitor can effect personal service (but not postal service). If the court is effecting service, service will be by first class post and will be deemed to have taken place on the seventh day after the summons was posted. The court will then send to the plaintiff a plaint note. This acts as (a) a receipt for the court fee and (b) informs the plaintiff of the date the court deems service to be effective.

Document 3

IN THE OLDCASTLE COUNTY COURT   Case No. OL794762

BETWEEN

RENT-A-TENT LIMITED   <u>Plaintiff</u>

and

HAWTHORN LIMITED   <u>Defendant</u>

PARTICULARS OF CLAIM

---

1.   The Plaintiff[1] is and was at all material times[2] a company whose business includes hiring for reward marquees and other items ancillary thereto. The Defendant is and was a company carrying on business as joiners and shopfitters.

2.   By an oral agreement ('the Agreement'[3]) made on 13th January 1997[4] the Defendant agreed to manufacture and supply to the Plaintiff 1,000 portable dancefloor tiles at a cost of £35.00 plus VAT per tile.

3.   The following were express or alternatively implied terms of the Agreement.[5]

  (a)   The tiles would be manufactured to comply with the specification of the sample tiles provided by the Plaintiff to the Defendant.

(b) The tiles would be fit for their purpose as made known by the Plaintiff to the Defendant.

(c) The Defendant would exercise all proper skill and care and would complete the manufacture of the tiles in a good and workmanlike manner.

(d) The tiles would be of a satisfactory quality.

(e) The first 300 tiles would be supplied to the Plaintiff by 28th February 1997.

4. In breach of the Agreement the Defendant failed to supply 300 tiles by 28th February 1997 and did not do so until 21st March 1997 and those tiles supplied are defective and/or do not comply with the specification of the sample tile and/or are not of satisfactory quality.

PARTICULARS OF DEFECTS[6]

(a) Locking latches — these have been manufactured without adequate pre-load. Furthermore the length of the latch member is 165mm as opposed to 300mm on the specimen tiles.

(b) Location strip — these have not been grub-screwed to the body of the tile and are therefore prone to become mis-aligned.

(c) Edge trims — these fail to interlock satisfactorily making assembly and disassembly difficult.

(d) Release access hole — brass ferrules have been omitted and with repeated usage the hole edges will fray.

(e) Cutting burrs — the cuts have been inadequately machined and finished and cause and/or contribute to malfunction.

(f) Cosmetically — the appearance of the tiles is inferior to the sample tiles in the following areas:

   (i)   Texture and quality of wood finish.

   (ii)   The finishing lacquer is rough affecting the frictional qualities of the dancefloor.

   (iii)   The surface quality of the aluminium extrusions.

   (iv)   The depth and colour of the anodising and dyeing of the aluminium extruded strips.

5. By reason of the Defendant's breach the Plaintiff has been unable to use the dancefloor system in connection with its business or otherwise market the system for hire or sale, and in particular the Plaintiff has lost a sale of 300 tiles to Oldcastle University at £40.00 plus VAT per tile.[7]

6. By letter dated 13th May 1997 the Plaintiff by its solicitors gave notice to the Defendant rejecting the tiles delivered.[8] Further it is averred that the Defendant is in repudiatory breach of the Agreement and by the issue and service of proceedings herein the Plaintiff accepts that repudiation.

7. By reason of the matters aforesaid the Plaintiff has suffered loss and damage, and further claims interest on such damages as it may be awarded pursuant to s. 69 of the County Courts Act 1984.[9]

AND the Plaintiff claims[10]

  (1) Damages limited to £50,000.

RENT-A-TENT LTD v HAWTHORN LTD

(2) Interest pursuant to s. 69 of the County Courts Act 1984 at the rate of 8% per annum on such sum as may be awarded and for such period as the Court thinks fit.

DATED this 26th day of May 1997

To the Court and to
The Defendant
Hawthorn Limited
4 Willow Vale
Oldcastle
OL9 2WN

....
Nixons
16 High Street
Oldcastle
OL1 2XL
Plaintiff's Solicitors

NOTES: PARTICULARS OF CLAIM

(1) When referring to a company it is acceptable to use the singular or plural, but whichever you adopt ensure consistency. In this case you will see Tom has adopted the singular.

(2) If the status of a party is relevant to the case then the phrase 'at all material times' is used to bring in that status in this opening paragraph to define the parties and avoids any need to repeat that status. In this case it is to be alleged that the plaintiff wanted the dancefloor tiles for use in conjunction with its business and it is therefore relevant to state that business here. Equally, with the defendant, the plaintiff will want to rely on its (apparent) expertise as joiners and shopfitters.

(3) Definitions are to be preferred when there are to be references to matters you have already described rather than having to repeat the description or use the phrase 'the said agreement' or 'the aforesaid agreement'.

(4) Quite often you will see the date referred to 'on or about ...' or even less precisely as 'in or about February 1997'. If you can be precise about the date then be so; if not then adopt one of the alternative phrases. All dates, sums and other numbers should be in figures, not words (RSC Ord. 18, r. 6).

(5) Given that the agreement was oral (and preceded by, to a lesser or greater extent, negotiation) it is likely that there will be some dispute and consequent difficulty in proving one or other term was expressly agreed. Therefore it is necessary to plead as an alternative that the terms should be implied, relying upon such matters as the status and other circumstances surrounding the making of the agreement and the implied statutory terms as to satisfactory quality. Needless to say, if the contract was written then you would plead express terms then, if necessary, plead whatever terms separately you may wish to rely on as implied terms.

(6) Note that in the personal injury case study (see page 69) Meg particularised the negligence of the defendant. In much the same way here, the plaintiff's solicitors particularise the defects of the tiles.

(7) Paragraph 8 sets out the result of the breach in the same way as the personal injury case study set out the result of the negligence.

(8) Note that the letter of rejection is referred to in the pleading.

(9) Interest must be claimed in the particulars of claim (CCR Ord. 6, r. 1A). If there was a contractual rate then that should be pleaded.

(10) See note (10) to the prayer in the personal injury case study at page 73.

RENT-A-TENT LTD v HAWTHORN LTD

STEP 2

Now that Tom has discussed matters in detail with Anne and the meeting is over, he prepares an attendance note to record the information obtained and other matters covered with Anne.

Document 4

Watkins & O'Dwyer

Attendance Note

Your name   Tom Wood   Date 6.6.97.

Client's name   Hawthorn Ltd

Person attended   Anne Francis

Time start 10.35 a.m.   Time finished 11.40 a.m.

Attending Ms Francis, managing director of Hawthorn Ltd. The company address is 4 Willow Vale, Oldcastle, OL9 2WN (registered office and trading) and that is where I shall contact her. The telephone number is 464 2731.

As a preliminary matter I informed Ms Francis of the basis on which her company would be responsible for our costs and that my involvement in the matter would be charged at £85 per hour + VAT. With regard to the overall cost of dealing with the matter I informed her that it would be very difficult to give any meaningful accurate estimate, but as an estimate we would probably spend 1 hour in interview today and then I would estimate a further 2 ½ hours to consider the file and prepare the defence and possible counterclaim. Thereafter it would depend on what reaction this brought from the plaintiff and the possibility of negotiating a settlement. I would send her a client care letter to confirm our discussions and this would, amongst other things, confirm the position on costs. I informed her that if her company was successful in defending the claim then she could expect to recover costs of perhaps up to 70 per cent of their own legal costs. I briefly explained the reason why a full cost recovery could not be expected and that any recovery is subject to being able to enforce an award against what may be an insolvent company. On this point I would consider, after we discussed the matter in detail, the prospect of applying for security for costs.

She had with her a summons and particulars of claim served against Hawthorn Ltd by Rent-A-Tent Ltd. The summons was issued on 29 May and Ms Francis says that this was received in the post on 3 June. She explained that Hawthorn Ltd is a specialist shopfitting company which was approached by Bob Dancer of Rent-A-Tent Ltd at the end of last year enquiring whether they could manufacture for him a portable dancefloor system. Apparently, Rent-A-Tent Ltd is a company which hires out marquees for various functions and in connection with that business he wanted to provide a flooring system which can be supplied with the marquee and laid to any size. He had at the time of the approach to our client already had a small number of wooden tiles manufactured as a prototype, but those had proved very expensive to manufacture. The idea was that the dancefloor would be made up from numbers of these wooden tiles being laid out and assembled to create a rigid secure dancefloor area by an interlocking mechanism on each tile. Mr Dancer had explained to our client that whilst similar floor systems did exist, none of them had an interlocking system which was either simple to operate or otherwise as secure as his system.

After the initial enquiry which had been by telephone a meeting had been arranged between Ms Francis, George Best (our client's production manager) and Bob Dancer. The meeting took place on 18 December 1996 at our client's offices and Bob Dancer brought with him four of his prototype tiles. The company which had manufactured these tiles as prototypes had quoted him a

---

156

manufacturing cost of £70 per tile and he wanted to know whether our client could manufacture them for less.

During discussions at that meeting Mr Dancer had said that provided the tiles he eventually ended up with were based on the prototype and particularly provided a similar secure rigid system that these prototypes provided, then he was not particularly concerned as to the overall appearance or quality of finish or the manufacture of the tiles being slavishly followed.

It was agreed that he would leave with the client the four prototype tiles, the client would look at them, disassemble one and then contact Mr Dancer during the course of the next two weeks to let him know whether they could manufacture tiles, and if so at what cost.

During the course of the next two weeks the production manager along with one of his joiners had looked at the tiles and disassembled one into its component parts and decided that our client could manufacture these at a cheaper cost to Rent-A-Tent Ltd than the £70 per tile, on the basis of minor modifications to the design and manufacture and by sourcing the aluminium edging and fittings which fitted around each wooden tile from a third party, who they would introduce to the plaintiff, on the basis that the plaintiff would contract directly with that third party for the supply of the aluminium extrusions.

On 13 January 1997 a further meeting took place at our client's office at which Mr Dancer was told that our client could manufacture the tiles at a cost of £35 per tile on the basis of:

(a) The plaintiff obtaining and providing the aluminium extrusions through Metal Ltd, a third party company to whom our clients would introduce Rent-A-Tent Ltd. (This would add approximately £10 per tile to the cost to the plaintiff.)

(b) The wood which our client would use would be a hardwood to be sourced by our clients from whatever source they decided on the basis that it would nevertheless be of a uniform colour.

(c) The tiles would have a lacquer finish though not to the same depth as the prototype.

(d) There would be minor modifications to the assembly system of the tile and interlocking mechanism which would not jeopardise the overall integrity of the system.

(e) The cost was based on the manufacture and supply of a minimum of 1,000 tiles.

Mr Dancer confirmed his agreement and at the meeting it was agreed that our client would write to him to confirm the agreement and commence manufacture immediately with a view to supplying the first batch of 300 tiles to the plaintiff by 28 February on the basis that the plaintiff had mentioned at the meeting he had in fact agreed to sell a number of tiles to provide a dancefloor system at Oldcastle University. In the meantime, the plaintiff would contact Metal Ltd and confirm the agreement with them for the supply of the aluminium extrusions to our client. Our client provided him with the name and telephone number of the production director at Metal Ltd.

Following the meeting our client began manufacture of the tiles and expected Metal Ltd to provide the extrusions by the end of January (Ms Francis had spoken to the production director at Metal Ltd and he confirmed that they would be able to supply the extrusions by that time for the first 300 tiles.) However, by then only sufficient aluminium extrusions had been supplied for 120 tiles and there was a delay until 24 February when the balance of the aluminium was supplied.

During that time there had been some argument between our client and the plaintiff as to who should be chasing the aluminium company. Ms Francis had spoken to Metal Ltd by telephone on two occasions to find out what the problem was, but had simply been told they were experiencing problems with their production line.

RENT-A-TENT LTD v HAWTHORN LTD

On 21 February our client had supplied the 120 tiles to the plaintiff and the balance of 180 were then supplied three weeks later on 21 March. Following the supply of the balance of 180 tiles, on 25 March Mr Dancer had telephoned Ms Francis and told her she should not manufacture any more tiles for the time being as he was having problems concerning the tiles with Oldcastle University. Nothing further was heard from the plaintiff for three weeks and our client decided to then send an invoice for the 300 tiles which had been supplied at £35 + VAT per tile. That invoice was sent on 15 April and nothing was heard from the plaintiff for four weeks and therefore on 9 May Ms Francis telephoned Mr Dancer to find out what the position was, and particularly to chase for settlement of the invoice. Mr Dancer had said that he would be dealing with their invoice and would be contacting her shortly about the remaining tiles.

The following week the client received a letter before action from Nixons Solicitors on behalf of Rent-a-Tent Ltd. This had arrived the first day of Ms Francis' absence on holiday and nobody had responded to it. Ms Francis had come back to the office from holiday on 3 June and on the same day the letter and summons arrived in the post.

I went through the Particulars of Claim with Ms Francis and she made the following specific comments:

<u>Para 1</u> — Agreed. We had not had dealings with the plaintiff before but we were aware of them and their business.

<u>Para 2</u> — Agreed save that the Plaintiff's letter suggested that this price included the aluminium which was being obtained from Metal Ltd. This was not the case — the Plaintiff contracted directly with Metal Ltd.

<u>Para 3</u> (a) Not correct — we were told by Dancer that provided the tiles could do the job they were not concerned with too much detail as to finish or method of manufacture.

(b) Purpose — this may be the case but we were only asked to manufacture dancefloor tiles in accordance with the sample tile — we were not asked to design and manufacture a dancefloor, only to manufacture tiles which were comparable to the prototype and functional.

(c) Agreed — we did.

(d) They were.

(e) Agreed but I do not recall there being any firm emphasis on this date by Dancer — he had simply said he would like the first 300 by that date as he had a sale agreed for them to the University — no date was mentioned as to when he was to supply the tiles to the University.

<u>Para 4</u> — The first 120 tiles were delivered by us to the Plaintiff's premises at Fetter Street on 21 February. The balance of 180 were more or less finished apart from awaiting the aluminium extrusions which needed to be cut and fitted when received from Metal Limited. If the extrusions had all been delivered by the end of January I think that we would probably have had the whole 300 tiles ready for 7 March. As it was, because we did not receive the remaining extrusions until 24 February, we did not complete the tiles until 20 March (working flat out) and delivered them to the Plaintiff at Fetter Street on 21 March (the driver told me that the other 120 were just where he had unloaded them!).

158

RENT-A-TENT LTD v HAWTHORN LTD

(a) The 'pre-load' refers to the 'springiness' of the latch and whether it has any play in it. There is some play in the latch but this does not affect its interlocking capability and we have used the same springs as on the prototype and therefore the difference must be due to different tolerances in the manufacture of the extrusions by Metal Limited.

The lengths mentioned are correct but the reduction does not adversely affect the interlocking capability. The reduction in length was a cost saving modification and was specifically mentioned by George Best as a modification we would make at the meeting with Dancer on 13 January — he did not object.

(b) The prototype was grub-screwed, but this was unnecessary — the glue we used was secure.

(c) The edge trims were manufactured by Metal Limited — all we did was cut them to size and fit them to the tiles.

(d) The omission was part of the cost saving — a hardwood was used and the edges do not fray with normal use.

(e) Denied insofar as the extrusions were cut to fit by us.

(f)(i) The prototype used oak, we used teak — certainly a different wood in appearance, but it had been agreed that we could use whatever hardwood we wanted provided it was uniform.

(ii) I do not understand this — a hard resin clear varnish has been used and it was fine.

(iii) Again I do not understand — the extrusions were in any event supplied by Metal Limited under the separate agreement with the Plaintiff.

(iv) Ditto.

<u>Para 5</u>. I do not now believe that Dancer ever had a firm order from the University; and that he was hoping to principally market the floor for sale rather than use it for hire with his marquee and he has not found any buyers — he is therefore trying to avoid paying us and intends to drop the idea.

I emphasised to Ms Francis that she should ideally let me have all the original documentation they have which is at all relevant to the case, to include any manuscript notes, or at the very least copies and ensure the originals are retained safely.

I concluded the interview with Ms Francis by agreeing that I would review the papers she had left with me, draft a defence and counterclaim and obtain a company search against Rent-A-Tent Ltd to better advise on the question of the application for security for costs. I told her that I would need to interview the company's production manager. I will send her our firm's standard client care letter, together with a copy of a note of the interview and a draft first proof of evidence. We also agreed that she would arrange to have a prototype tile and one they had manufactured dropped off at my office that afternoon.

Engaged in preparation of this note — 25 minutes.

RENT-A-TENT LTD v HAWTHORN LTD

Commentary: The Attendance Note

An attendance note is important in many respects and consequently you should take steps to ensure it is a full, concise, accurate and contemporaneous record of what it contains.

An attendance note can range from, as in this case, a full and accurate record of the initial client interview and the basis upon which you are instructed, through to a simple record of how long you have been engaged in dealing with some aspect of the matter. For example, note at the foot of this attendance note that we have recorded how long Tom has been engaged in dictating this note from his manuscript notes — in practice this record may itself form a separate attendance note. An attendance note will assist you in the following ways:

(a) It will be a record of what it contains.

(b) An attendance note of a meeting, telephone, conference etc. can be sent to the client or other parties to confirm instructions, advice etc.

(c) It will remind you of what has taken place.

(d) It will be essential for any other person who needs to become acquainted with the file.

(e) It will be very important on taxation (or other justification of costs) as both a necessary record of time involved (to date the taxing office will not simply accept evidence of time from formal time recording systems) and a justification as to how long you were involved.

(f) In this day and age, unfortunately, you may well find yourself in disagreement with perhaps a solicitor or even your client as to what has been discussed — your attendance note will be invaluable. This equally goes for countering potential allegations of negligence in, e.g., failing to follow client's instructions — if you have a proper record of all matters discussed then that record will be very persuasive as to the accuracy of its content.

For all these reasons it is important that, in compiling your note, you ensure:

(a) it is as comprehensive as possible;

(b) it accurately records time — if of a meeting then by reference to time start and finish, if of a task, e.g., preparing proof of evidence, then a record of the actual time involved is sufficient;

(c) ideally it should be typed — you will usually find a handwritten note of a meeting will be illegible to everybody else (and even yourself a few days later) although if it is fairly brief and apparently uncontentious then a handwritten note will suffice;

(d) it is contemporaneous — this obviously applies to your handwritten note made at the time but additionally ensure you have a typed note made as soon as possible, not only because of the rule of increasing illegibility, but also it is far easier to dictate it fluently when it is fresh in your mind than some days later.

STEP 3

Tom writes to Anne enclosing a copy of the attendance note and a client care letter. He also proceeds to obtain a company search against Rent-A-Tent Limited, to file a holding defence at court and inform the other side of his interest.

160

Document 5

Watkins & O'Dwyer
Solicitors

17 Sycamore Avenue
Oldcastle OL10 1BR
Tel. 011-111-1111
Fax 011-111-1111
DX Oldcastle 1000

Partners: J. Watkins
A. O'Dwyer

9 June 1997

Our ref: TW/DR/623

Ms Anne Francis
Hawthorn Limited
4 Willow Vale
Oldcastle OL9 2WN

Dear Ms Francis

Re: Rent-A-Tent Limited

Further to our meeting on Friday I enclose:

1. Attendance note of our meeting.[1]

2. Client care letter plus copy.[2]

With regard to the attendance note, I hope you will find this accurately records those matters addressed at our meeting, but if you feel there are any points not adequately covered then please let me know.

The client care letter is self explanatory and sets out the main terms of our retainer, to include the basis upon which we will charge you for dealing with this matter. You should read through this letter and, assuming you accept its terms, sign and return the copy to me by way of acknowledgment.

I have now filed a holding defence to the claim and indicated a counterclaim. I will shortly, when I have considered the papers you left with me, let you have a draft defence and counterclaim together with a proof of evidence (a statement) which will set out the detail of your agreement etc. with Mr Dancer.

I should also at that time have the result of our company search[3] and be better able to advise you on the merits of an application for security for costs against Rent-A-Tent.

As mentioned at our meeting, it is important that you let me have the original documents which may be relevant to the case and, if you are at all in doubt about the relevancy of any particular document, let me have that document so I can decide whether it is relevant. If for any reason you cannot let me have the originals then you should let me have copies together with a note as to why the originals cannot be provided and, insofar as those originals are still with you, ensure they are retained safely. You do have a duty in legal proceedings of disclosure of all relevant documentation and, when it becomes necessary to disclose the documents, if for any reason documents which should exist are no longer available to you, then the court may well infer such documents to be detrimental to your case and you should bear in mind the other side will certainly press hard for such an inference to be drawn.[4]

Finally, whilst I appreciate that you feel strongly about defending this claim, it is almost inevitable that at some point there will be a suggestion, perhaps from the other side, as to compromising the claim without going to trial. I do feel it is important to appreciate that it can often be commercially more beneficial to settle rather than proceeding to trial, having in mind the costs, time and inconvenience of your company involvement as well as the risk factor involved. I will of course advise you on the merits (I may suggest seeking advice from counsel) and it will then be your decision, with such advice, as to whether you wish to consider a settlement, either reacting to an offer from the other side or by making our own proposal.[5]

I will of course be happy to discuss any matters raised in this letter with you.

Yours sincerely

Tom Wood

NOTES: LETTER TO ANNE FRANCIS

(1)   By sending Anne a copy of the attendance note, Tom ensures that Anne has a clear record of events, and that if he has misunderstood any matter, Anne can correct it. It also may prompt the client to remember further information.

(2)   The client care letter is discussed below at page 165.

(3)   Before beginning proceedings against a company, the solicitor should ideally obtain a company search, first to check the correct name and registered office of the company, and second to check the company's financial status re enforcement. In this case, as Tom is defending proceedings, he requires a company search to ascertain the company's financial position, re the intended security for costs application (see pages 194 *et seq.*).

(Note that the company search is not reproduced.)

(4)   Tom stresses in the letter the obligation on the client to disclose all documentation it has relevant to the case. It is vital that the solicitor obtains all the documentation at an early stage and to put it into chronological order for the purpose of discovery (see pages 221–223). Note that Tom has stated that the client should let him have all the documentation, whether or not it thinks it is relevant. Frequently the client may not consider a document relevant and will fail to disclose it.

(5)   The letter also indicates that it may be more advantageous to settle the matter. It is wise to introduce the possibility of settlement at an early stage in a commercial matter, as often the client will be blinkered and cannot see any other alternative than taking the matter to trial.

RENT-A-TENT LTD v HAWTHORN LTD

Document 6

Watkins & O'Dwyer
Solicitors

17 Sycamore Avenue
Oldcastle OL10 1BR
Tel. 011-111-1111
Fax 011-111-1111
DX Oldcastle 1000

Partners: J. Watkins
A. O'Dwyer

9 June 1997

Our ref: TW/DR/623

Ms Anne Francis
Hawthorn Limited
4 Willow Vale
Oldcastle OL9 2WN

Dear Ms Francis

Re Professional terms of Engagement

Further to our recent meeting, I should like to thank you for your instructions in this matter and I can of course confirm that this practice is happy to act on your behalf. The purpose of this letter is to record the main terms of the retainer.

1. <u>The work</u>

The work in which we are instructed relates to Rent-A-Tent Limited.[1]

2. <u>Responsibility for work</u>[2]

I will have the overall conduct and responsibility of this matter on your behalf although I will of course, as and when necessary, call upon the assistance of other staff within the office. The partner with overall responsibility for this matter is Alan O'Dwyer.

3. <u>Fees</u>[3]

Our charges will be based upon the time spent by the fee earner dealing with your matter. We can at all times provide you with a detailed breakdown of time involved and description of the activity. The applicable hourly rates are shown in the Schedule of Fee Earners annexed to this letter and in addition there will be VAT on our fees together with any disbursements which may arise, such as Court fees, Counsel's fees, travelling expenses and expert's fees. Travelling and waiting time is charged at reduced rates. You may, if you wish, impose a limit on the fees and disbursements which we would then not exceed without first consulting you. If you wish to impose such a limit, please confirm this in writing.

163

RENT-A-TENT LTD v HAWTHORN LTD

4. Counsel and experts[4]

It may well be necessary in a case of this nature to involve Counsel in order to advise or to represent you at any court attendances. However, before I instruct Counsel I will discuss the matter with you and obtain your agreement.

In addition, in this case, it may well be necessary to appoint experts to prepare a report and, if necessary, attend any court hearing as an expert witness on your behalf. However, before instructing such an expert, I will discuss the matter with you and obtain your agreement and the expert's fees will be payable by you as a disbursement.

5. Matters of complaint[5]

If at any time you are at all unhappy with any aspect of our handling of this matter then I would ask you to raise it with John Watkins, our senior partner, and he will endeavour to resolve the problem with you. If, however, your concern continues then it may be referred to the Solicitor's Complaints Bureau (I will provide you with details on request).

6. Billing[6]

Dependent on the amount of work involved over the period and consequently the level of fees and disbursements incurred, I intend to deliver to you monthly or quarterly bills which I would then ask you to settle within 30 days. If you require any details as to costs, these can be provided by way of an itemised schedule.

Additionally, I intend delivering to you a bill when the value of the outstanding work on this matter exceeds £200.

Under the Solicitors' (Non-Contentious Business) Remuneration Order 1994, we have the right to charge interest on the amount outstanding under any bill delivered to you after the expiry of one month from the delivery of the bill. Whilst the right under that order is restricted to non-contentious matters, as a matter of agreement with you, we will have the right to charge interest on any bill which we deliver to you and which remains unpaid for a period in excess of one month from the date of delivery, the interest applied will be that equivalent to the statutory judgment rate, presently being 8% per annum.

7. Payment on account[7]

I have already mentioned that I may incur certain disbursements on your behalf. Prior to our firm paying such disbursements for you it is now our policy to obtain a payment on account to cover those disbursements.

In anticipation of these disbursements, I must ask you to make a payment on account of £300 and this will of course be taken into account on delivery of a first invoice to you. However, at that stage, I may need to request in addition to payment of the invoice, a further payment on account of costs and disbursements.

8. Estimate as to overall costs[8]

I will endeavour at all times to keep you informed of the overall costs position, although providing an estimate for the total costs which may be incurred is extremely difficult, given that the only certain factor is the hourly rate. All other matters are dependent on the outcome of the case and whether any settlement is possible.

9. <u>Order for costs</u>[9]

In the event of this matter being subject to court proceedings, then it is usual for the successful party to recover their costs from the loser. However, it is important that you are aware of the following:

(a) If the matter is settled out of court then you should ensure that you are happy with the terms of the agreement and you will need to take into account the costs position.

(b) Even if a costs order is made in your favour, in court proceedings it rarely results in a complete costs recovery but probably only 60 to 70% of the costs incurred. Such a recovery is in turn subject to the other party having the means to satisfy any court order.

(c) You will be personally liable for our costs and disbursements incurred notwithstanding any costs order made in your favour by the court.

(d) If you are unsuccessful in the matter you will of course not recover any costs from the other side and you will also have to pay the other side's costs.

I shall forward to you copies of all material correspondence. This is to keep you informed of all recent developments where the copy correspondence is self-explanatory. This service is provided free of charge.[10]

If there are any matters raised in this letter that you wish to discuss with me please do not hesitate to contact me. In the meantime I would be grateful if you could sign and return to me the enclosed copy of this letter by way of acceptance of these terms.

Yours sincerely

Tom Wood

NOTES: CLIENT CARE LETTER

(The client care letter is required by the Professional Conduct Rules on Good Practice — see The Law Society's *Guide to Professional Practice*.)

(1) Paragraph 1 sets out the work the solicitor has been instructed to do. This is simply to avoid any confusion. The client may have several matters ongoing at any one time either with your firm or different firms.

(2) In accordance with the Law Society's Written Professional Standards: Communications With The Client (see *Civil Litigation: A Guide to Good Practice*, published by the Law Society) the client should be told the name and status of the person responsible for the day to day running of the matter and the partner (if different) responsible for the overall supervision of the matter. Note here that the letter explains that it may be appropriate to delegate certain matters to other persons in the office. This is so the client is aware that other parties may be dealing with the matter and is not taken by surprise.

(3) The solicitor must inform the client how the firm's charges are calculated. This letter leaves the client under no illusions by attaching a schedule of the charge out rate. Additionally the letter explains whether the fee includes VAT and disbursements. By imposing a fixed hourly rate the costs conform with

the terms of a Contentious Business Agreement (see s. 59 of the Solicitors Act 1974, as amended). The client must also be told that a limit can be placed on the total costs. Now of course the solicitor has the additional option of suggesting a conditional fee arrangement (see the commentary immediately below these notes).

(4) The letter then continues by informing the client what other costs could arise, e.g., counsel's fees. Again this is so the client is made aware at the outset that fees to third parties may arise.

(5) The client should always be told who to contact in the event of complaint pursuant to the Solicitors' Practice Rules 1974 and the nature of the complaints handling procedure.

(6) The client must be told how he is to be billed. The solicitor must tell the client how his fees are to be met.

(7) A solicitor may agree with his client that the client shall make payments on account. Further, pursuant to the Solicitors Act 1974, s. 65(2) the solicitor can make reasonable demands for payments on account from the client even if there was no agreement between the solicitor and the client that he will make such payments and if the client fails to make such payment the solicitor can withdraw from the retainer.

(8) It is in most cases impossible to accurately estimate the overall costs of the matter at the beginning of the matter. However, by enclosing the charge out rate and billing the client when fees reach £200 or more by way of interim bills, the client should at all stages be aware of what fees have been incurred.

(9) The client must be made aware that even if he is successful, he may not recover all of his costs and in any event the other side may not have the means to pay. Additionally the client should be informed that if he loses the action he will have to pay not only your costs but the costs of his opponent.

(10) Forwarding the client copy correspondence is undoubtedly the easiest way to keep the client informed.

Note that if appropriate, the letter should also include a paragraph that the other side may be legally aided and the effect on costs. This is not appropriate in this letter where Tom knows that the other side is not legally aided.

Commentary: Conditional Fees

Since 5 July 1995 pursuant to the Conditional Fee Agreements Order 1995 (SI 1995 No. 1674) and the Conditional Fee Agreements Regulations 1995 (SI 1995 No. 1675) a client in some cases has the option of making a conditional fee arrangement with his solicitor. To date the order only applies to proceedings for personal injuries, proceedings by companies in administration or winding up or by their administrators or liquidators and by trustees in bankruptcy and proceedings before the European Commission of Human Rights and the European Court of Human Rights. Proceedings do not include those actions where the client is legally aided. Essentially the nature of the agreement is that if the client should win the case he is liable to pay his solicitor's basic costs, disbursements and a success fee, but should he lose the case then he is only responsible for his solicitor's disbursements together with his opponent's costs and disbursements. The maximum percentage by which the fees may be increased is 100 per cent. Note that a conditional fee agreement should be distinguished from a contingency fee agreement. The latter is also known as a 'no win no fee' arrangement and is prevalent in the United States where the lawyer agrees that if he is unsuccessful he will not charge the client. If, however, he wins the case he will deduct an agreed percentage from the client's damages in respect of his fee. In a conditional fee arrangement the solicitor's fee is enhanced by a percentage of the taxed costs.

A conditional fee arrangement does not materially affect the solicitor/client relationship. The level of the success fee reflects the risk the solicitor is taking in not earning anything if he should lose the case together with the fact that the solicitor is not being put in funds in advance. The Law Society Model Conditions suggest that the total of the solicitor's success fee plus any barrister's uplift should not exceed 25 per cent of the damages recovered. Note that the rules as to who pays what at the end of the case remain unaffected, i.e., either the parties will agree costs or there will be a taxation, the only difference being is that the client is responsible for the success fee and not his opponent. Clearly the client is still at risk should he lose the case; however, that may be mitigated by taking out Accident Line Protection Insurance. To date this is only available for personal injury cases and the client's solicitor must be a member of the Accident Line Scheme. For a premium of £100 the client will be insured for his opponent's costs if he loses the case. The insurance will come into effect in two instances:

(i)   if the court orders the insured to pay his opponent's costs following judgment against him;

(ii)   if the insured is ordered to pay by consent or otherwise his opponent's costs.

In addition the policy will also cover the insured solicitor's own disbursements but will not cover those disbursements incurred before proceedings are issued. The limit of the indemnity is currently £100,000. Not all personal injury actions come within the ambit of the scheme; actions which are excluded are those for medical negligence, pharmaceutical, drug and tobacco related actions and in addition the scheme does not cover the insured's barristers' or advocates' fees. For more information on conditional fees and the Accident Line Protection Insurance consult the Law Society and the Accident Line Protection Unit, Tel: 0171 845 7667.

Finally, a client still has the right to challenge the costs payable under a conditional fee arrangement either between himself and his solicitor or between the solicitor and counsel. The client may challenge the hourly rate plus mark up (the base costs) or the percentage increase (the success fee) or both (see RSC Ord. 62, r. 15A and RSC (Amendment) 1995 (SI 1995 No. 2206 (L.9)).

RENT-A-TENT LTD v HAWTHORN LTD

Document 7

Watkins & O'Dwyer
Solicitors

17 Sycamore Avenue
Oldcastle OL10 1BR
Tel. 011-111-1111
Fax 011-111-1111
DX Oldcastle 1000

Partners: J. Watkins
A. O'Dwyer

9 June 1997

Your ref: PT/4/101
Our ref: TW/DR/623

Nixons
16 High Street
Oldcastle
OL1 2XL

Dear Sirs

Re: Rent-A-Tent Limited v Hawthorn Limited

We act for Hawthorn Limited and have been passed the summons and supporting papers you have issued on behalf of Rent-A-Tent Limited.

We have filed Form N9 with the Court stating, briefly, the claim is to be defended and a counterclaim pursued. We enclose a copy for your information. We do propose filing a fully pleaded defence and counterclaim and hope to be able to effect service upon you within the next 14 days.

Yours faithfully

Watkins & O'Dwyer

RENT-A-TENT LTD v HAWTHORN LTD

Document 8

Form for Replying to a Summons

- *Read the notes on the summons before completing this form*
- *Tick the correct boxes and give the other details asked for*
- *Send or take this completed and signed form immediately to the court office shown on the summons*
- *You should keep your copy of the summons*

- **For details of where and how to pay see the summons**

What is your full name? (BLOCK CAPITALS)

Surname .... HAWTHORN LIMITED ....

Forenames ....

Mr ☐ Mrs ☐ Miss ☐ Ms ☐

How much of the claim do you admit?

☐ **All of it** *(complete only sections 1 and 2)*

☐ **Part of it** *(sections 1,2,3,4,5)* **Amount** £   :

☑ **None of it** *(complete sections 3,4 and 5 overleaf)*

In the	OLDCASTLE	County Court
Case Number	*Always quote this*	OL794762

Plaintiff *(including reference)*
RENT-A-TENT LIMITED

Defendant
HAWTHORN LIMITED

Section 1   Offer of payment

I offer to pay the amount admitted on (date) ....

or for the reasons set out below

I cannot pay the amount admitted in one instalment

but I can pay by monthly instalments of   £   :

Fill in the next section as fully as possible. Your answers will help the plaintiff decide whether your offer is realistic and ought to be accepted. Your answers will also help the court, if necessary, to fix a rate of payment that you can afford.

Section 2   Income and outgoings

a. Employment I am

☐ Unemployed

☐ A pensioner

☐ Self employed as ....

☐ Employed as a ....

My employer is ....

Employer's address:

b. Income *specify period: weekly, fortnightly, monthly etc.*

My usual take home pay	£	:
Child benefit(s) total	£	:
Other state benefit(s) total	£	:
My pension(s) total	£	:
Other people living in my home give me	£	:
Other income *(give details)*	£	:

SPECIMEN

c. Bank account and savings

☐ I do not have a bank account

☐ I have a bank account

The account is ☐ in credit ☐ overdrawn by £   :

☐ I do not have a savings account

☐ I have a savings account

The amount in the account is   £   :

d. Dependants *(people you look after financially)*

Number of dependants

(give ages of children) ....

e. Outgoings

I make regular payments as follows:

	weekly	monthly		
Mortgage		☐	£	:
Rent	☐	☐	£	:
Mail order	☐	☐	£	:
TV rental/licence	☐	☐	£	:
HP repayments	☐	☐	£	:
Court orders	☐	☐	£	:

specify period: yearly, quarterly, etc.

Gas		£	:
Electricity		£	:
Council tax		£	:
Water charges		£	:

Other regular payments *(give details below)*

£   :

Credit card and other debts *(please list)*

£   :

Of the payments above, I am behind with payments to

£   :

continue on a separate sheet if necessary – put the case number in the top right hand corner

Give an address to which notices about this case should be sent to you	I declare that the details I have given above are true to the best of my knowledge
	Signed *(to be signed by you or by your solicitor)*
	Position *(if signing on behalf of firm or company)*
Postcode	**Dated**

N9 Form of admission, defence and counterclaim to accompany Forms N2, 3 and 4 (Order 3, rule 3(2)(c))   11.95

Printed by Satellite Press Limited

169

RENT-A-TENT LTD v HAWTHORN LTD

Case No. OL794762

Section 3	Defending the claim: defence

Fill in this part of the form only if you wish to defend the claim or part of the claim.

a. How much of the plaintiff's claim do you dispute?

All of it ☑

Part of it ☐   *give amount*   £ ....

If you dispute only part of the claim, you must complete sections 1 and 2 overleaf and part b. below.

b. What are your reasons for disputing the claim?

A FULLY PLEADED DEFENCE AND COUNTERCLAIM WILL BE FILED SHORTLY

Section 4	Making a claim against the plaintiff: counterclaim

Fill in this part of the form only if you wish to make a claim against the plaintiff.
If your claim against the plaintiff is for more than his claim against you, you may have to pay a fee. Ask at the court office whether a fee is payable.

a. What is the nature of the claim you wish to make against the plaintiff?

MONIES DUE FOR GOODS SUPPLIED AND LOSS OF PROFIT

b. If your claim is for a specific sum of money, how much are you claiming?

£ ....

c. What are your reasons for making the claim?

THE PLAINTIFF FAILED TO FULFIL ITS AGREEMENT TO PAY FOR GOODS SUPPLIED AND TO TAKE FURTHER QUANTITIES OF GOODS AT AN AGREED PRICE

SPECIMEN

continue on a separate sheet if necessary – put the case number in the top right hand corner

Section 5 Arbitration under the small claims procedure

How the claim will be dealt with if defended

If the total the plaintiff is claiming is £3,000 or less, it will be dealt with by arbitration (small claims procedure) unless the court decides the case is too difficult to be dealt with in this informal way. Costs and the grounds for setting aside an arbitration award are strictly limited. If the claim is not dealt with by arbitration, costs, including the costs of help from a legal representative, may be allowed.

If the total the plaintiff is claiming is more than £3,000, it can still be dealt with by arbitration if you or the plaintiff ask for it and the court approves. If your claim is dealt with by arbitration in these circumstances, costs may be allowed.

Please tick this box if you would like the claim dealt with by arbitration ☐

Give an address to which notices about this case should be sent to you 17 SYCAMORE AVENUE OLDCASTLE Postcode: OL10 1BR	**Signed** *(to be signed by you or by your solicitor)* Watkins & O'Dwyer **Position** *(if signing on behalf of firm or company)* SOLICITORS **Dated** 9 JUNE 1997

Commentary: N9

1.   The practice in the county court is, where an obvious holding defence has been filed on form N9, to allow (and usually require on the plaintiff's application) the defendant to file and serve a fully pleaded defence without the need for it, in form or description, to be viewed as an amended defence.

2.   The N9 is either posted or taken to the court. Strictly it should be filed within 14 days after service but, assuming the court has effected service, in practice the court will allow 21 days from the date of the postmark on the summons.

3.   If the defendant admitted liability but disputed quantum then the plaintiff would still enter judgment, but there would be a subsequent hearing where damages are assessed. If the defendant admitted the claim but required time to pay then the defendant should send back the N9 with its proposals for payment.

4.   Note that if the claim was only for a liquidated sum then on filing a defence the proceedings will be automatically transferred to the defendant's home court, being the county court for the defendant's address for service as stated on the defence — see CCR Ord. 9, r. 8 (as amended by County Court (Amendment No. 3) Rules 1994 (SI 1994 No. 2403)).

STEP 4

Tom then considers the file of correspondence left by Anne. He prepares a draft proof of evidence, and defence and counterclaim. (Included in the following documents you will see extracted letters between the client and Rent-A-Tent Ltd.)

Document 9

Watkins & O'Dwyer

Note

Your name   Tom Wood   Date 11 June 1997

Client's name   Hawthorn Ltd

Person attended

Time start 10.15 a.m.   Time finished 12.57 p.m.

Tom Wood considering client correspondence. Particularly noting letters of 15 January (client to Rent-A-Tent) and 17 January (Rent-A-Tent to client) re payment by Rent-A-Tent — indicative of weak financial position — support for security for costs application.

Engaged 30 mins.

Preparing draft Proof of Evidence for Anne Francis — 1 hr 12 mins

Preparing draft Defence and counterclaim — Engaged 1 hr

RENT-A-TENT LTD v HAWTHORN LTD

Commentary: Attendance Note

It is important at all stages of the action to keep an accurate record of time. In addition to the time recording system, if you are engaged for a period in an activity, e.g., looking at a file, preparing a pleading, you should make a note of this. This is because if the case went to taxation, you will have to account for why you spent so long on the file. A time recording system often does not record the actual details of what you were doing.

In addition, this information will be useful if the client queries the bill.

Document 10

CLIENT CORRESPONDENCE

BY FAX

3 January 1997

Dear Anne

Further to our telephone conversation, I have now been able to find out from Regal Oak who supplied the springs, and this is a company called High Tension Limited in Bristol, telephone 0117 965475.

I look forward to hearing from you on the costing for the tiles.

Yours sincerely

Bob Dancer

Document 11

CLIENT CORRESPONDENCE

Hawthorn Limited

4 Willow Vale
Oldcastle
OL9 2WN

15 January 1997

R Dancer, esq
Rent-A-Tent Limited
76 Fetter Street
Oldcastle
OL16 2SU

Dear Bob

I am pleased to confirm the agreement at our meeting on 13 January for the manufacture of the wooden dancefloor tiles.

For the record we are to manufacture for you a minimum of 1,000 tiles at a cost per tile of £35 plus VAT. These tiles will be based on the prototype you left with us but, obviously bearing in mind the costs savings, we will use the most economical but suitable hardwood we can source and there will be slight modifications in manufacture as discussed but which will not affect the overall integrity of the system.

In addition, you will be contacting John Irons at Metal Limited to arrange with him the supply of the aluminium extrusions. If you have not already done so, I would suggest you contact him straightaway as obviously we cannot complete the manufacture and assembly until we have the extrusions.

We have already started work on the first batch of 300 tiles and these should be ready for delivery by 28 February.

With regard to payment, we omitted to agree payment dates at our meeting. Our normal policy would be to require an advance payment of 20 per cent. However, in this case I would propose invoicing you for payment on delivery of the first 300 tiles and do the same on delivery of the second and third batches of 350 each.

Yours sincerely

Anne Francis
Managing Director

RENT-A-TENT LTD v HAWTHORN LTD

Document 12

CLIENT CORRESPONDENCE

Rent-A-Tent Limited

76 Fetter Street
Oldcastle
OL16 2SU

17 January 1997

Ms Anne Francis
Hawthorn Limited
4 Willow Vale
Oldcastle
OL9 2WN

Dear Anne

Thank you for your letter of 15 January and I am happy that you will proceed as agreed.

I have spoken to John Irons but, to be on the safe side, perhaps you would give him a call to confirm the extrusions will be ready for the first 300 tiles — he has assured me he has sufficient metal in stock to get started and should let you have the first batch shortly.

With regard to payment, I am bound to say that I have assumed you will be paid in full on completion of the 1,000 tiles. I have worked on this basis in dealing with cashflow and my bankers are providing a facility for part of the total cost. I would therefore like to keep to this arrangement.

Yours sincerely

Bob Dancer

STEP 5

Tom receives the automatic directions from the court. He writes to Anne enclosing the draft proof of evidence, defence and counterclaim and the results of the company search. (Note: We have not reproduced the company search but you will see the relevant information extracted by Tom.)

RENT-A-TENT LTD v HAWTHORN LTD

Document 13

Notice that automatic directions apply (Order 17, rule 11)

Plaintiff

| RENT-A-TENT LIMITED |

Defendant

| HAWTHORN LIMITED |

In the	OLDCASTLE
	County Court
Case No.	OL794762
Plaintiff's Ref.	PT/4/101
Defendant's Ref.	TW/DR/623
Date	11 JUNE 1997

The court has received a defence in this case which is one to which automatic directions apply.
This means you will not have to come to a court hearing for a District Judge to give directions, that is, to tell you what you have to do to prepare your case for trial.
Instead these notes tell you what you must do and the timetable you must follow.
If you want to change any of these directions you must apply to the court.
The timetable begins 14 days after the date given above, or 28 days if a counterclaim was filed with the defence.

Step 1 *(Both parties)*
Not later than 28 days from the start of timetable.

Make a list of all documents you have ever had which contain information about the dispute between you and the other party. You can do this in the form of a letter or use form N265 which you can get from any county court. If the defendant has accepted responsibility for the claim, but is disputing the amount of damages you should receive, only documents relating to the amount of damages need be included in your list. Send your letter (or form N265) to the other party. Tell them where and when they can look at all the documents listed and take copies if they wish. The date(s) you suggest must be within 7 days after the day they get your list. Alternately, the other party can ask you to send them copies of the documents they want. They must ask for these within 7 days of getting your list. You must send the copies within 7 days of receiving their request. The other party must repay you any cost involved e.g. postage, copying charges.

Step 2 *(Both parties)*
Not later than 10 weeks from start of timetable.

Agree with the other party when you will exchange copies written witness statements (including the written report of any expert witness) you are going to use at the trial. If you don't do this you may not be able to use your witnesses' evidence at the trial. All statements should be signed and dated by the witness. You may not have more than two expert witnesses unless the other party, or the court, agrees.

Step 3 *(Both parties)*
Any time before the start of the trial.

If you are to use photographs or sketch-plans to support your claim, you should, if possible, agree with the other party that they are accurate. The person who took the photographs or made the sketch-plan need not be at the trial.

Step 4 *(Plaintiff only)*
Not later than 6 months from start of timetable.

Write to the court, asking that a date be fixed for the trial (unless the court has set a date already). Tell the court how long you think the case will last and how many witnesses you and the other party will have at the trial. The court will tell you when the trial will begin, giving you at least 21 days notice.

Step 5 *(Defendant only)*
Not later than 14 days before the date fixed for trial.

Write to the plaintiff saying what documents you are going to use at the trial.

Step 6 *(Plaintiff only)*
Not later than 7 days before date fixed for trial.

Send the court a bundle of the documents both you and the defendant are going to use at the trial. You should make a numbered list of them, and number each page to correspond with the list. In addition, you should send two copies of the following (if applicable):

- any witness statements (including expert reports) exchanged under Step 2. Say whether or not they were agreed with the other party;

- any legal aid certificate, if not already filed;

- any request for particulars and the particulars given in reply, and the answer to any interrogatories.

Notes

SPECIMEN

1. **Personal Injury Claims** - In personal injury actions, the Steps are varied as follows:

   Step 1 - Where the injury arises out of a road accident, you need only list documents relating to the amount of damages.
   Step 2 - Each party will be limited to two medical experts and one further expert of any kind unless the parties agree otherwise.
   Step 3 - In an action involving a road accident, you may use any police accident report at the trial without the policeman who made it having to be there. You should agree its contents with the other party if possible.

2. **Changes to the Timetable** - You and the other party may agree a longer period for Steps 1, 2 and 4 but the plaintiff must ask for a date for trial within 15 months from the start of the timetable. If you (the plaintiff) believe you may not be able to request a date within 15 months, you must apply to the court and obtain a new timetable.

3. **Automatic striking out** - if a date for trial has not been requested within 15 months (or within 9 months of the date set for requesting a date for trial given in any new timetable) the case will be automatically struck out and you will not be able to proceed with it.

N450 Notes for guidance on automatic directions (Order 17 rule 11) (6.95)

Commentary: Directions

1. From 1 October 1990 automatic directions under CCR Ord. 17, r. 11 were extended to all default or fixed date actions with the limited exceptions set out in paragraph (1) to the Rule. Prior to the introduction of the automatic directions the court, on receipt of a defence, would have fixed a pre-trial review at which time both parties would have attended before the district judge and obtained directions. Now, upon receipt of a defence, the court will automatically issue automatic directions to the parties on form N450.

2. The automatic directions will be issued by the court upon receipt of the defence notwithstanding any application being made by either party. Accordingly, in this case, automatic directions apply. It is still possible to obtain specific directions from the court and it is not uncommon, on an application before the court by either party, for the court to make particular directions or vary the timetable under the automatic directions, if only to cater for the delays which have occurred as a result of that application being brought before the court (see order at page 215). However, as is often the case, neither party will comply strictly with the timetable but will proceed at its desired pace unless, and until, forced into action by the other side through an application for an order by the court. (But note the automatic striking out provision in cases of extreme delay — see point 5(e) below.)

3. The directions stage occurs after the close of pleadings (see CCR Ord. 17, r. 11(11)). This is 14 days after delivery of a defence or 28 days after delivery of a defence and counterclaim.

4. In the county court the automatic directions apply in most cases save those where a pre-trial review is held (e.g., third party proceedings), or where neither the automatic directions nor the pre-trial review is appropriate (e.g., cases proceeding to arbitration).

5. Form N450 sets out the full content of the automatic directions. They are very similar to the automatic directions in the High Court. For convenience we have again listed the directions below with notes on each. However you should also refer back to the relevant section in the personal injury case study at page 107.

    (a) <u>Discovery and inspection</u>   Discovery is made within 28 days of close of pleadings, and inspection seven days thereafter. For commentary on the meaning of discovery and on the list of documents see page 224 and the personal injury case study at page 107.

    (b) <u>Experts</u>   The parties must within 10 weeks of close of pleadings (14 weeks in the High Court) disclose their expert's report on which they intend to rely at trial. In this case the parties will each be able to adduce two expert reports. Exchange will be simultaneous and you should refuse to disclose your report unless the other side agrees they are also ready to disclose their report. As this is a contract action the plaintiff is not under the disadvantage a plaintiff is under in a personal injury action where the plaintiff must disclose their expert evidence first on service of the statement of claim (see personal injury case study at page 69, note 2).

    (c) <u>Exchange witness statements</u>   Exchange should be effected within 10 weeks of close of pleadings and must be exchanged simultaneously (see CCR Ord. 17, r. 11(3A) and Ord. 20, r. 12A(4)(c)). For an example of witness statement see pages 226 *et seq.* and the commentary in the personal injury case study at pages 117 *et seq.* Note the decision in *Beachley Property* v *Edgar* (1996) *The Times*, 18 July. Initially both parties had failed to comply with the automatic directions timetable and the plaintiff applied for an order for exchange. Subsequently the plaintiff then wished to exchange a further three witness statements a few weeks before trial. These statements contained an important piece of evidence. The Court of Appeal refused to admit the witness statements on the grounds that as they contained important evidence there was no excuse for their late exchange despite the plaintiff's argument that the defendant had not been prejudiced by the late exchange. *Beachley* therefore appears to be authority for stating that, even though the other party is not prejudiced by late exchange, witness statements that are served late will not be admissible unless a very good reason is given for their late exchange. Note the wording of CCR Ord. 17, r. 11(3) which states that witness statements should be exchanged within 10 weeks of close of pleadings 'except with the leave of the court *or where all parties agree*'.

Recently, however, the Court of Appeal has taken a more lenient approach to that in *Beachley* in *Mortgage Corporation* v *Sandoes* (1996) *The Times*, 27 December. Here neither party had exchanged its witness statements or expert reports in accordance with RSC Ord. 38 and a further direction of the court. At first instance the plaintiff's applications to extend time for service of these documents, for leave to vacate the trial date and to call additional expert evidence were refused. The Court of Appeal allowed the plaintiff's appeal on the grounds that as both parties were equally at fault it would be unfair solely to penalise the plaintiff. Had the decision been otherwise the plaintiff would have been unable to prove his case. The Court of Appeal distinguished this case from *Beachley* as in the latter the plaintiff was solely in default.

The Court of Appeal then went on to issue the following guidelines:

(i)   time requirements specified by either the rules or directions given by the court are to be observed and not simply targets to be attempted;

(ii)   at all times the overriding principle is that justice should be done;

(iii)   litigants are entitled to expect that their cases are dealt with with reasonable expedition and a failure by one party to comply with time limits can cause prejudice to one or more of the parties to the litigation;

(iv)   the vacation or adjournment of the trial date additionally prejudices the other litigants and disrupts the administration of justice;

(v)   hence applications for extensions of time which affect the trial date should be granted only as a last resort;

(vi)   if time limits have not been complied with then the parties should endeavour to reach an agreement as to new time limits which will not affect the date of the trial;

(vii)   where such agreement is made between the parties then there is no need for a separate application to the court solely for the court's approval as the court would ordinarily give approval at the trial;

(viii)   a party who seeks to gain tactical advantage for the failure of another party to comply with the time limits will not be looked on favourably by the courts;

(ix)   where the parties fail to reach an agreement as to a new timetable then a prompt application should be made to the court;

(x)   finally, in considering whether or not to grant an extension of time to a party who was in default the court will consider all of the circumstances of the case including those matters outlined above.

(d)   <u>Photographs, sketch plans</u>   These are receivable in evidence provided that at least 10 days before the trial the other party has had the opportunity to inspect them (see RSC Ord. 38, r. 5: there is no equivalent rule in the county court).

(e)   <u>Date for trial</u>   The plaintiff must within six months of close of pleadings request the court to fix a date for trial. If the plaintiff fails to apply for a date for trial within 15 months of close of pleadings the action shall be automatically struck out (see CCR Ord. 17, r. 11(9)). Note that no notice is given to the parties either before or after it happens. Under CCR Ord. 13, r. 4 the court may extend such a period though if possible the application for an extension should be made before the expiry of the 15 month period. The court will look at the interests of justice and the balance of hardship. The plaintiff must show that he/she had prosecuted the case with the utmost diligence. See further *Rastin* v *British Steel plc* [1994] 2 All ER 641 and *Gardner* v *London Borough of Southwark* noted at [1996] 1 WLR 571. In *Gardner* the court emphasised that the responsibility for progressing a case with due diligence lies with the plaintiff because he always has a remedy to force the defendant to comply with their obligations. It is therefore irrelevant that the defendant has been dilatory. Note that a decision to strike out under CCR Ord. 17, r. 11(9) does not amount to a dismissal for want of prosecution (see *Rastin* above).

As there has been a number of automatic striking out cases and because of the importance of the issue we thought it useful to list some of the more significant points which appear to have emerged.

1. When a case has been automatically struck out the commencement of a second action is not an abuse of process (*Gardner* v *London Borough of Southwark No. 2* [1996] 1 WLR 561).

2. Where the court makes specific interlocutory directions these supersede the automatic directions timetable (*Downer & Downer Ltd* v *Brough* [1996] 1 WLR 575).

3. Where the plaintiff's solicitors had conducted the case with reasonable diligence and had simply missed the hearing date because of an oversight this in itself was not excusable (*Hackwell* v *Blue Arrow plc* (1996) *The Times*, 18 January).

4. With regard to the commencement of the timetable:

    (i)   it begins when the defence is lodged at court (*Lightfoot* v *National Westminster Bank* (1996) *The Times*, 18 January);

    (ii) where there is more than one defendant the timetable will commence on the lodgment of the latest defence (*Peters* v *Winfield* [1996] 1 WLR 604);

    (iii) the issue of the form N450 by the court is purely an administrative act and does not vary the operation of the rule (*William* v *Globe Coaches* [1996] 1 WLR 553).

5. With regard to costs, in *Jackson* v *Slater Harrison* and *Reville* v *Wright* [1996] 1 WLR 597, both cases where the plaintiffs' actions were struck out, cost orders were made against the plaintiffs 'not to be enforced unless the plaintiffs received an indemnity'. In reality this was a costs order against the plaintiffs' respective solicitors although this was only because the plaintiffs were legally aided.

6. Recently the Court of Appeal in *Burgess* v *Stratton* (1996) *The Times*, 15 October emphasised that where such directions are given they ought to be expressed in clear and specific terms. In *Burgess* the district judge had ordered that 'the automatic directions be extended for a period of three months from today'. The plaintiff had argued that the effect of this direction was that time began running afresh for all purposes. The Court of Appeal upheld the district judge's ruling that the order merely postponed the guillotine date and allowed the plaintiff a further three months to request a hearing date. Common sense dictated that a restrictive interpretation was applied.

(f) <u>Length of trial</u> The parties must agree an estimate of the length of the trial and the number of witnesses called. The obligation for filing the note detailing the parties' agreement rests with the plaintiff whether the parties are in agreement or not.

Document 14

Watkins & O'Dwyer
Solicitors

17 Sycamore Avenue
Oldcastle OL10 1BR
Tel. 011-111-1111
Fax 011-111-1111
DX Oldcastle 1000

Partners: J. Watkins
A. O'Dwyer

12 June 1997

Our ref: TW/DR/623

Ms Anne Francis
Hawthorn Limited
4 Willow Vale
Oldcastle
OL9 2WN

Dear Ms Francis

Re: Rent-A-Tent Limited

Further to my letter of 9 June I enclose:

1. Draft proof of evidence.

2. Draft defence and counterclaim.

3. Company search result on Rent-A-Tent.

With regard to each of these documents:

1. Draft Proof of Evidence

This is simply your statement which ideally will contain details of all the relevant facts known to you and any other information which you consider relevant, to include matters of opinion. I will use this statement throughout the case for various purposes and it is important at this early stage to get all of the information down on paper, for your own benefit in directing your mind to it now as well as mine. Eventually it is likely this statement will go to Counsel when it becomes necessary to instruct Counsel for you, and additionally I will need to prepare a witness statement (which we will need to exchange with the other side's witness statements) and will base this on your proof of evidence.

RENT-A-TENT LTD v HAWTHORN LTD

It is therefore very important that you read through this draft carefully, let me have any outstanding information which is apparently needed and let me know of any amendments/additions you feel should be made.

I will then let you have a final original and copy which you will need to sign and return the original to me.

2. Draft Defence and Counterclaim

This is our detailed response to the Plaintiff's Particulars of Claim and you will see it basically denies Rent-A-Tent's claim and then sets out our claim for the unpaid tiles and loss of profit on the balance of the 700 tiles. You should read through this and ensure the facts as to dates, amounts etc. are correct. Again, please let me know any amendments/additions which you feel should be made.

3. Company Search Result

You may be accustomed to interpreting company search results and, if so, you will see that from the limited information available Rent-A-Tent does not appear to be in an enviable financial position. It seems that from the last filed accounts for the period to 31 December 1996:

(a) The turnover has decreased by nearly 30%.

(b) The cost of sales has increased by nearly 20%.

(c) The trade creditors have increased by 15% to £140,000 whereas the debtors' figure has remained fairly static.

(d) The company has a net loss for the year of £12,000 against a net profit the year before of £42,000.

Additionally, you will see from the Charges Register that the company granted a second fixed and floating charge over its assets to Forcem Factors Limited on 17 February 1997.

On this basis it does appear that Rent-A-Tent may well be in some financial difficulty and referring to Bob Dancer's letter to you of 17 January concerning a bank facility to pay you, a reason (if not the only reason) why they are now attempting to avoid agreement with you may be that the bank have withdrawn the facility.

I therefore consider there is a real risk that, if you successfully defend the claim, Rent-A-Tent will not be able to comply with the almost inevitable costs order that will be given in your favour and it is for this reason that I recommend we make an application for security for costs.

This application will be heard before a District Judge and dealt with on the basis of affidavit evidence and representations at the hearing. There will not be any need for you to attend. If we are successful, Rent-A-Tent will be required to provide security for your costs and the action will be stayed in the meantime.

There will not be a court fee payable but there will be oath fees of about £15.00 to pay plus, of course, our costs involved in preparing the application and evidence, dealing with any evidence served by the other side and then attending on the hearing. Assuming the hearing will last for perhaps 1 hour (this will of course depend on the other side's evidence) I anticipate further work involved of about 2½ hours, thus giving costs of about £300 (although you must appreciate that this is a rough estimate and it may be exceeded dependent upon the reaction of the other side). If we succeed then it is likely the other side will be ordered to pay the costs involved (on the basis as set out in our client care letter). If, however, we do not succeed it is equally likely you will be ordered to pay their costs involved in defending the application.

On balance I consider that we will succeed although I cannot guarantee this. It will depend to a large extent on the particular District Judge's view of the merits of the case (although he should not be involved in an in-depth analysis of this) and whether, if he were to order security to be given, this would unfairly prevent the plaintiff from pursuing the claim because it could not provide the security.

If we are to make the application then I will first write to the other side putting our reasons to them and asking them to assure us on our fears or provide security voluntarily. Assuming, as is likely, that they do not respond satisfactorily I will then make the application, although in the meantime I will also serve our defence and counterclaim.

Finally, if the claim against you is to continue then I feel we should consider joining in Metal Ltd on the basis that the delays complained of were caused by Metal and also some of the defects are clearly defects in the aluminium extrusions supplied by Metal. Whilst primarily our case is that Rent-A-Tent contracted directly with Metal and therefore you cannot be held responsible for any problem with the aluminium, nevertheless to ensure you are fully covered I suggest Metal is joined so that if the court does consider you are liable for these particular problems, you can seek an indemnity from Metal because it was Metal's fault.

I look forward to hearing from you once you have had an opportunity of considering this letter and enclosures and if you have any queries please do not hesitate to contact me.

Yours sincerely

Tom Wood

Commentary: Letter to Anne Francis

Note that at the onset of the action, Tom points out that there is a real risk that even if Hawthorn successfully defends the action then it may not recover all of its costs. Obtaining a company search is something you may associate with acting for the plaintiff and checking that you will be able to enforce judgment against a defendant company. However as the defendant's solicitor, Tom must consider how his client will recover its costs should it successfully defend the action. As Rent-A-Tent are in a precarious financial position, Tom advises Anne that a security for costs application should be made. Also note Tom is raising the prospect of a third party claim against Metal Ltd. As you will see below this is eventually pursued.

Document 15

PROOF OF EVIDENCE

I Anne Francis of 7 Burlington Mews, Oldcastle, OL3 4JW Company Director will say as follows:

1. I am the Managing Director of Hawthorn Limited, a company I established with my husband six years ago as a small specialist joinery company but which has now grown to be a successful joinery and shopfitting company with twenty-five employees, including myself. I am responsible for the administration and marketing of the company.

2. In early December 1996 I took a telephone call from Robert Dancer who informed me that he had a company, Rent-A-Tent Limited, and he wanted to know if we would be interested in manufacturing for him some portable dancefloor tiles. He briefly explained on the telephone what

these were and that he had a number of prototypes manufactured but they were proving to be too expensive. What he wanted was to bring some of his prototypes to us and basically get a quote from us to manufacture them for him.

3.   I agreed to a meeting with Mr Dancer and this was arranged for 18 December at my office.

4.   At that meeting, which took place in the morning, I met with Mr Dancer and additionally my Production Manager, George Best, was present. Mr Dancer brought with him four of his prototype tiles which I understood had been manufactured by Regal Oak Limited, a company based in Edinburgh known to me as a high class joinery company particularly specialising in quality reproduction and modern furniture.

5.   Mr Dancer had explained on the telephone that he had designed these tiles which he regarded as better than anything else available, principally due to the ease of assembly and secure locking system. Neither I nor George Best had any experience of such a portable dancefloor system and at the meeting Mr Dancer elaborated and, by reference to the prototypes, explained how each tile had, on two adjacent edges, a 'male' locking mechanism and on the other two adjacent edges a 'female' locking mechanism. When the tiles were assembled into a complete dancefloor, the male sides would slot into the female sides on adjoining tiles and the complete floor would then be surrounded by aluminium edges which would add to the strength of the floor.

6.   The tiles were made up of wooden strips approximately two inches wide and two feet long. Twelve of these strips would be bound together by glue with a rubber backing and then this would be surrounded by aluminium edging which would be cut from extruded aluminium and assembled on the tile, being secured in place by glue and grub-screwed, to form the male and female locking system. Each female edge had a drill hole into which was affixed a brass ferrule and this hole was used to release the tiles by inserting a simple release tool which would push down the inserted male mechanism and allow the tiles to be pulled away from each other.

7.   The quality of manufacture of these prototype tiles was very high — the wood was good quality oak, there was a high quality lacquer finish which had obviously been achieved with perhaps four or five separate coats, the aluminium was clearly very well machined and the overall impression was one of great quality which could only be achieved by the use of top quality materials and craftsmanship. I was not surprised when Mr Dancer told us that Regal Oak Limited wanted to charge £70 per tile to manufacture these. He wanted to know if we could manufacture them at a cheaper price and he said he was thinking of something around £40 per tile.

8.   George Best said that he was sure we could manufacture the tiles although the aluminium extrusions would have to be supplied from an outside contractor and if we were to do it at the price Mr Dancer was talking about, then he couldn't expect them to be of the same quality as the prototypes. Mr Dancer accepted this and said that provided that the tiles would do the job and looked OK, then he did not mind if they were not exact replicas of the prototype. It was agreed that he would leave the four prototype tiles with us for two weeks during which time George would disassemble one and we would see what we could do to keep the costs down. We agreed to contact him again in two weeks' time.

9.   During the next two weeks George disassembled one of the prototypes although this only meant taking the aluminium edges off and disassembling these into their component parts to see how they were made up. I discussed the project with George and we agreed that we could manufacture the tiles and make costs savings as follows:

(a)   use a cheaper wood;

(b)   only apply two coats of lacquer finish;

(c)   dispense with the grub screws;

(d)   shorten the male interlocking latches;

(e)   dispense with the brass ferrules.

RENT-A-TENT LTD v HAWTHORN LTD

10. With regard to the aluminium extrusions George suggested that we put Mr Dancer in touch with Metal Limited, a metal furnishing company who we had used before to supply us with aluminium frames for shopfitting projects. The other parts, being screws and the springs for the assembly of the interlocking system, we would obtain ourselves although we would need to obtain the springs from an outside source, ideally the same source that had supplied them for the prototype.

11. I telephoned Mr Dancer about the springs and he said he would have to find out who supplied them, discreetly, from Regal Oak. That same day he sent me a fax to confirm the supplier of the springs was a company in Bristol, High Tension Limited, and he gave me their telephone number. I telephoned and spoke to their Sales Director, a Mr Jarvis, and he recalled the supply to Regal Oak and confirmed he could supply us with as many of the springs as we wanted at a cost of £200 per 1,000. I told Mr Jarvis that we would probably want 4,200 but I would get back to him during the course of the next week.

12. George contacted John Irons at Metal Limited and, one afternoon, went over to see him, taking one complete prototype tile with him and the aluminium edge parts from the disassembled one. When George came back he told me that Metal Limited could supply the aluminium extrusions and it would probably work out at a cost of £10 per tile.

13. On the basis of all this information George and I then worked out a costing for each tile. Taking into account the material and labour cost and contribution to overheads we came out with a figure of £6.00 for the materials, £16.00 labour cost and £2.00 contribution to overheads, giving a total manufacturing cost of £24.00 per tile, but this did exclude the aluminium supply, which would have to be dealt with as a separate matter between Rent-A-Tent Limited and Metal Limited.

14. We generally have a profit mark up on most items of around 50%. In this case and bearing in mind the figure mentioned by Mr Dancer of 'around £40' we decided to mark the price up to £35.00 per tile on the basis of the additional cost of the aluminium of £10.00 per tile. We did say that we would be prepared to come down on this price by up to £2.00 per tile if Mr Dancer was unhappy, but as it was he didn't try and negotiate this price down.

15. I telephoned Mr Dancer and an appointment was made for him to come and see us on 13 January. I told him on the telephone that we could manufacture the tiles at £35.00 plus VAT, but this would be on the basis of the aluminium being supplied under a separate contract at a cost of about £10.00 per tile, and modifications for the prototype, which I felt George would need to explain to him at the meeting.

16. The meeting took place when George and I met Mr Dancer. George explained the modifications to him. I can specifically recall George mentioning the following:

(a) we would not use oak but whatever hardwood was generally available to us at a competitive price. Teak was mentioned but George did not say we would definitely use teak. It was left open to us to use whatever hardwood we liked although on the understanding that it would be uniform in final appearance;

(b) the prototype tiles appeared to have about five coats of lacquer finish. We would only apply two and this would be sufficient;

(c) we would not use grub screws — they were superfluous. Modern glues are very secure;

(d) the brass ferrules would be dispensed with;

(e) the length of the locking latches would be shortened.

RENT-A-TENT LTD v HAWTHORN LTD

17. I told Mr Dancer that we had spoken to Metal Limited about the supply of the aluminium extrusions and George told him of his visit to see John Irons with a tile and the aluminium edging. He said that John Irons had confirmed Metal Limited could produce the extrusions and the additional cost would be about £10.00 per tile.

18. Mr Dancer asked us whether we would sort out the supply of the extrusions directly with Metal Limited. I responded by saying that whilst we would of course liaise with them on the question of delivery and quantities, he would have to contract with Metal Limited directly given the volume and money involved. He agreed and I provided him with Metal Limited's address and telephone number on the basis that George was to immediately telephone John Irons and tell him to expect a call from Mr Dancer and George would drop off with John Irons the tile and separate aluminium edging that he had previously seen so that they could work from it.

19. I'm not sure at what point we had a definite agreement to manufacture the tiles but it was undoubtedly accepted by this stage that we would do so. Mr Dancer was happy with our proposals and certainly didn't argue about the price. In fact he said that this was about what he had been hoping for.

20. I told Mr Dancer that the minimum initial manufacturing run would be 1,000 but thereafter he could have them in multiples of 100. He said that was fine and we should start with 1,000 minimum although he anticipated that he would need more.

21. It was at this point that he said he had a contract to supply 300 tiles to Oldcastle University, and would it be possible to have these 300 ready by the end of February. I told him that this should be possible and we'd better get started. At this the meeting concluded with Mr Dancer saying he would contact John Irons straightaway.

22. We started manufacture straightaway, using teak hardwood that we had in stock initially and ordering further amounts. The first thing we had to do was to cut the strips and then bind these together, gluing them onto the rubber backing sheet. Once this had been done then the aluminium edging was to be added.

23. The edging would be received in continuous lengths from Metal Limited being extruded by them in one continuous process. The lengths were, individually, the edging strips and in addition the strips which, when cut to size, would be fitted into the edging strip to form the 'male' locking latch and location strips.

24. The edging strips were cut to the length required for each tile and these (as they were) formed the 'female' sides and could be affixed to the tile by slotting them along the length of the tile and secured by glue.

25. The 'male' side however had to be assembled by insertion into the outside edge of the strip of three separate pieces, being (in order) a location strip, the locking latch and then a further location strip. The first location strip was inserted using glue and a single screw to secure it. The locking latch mechanism was then inserted. This was constructed first by inserting two springs, compressing these and then inserting the locking latch strip and then releasing the springs. The second location strip would be inserted and secured as before. The effect of being between the two secure location strips and the effect of the two springs held the locking latch secure. The completed 'male' side was then affixed to the tile as before and the tile was then complete (the lacquer had been applied to the wood prior to the edging being affixed).

26. To complete 300 tiles by the end of February would have needed the aluminium being supplied by the end of January. I spoke to John Irons at Metal Limited who telephoned me, saying that he had briefly met with Mr Dancer and agreed a price with him and when did we want the aluminium for, mentioning that Mr Dancer had told him the first 300 tiles should be ready by

RENT-A-TENT LTD v HAWTHORN LTD

the end of February. I told Mr Irons that we would need the aluminium for the end of January. He did say that might be a bit tight but he should be able to do it.

27. However, by the end of January, only sufficient metal had been received for us to complete 120 tiles. These were completed by the 19 February. I telephoned and spoke to John Irons on two occasions during February to find out when the rest of the metal would be available. He was evasive and simply said that it was more complicated than he first thought. I did not chase more than this because I considered it was up to Mr Dancer. I spoke to him on the telephone on two or three occasions, the first at the beginning of February when I told him that the tiles would not be ready for the end of February due to the delay in delivery by Metal Limited. His response was to the effect that I should sort the problem out. Following this I telephoned John Irons (the first time I telephoned him — the Production Manager had originally told George Best that there would be a delay) and he told me of his problem.

28. I telephoned back to Mr Dancer (not immediately, perhaps a day or so later) and told him of my conversation with John Irons. Mr Dancer said, effectively, that he was not happy and that he had an agreement with us for delivery by the end of February. I told him it was not our fault and if the metal was available we could give him the tiles by then. I suggested he sort it out with John Irons.

29. About a week later Mr Dancer telephoned me and said he had spoken to John Irons and had been promised the metal would be available at the beginning of next week. The metal did not arrive and I again telephoned John Irons who more or less told me the same thing as before, but he said that he should be able to get the metal to us by next week.

30. I telephoned Mr Dancer and told him of my conversation. He said he had been let down again. I told him he had not been let down by us and if the metal was supplied next week then we should be able to let him have the tiles for mid-March. He asked me whether we had any finished and I told him we had 120. He asked us to let him have those and I agreed, arranging delivery with him to his premises for 21 February.

31. The metal finally arrived from Metal Limited on 24 February. We completed the remaining 180 tiles and delivered them to Mr Dancer on 21 March.

32. With regard to payment, when we agreed to manufacture the tiles at the meeting on 13 January, unfortunately I overlooked agreeing payment terms. I therefore wrote to Mr Dancer on 15 January when I confirmed the agreement and also raised the question of payment, suggesting payment for the first 300 on delivery and the payment for the balance of 700 on completion and delivery of 350 lots. Mr Dancer wrote back on 17 January effectively saying he was not happy with my proposal and saying he wanted to pay on completion and delivery for the whole 1,000 tiles, as this had been his understanding. I was not happy with this but, as I considered it was my own fault in not dealing with payment at the meeting (which is very unlike me) I did not respond but simply accepted this.

33. Having delivered the total 300 tiles, I received a telephone call from Mr Dancer on 25 March when he said we should not manufacture any more tiles for the time being as he was having problems in Oldcastle University taking the 300 he had. I obtained the impression that this was simply a temporary delay and he would telephone in the next few days to confirm we should continue. I did not ask him what the problem was but simply said OK, we would put a hold on it for a few days.

34. However, nothing further was heard from Mr Dancer for about three weeks and so, on 15 April, I raised and sent out to Mr Dancer an invoice for the 300 tiles at £35 each, totalling £10,500 plus VAT.

RENT-A-TENT LTD v HAWTHORN LTD

35. Again nothing was heard from Mr Dancer and so on 9 May I telephoned him to clarify the position and to ask for payment of our invoice. He was quite short on the telephone, saying that he would contact me shortly about the remaining tiles and he would deal with our invoice. I did not press but understood this to mean that he would be asking us to re-commence manufacture of the tiles in the next few days and he would be arranging for payment of our invoice.

36. I went away on holiday on 17 May and on that date the letter from Mr Dancer's solicitors, Nixons, arrived at the office. Unfortunately, nobody had bothered to respond to it, deciding to leave it for me to deal with on my return. I came back to the office on 3 June and on that same day the summons arrived in the post.

37. With regard to the summons I would like to make the following points:

[Note: The proof of evidence then continues as per the attendance note at pages 156 *et seq.* where Tom went through the particulars of claim with Anne Francis and she commented on it with obvious amendments (see the witness statement at pages 226 *et seq.* onwards).]

<u>Signed</u>   Anne Francis   <u>Date</u>   19 June 1997

Commentary: Proof of Evidence

You should refer to the notes and commentary on the proof of evidence in the personal injury case study at pages 31 *et seq.*

The proof of evidence should be as full as possible and should contain all the information which Tom can glean at this stage. From the proof Tom will consider what areas to make further enquiries and generally advise Anne on the strength of her company's defence and possible counterclaim. We have in fact reproduced the proof in its final form after Anne made certain minor amendments to the draft and supplied more details.

Document 16

<u>IN THE OLDCASTLE COUNTY COURT</u>   Case No. OL794762

BETWEEN

RENT-A-TENT LIMITED   Plaintiff

and

HAWTHORN LIMITED   <u>Defendant</u>

DEFENCE AND COUNTERCLAIM

<u>DEFENCE</u>

1. Paragraphs 1 and 2 of the Particulars of Claim are admitted.[1]

2. As to the terms of the Agreement as set out in paragraph 3, it is averred that:[2]

(a)   The sample tiles provided by the Plaintiff were prototypes manufactured for the Plaintiff by Regal Oak Limited at a cost of £70.00 per tile. The Plaintiff enquired of the Defendant whether the Defendant could manufacture them at a cheaper cost. The Defendant confirmed it could do so but the tile would be modified in certain respects as set out in paragraph 4 below and, subject to them, sub-paragraph (a) is admitted.

(b)   As to sub-paragraph (b) such purpose as was made known to the Defendant for the dancefloor tiles was for use, when assembled together, as a dancefloor. The Agreement required the Defendant to manufacture individual dancefloor tiles similar to the sample produced by the Plaintiff. It was not the Defendant's responsibility to ensure the tiles thus manufactured would be fit for use as a dancefloor system.

(c)   Sub-paragraph (c) and (d) are admitted.

(d)   Sub-paragraph (e) is admitted save that it is denied time was of the essence (if it is so alleged by the Plaintiff) and further such delivery was dependent upon the supply by a third party, Metal Limited, of aluminium extrusions under a separate agreement between the Plaintiff and Metal Limited.

3.   Whilst it is admitted that the 300 tiles were not supplied until 21st March 1997 it is denied that the Defendant was thereby in breach of the Agreement as alleged in paragraph 4. As was well known to the Plaintiff, such late delivery was solely caused by the late delivery by Metal Limited of the aluminium extrusions.[3]

4.   As to the Particulars of Defects alleged in paragraph 4 it is denied that any such defects exist or, if there be such defects, that they arise through the Defendant's default.[4] With regard to each particularised defect it is averred that:

(a)   Locking latches — the pre-load is dependent upon the spring. The springs used by the Defendants are the same springs as used in the sample tile and provide adequate pre-load in comparison to the sample tile. The reduction in length is a modification agreed between the parties and in any event does not affect the function of the tile in comparison to the sample.

(b)   Location strips — it was agreed that these would not be grub-screwed. They are secure and it is denied they are prone to become mis-aligned.

(c)   Edge trims — it is denied that they fail to interlock satisfactorily, or, if there is such a fault that it is due to any default by the Defendant. The edge trims were manufactured by Metal Limited, being part of the aluminium extrusions supplied by them and if, which is denied, there are any defects these are due to a fault in manufacture by Metal Limited.

(d)   Release access hole — it was agreed that the brass ferrules would be omitted and it is denied that with proper use the hole edges will fray.

(e)   Cutting burrs — this is denied and in any event, insofar as the alleged defect relates to the aluminium extrusions supplied by Metal Limited, it is denied the Defendant is at fault.

(f)   Cosmetically.

(i)   Texture of quality of wood finish — it was agreed the Defendant could use any hardwood in manufacturing the tiles provided the overall appearance was uniform. The Defendant has used teak, as opposed to oak in the sample tile, and whilst the appearance and texture is different to oak, it is not admitted it is inferior to the sample tile or a breach by the Defendant.

RENT-A-TENT LTD v HAWTHORN LTD

    (ii)   Finishing lacquer — 2 coats of finishing lacquer have been applied (as opposed to 4 coats on the sample tile) as agreed and this provides a smooth finish.

    (iii)   Surface quality of aluminium — this is denied but any defect which does exist is due to manufacture by Metal Limited.

    (iv)   Depth and colour — this is denied but any defect which does exist is due to manufacture by Metal Limited.

5.   Paragraph 5 is denied.[5]

6.   Save that it is admitted the Plaintiff's solicitors sent the stated letter, the Plaintiff's right to reject the tiles and the remainder of paragraph 6 is denied.[6]

7.   Paragraph 7 is denied.

8.   Save as aforesaid each and every allegation in the Particulars of Claim is denied as if the same were set out herein and specifically traversed.[7]

COUNTERCLAIM

9.   The Defendant repeats paragraphs 1 and 2 of its Defence herein.[8]

10.   On 21st March 1997 the Defendant delivered the balance of 300 tiles to the Plaintiff, the first 120 having been delivered on 21st February 1997.

11.   By an invoice dated 15th April 1997 the Defendant invoiced the Plaintiff for payment of the 300 tiles delivered at £35.00 per tile plus VAT, totalling £12,337.50 (inclusive of VAT). In breach of the Agreement the Plaintiff has failed and refuses to pay the same.

12.   Further, the Plaintiff has by its action repudiated the Agreement and thereby waived and excused the Defendant from manufacturing the remaining 700 tiles under the Agreement and caused the Defendant loss of profit on these 700 tiles equating to £28,787.50.

13.   The Defendant additionally claims interest on such sums as shall be awarded pursuant to s. 69 County Courts Act 1984.[9]

And the Defendant Counterclaims

    (1)   Under paragraph 11, £12,337.50.

    (2)   Under paragraph 12, £28,787.50.

    (3)   Further or alternatively damages.

    (4)   Interest on such sum as shall be awarded to the Defendant at the rate of 8% per annum pursuant to s. 69 County Courts Act 1984 for such period as the Court thinks fit.

Dated this 17th day of June 1997

(signed)

TO: The Court and to
Nixons
16 High Street
Oldcastle OL1 2XL
Plaintiff's Solicitors

. . . .
Watkins & O'Dwyer
17 Sycamore Avenue
Oldcastle OL10 1BR
Defendant's Solicitors

RENT-A-TENT LTD v HAWTHORN LTD

NOTES: DEFENCE AND COUNTERCLAIM

Generally see comments on the defence in the personal injury case study at page 85.

(1)   Paragraphs 1 and 2 of the particulars of claim are uncontroversial and as such can be admitted.

(2)   At paragraph 2 the defendant puts forward its case. As this case centres around what was the nature of the alleged agreement, the defendant pleads what it alleges are the terms of the agreement. Note that the defendant does not simply deny the terms as pleaded in the particulars of claim, rather the defendant admits that which is accepted but qualifies it (see paragraph 2(d)).

(3)   At paragraph 3 the defendant explains why the tiles were delivered late. As the plaintiff is alleging that the defendant was in breach by failing to supply the tiles by the agreed date then the defendant should put forward any reason excusing the late delivery in its defence.

(4)   At paragraph 4 the defendant pleads in the alternative. Essentially not only does the defendant deny the existence of any defects, but even if they do exist then the defendant makes no admissions as to their causation. This is important — it may be that the tiles are defective, but by pleading in this way the defendant denies any responsibility for the alleged defects. The defence then goes on to deal with each 'particular' individually. It is not wrong to simply deny each allegation and leave it at that. However, where the crux of the case centres around what was agreed with regard to the tiles, it will add more weight to the defence if the defendant pleads positively to each allegation.

(5)   There is not much to say with regard to paragraph 5. The defendant simply denies the breach of contract and the consequences alleged.

(6)   There would be little point in denying that the letter was sent, but the defendant can deny it is of any consequence.

(7)   At paragraph 9 the defence includes a general denial. The defendant includes this to basically say that if the defence has failed to deny a particular allegation, then this phrase acts as a catch all provision, by denying that which has not already been denied. If the defence is properly pleaded it should not be necessary to include this phrase; however, you will often see it (particularly in complex defences).

(8)   With regard to the counterclaim, the only difference from the particulars of the claim in style is the first paragraph. As some of the material facts have already been pleaded there is no need to repeat them again in the counterclaim, hence paragraph 9 of the defence and counterclaim simply relies on paragraphs 1 and 2 of the defence.

(9)   Thereafter the counterclaim is similar to the particulars of claim. The defendant claims interest on the counterclaim as for the particulars of claim.

Commentary: The Counterclaim

As Hawthorn Ltd has a claim against Rent-A-Tent it has raised it by way of a counterclaim. A defendant in any action which alleges that it has a claim or is entitled to relief/remedy may make a counterclaim. For further commentary on a counterclaim see RSC Ord. 15, r. 2. The counterclaim although included in the defence is to all intents and purposes a separate action and may continue in its own right. Again it must be served within 14 days of service of the summons. Note that a fee is also payable on a counterclaim and, as for the plaintiff's claim, the fee is dependent on the amount of the claim. The fee is calculated on the *whole* of the counterclaim and not just the excess (see further page 153, note (6) for examples of the possible fees).

RENT-A-TENT LTD v HAWTHORN LTD

STEP 6

Following approval from Anne, Tom serves the defence and counterclaim and raises the question of security for costs with the other side. The other side respond.

Document 17

Watkins & O'Dwyer
Solicitors

17 Sycamore Avenue
Oldcastle OL10 1BR
Tel. 011-111-1111
Fax 011-111-1111
DX Oldcastle 1000

Partners: J. Watkins
A. O'Dwyer

17 June 1997

Your ref: PT/4/101
Our ref: TW/DR/623

Nixons
16 High Street
Oldcastle OL1 2XL

Dear Sirs

Re: Rent-A-Tent Limited v Hawthorn Limited

We enclose by way of service a defence and counterclaim.

We are concerned as to your client's ability to abide by adverse costs orders. We have obtained a company search from which the following are apparent from the last filed accounts for the period to 31 December 1996:

(a) The turnover has decreased by nearly 30%.

(b) The cost of sales has increased by nearly 20%.

(c) The trade creditors have increased by 15% to £140,000 whereas the debtors' figure has remained fairly static.

(d) The company has a net loss for the year of £12,000 against a net profit the year before of £42,000.

Additionally, from the Charges Register the company granted a second fixed and floating charge over its assets to Forcem Factors Limited on 17 February 1997.

Additionally, your client stated, in its letter to ours of 17 January, that a bank facility was needed to pay for the wooden tiles. We assume that facility has now been withdrawn and presumably your client equally does not have access to funds to pay our client's costs of this action.

In the circumstances we require you to either satisfy us, by evidence, of your client's means and consequent ability to meet our client's costs or, alternatively, voluntarily provide security for those costs. If you fail to do so within 14 days we are instructed to make an application for security for costs.

We look forward to hearing from you.

Yours faithfully

Watkins & O'Dwyer

190

Commentary: Security for Costs

See RSC Ord. 23; CCR Ord. 13, r. 8; Companies Act 1985, s. 726(1).

You must bear in mind the purpose of this case study is to illustrate how a case may proceed from start to finish, the steps you may find it necessary to take and illustrate the documents. It is not intended that the example documents can be slavishly followed in all cases and, in particular, allowances must be made when considering the facts and merit to any application you make.

Therefore, in writing to Anne about security for costs and the merits of the application (see page 179) this is to illustrate to you that the client is entitled to be kept informed and given some explanation of what you are doing (you should confirm this in writing) and your own thoughts on the merits, even if you do hedge your bets! The letter and subsequent application ignores and does not consider in depth the arguments that will be raised by the other side over and above the illustrated documents.

Apart from seeing the points raised by the other side we do not go into the merits of the application and argument in chambers which ultimately leads to the application failing. Tom has not addressed, so far, the consequence of Hawthorn Limited being in the position of plaintiff on its counterclaim which we will see in the letter from the other side.

Document 18

Nixons

16 High Street
Oldcastle
OL1 2XL

20 June 1997

Your ref: TW/DR/623
Our ref: PT/4/101

Watkins & O'Dwyer
17 Sycamore Avenue
Oldcastle
OL10 1BR

Dear Sirs

<u>Re: Rent-A-Tent Limited v Hawthorn Limited</u>

Thank you for your letter of 17 June.

Whilst we are taking our client's instructions as to the points you make on its financial standing, we are bound to say that in any event we consider your proposed application for security is ill-founded when your client is making a substantial counterclaim. Unsurprisingly the defence to that counterclaim will be on the basis of the breaches by your client complained of in the particulars of claim.

As such, your client being in the position of Plaintiff on its counterclaim, our client is entitled to defend that counterclaim without being subjected to an order for security.

RENT-A-TENT LTD v HAWTHORN LTD

If you do therefore proceed with your application, we will invite the court to agree that your client is no more at risk on costs in defending and counterclaiming than it would be in only pursuing the defended counterclaim, whereas there would clearly be prejudice to our client in being subjected to an order for security which it may not be able to comply with.

We would therefore ask you to confirm that you do not propose pursuing your application or otherwise, if you do so propose, confirm we may have a general extension of time until after that application has been heard to serve our reply and defence to counterclaim.

Yours faithfully

Nixons

Partners: J. D. Nixon, P. T. Turner, H. A. Tubby

Document 19

Watkins & O'Dwyer
Solicitors

17 Sycamore Avenue
Oldcastle OL10 1BR
Tel. 011-111-1111
Fax 011-111-1111
DX Oldcastle 1000

Partners: J. Watkins
A. O'Dwyer

23 June 1997

Your ref: PT/4/101
Our ref: TW/DR/623

Nixons
16 High Street
Oldcastle
OL1 2XL

Dear Sirs

Re: Rent-A-Tent Limited v Hawthorn Limited

Thank you for your letter of 20 June.

We do not accept what you say as to the lack of prejudice to our client, but do not intend to litigate this matter in correspondence with you.

In the absence of having received your response to the specific points raised, we have now forwarded our application to the Court for issue and service on you. We will let you have a copy of our affidavit in support shortly.

> In the meantime, we confirm you may have the extension requested for service of your pleading subject to seven days' written notice from us requiring service.
>
> Yours faithfully
>
> Watkins & O'Dwyer

STEP 7

Tom issues a notice of application regarding the application for security for costs.

RENT-A-TENT LTD v HAWTHORN LTD

Document 20

IN THE OLDCASTLE COUNTY COURT   Case No. OL794762

BETWEEN

RENT-A-TENT LIMITED   <u>Plaintiff</u>

and

HAWTHORN LIMITED   <u>Defendant</u>

I WISH TO APPLY FOR an Order that the Plaintiff do provide security for the Defendant's costs of this action to the satisfaction of the Court and that in the meantime all further proceedings on the Plaintiff's claim be stayed.

And that the Plaintiff do pay the costs of this application in any event.

Dated 23rd June 1997

Signed...............   Address for service:
Defendant's Solicitor

           17 Sycamore Avenue
           Oldcastle
           OL10 1BR

Time estimate: 1 hour

THIS SECTION TO BE COMPLETED BY THE COURT

To the Plaintiff/Defendant

TAKE NOTICE that this application will be heard by the District Judge at
          on   at   o'clock.

If you do not attend the Court will make such Order as it thinks fit.

Document 21

Watkins & O'Dwyer
Solicitors

17 Sycamore Avenue
Oldcastle OL10 1BR
Tel. 011-111-1111
Fax 011-111-1111
DX Oldcastle 1000

Partners: J. Watkins
A. O'Dwyer

23 June 1997

Our ref: TW/DR/623

The Chief Clerk
Oldcastle County Court
The Courthouse
Priory Street
Oldcastle
OL2 4TP

Dear Sir

<u>Re: Rent-A-Tent Limited v Hawthorn Limited — Case No. OL794762</u>

We enclose a notice of application in triplicate for issue before the district judge on the first available date after 1 July with a time estimate of 1 hour and look forward to the return of a sealed copy notifying us of the hearing date.

Kindly effect service of a sealed copy directly upon the Plaintiff's solicitors.

Yours faithfully

Watkins & O'Dwyer

Commentary: Notice of Application

See notes on the summons and interlocutory application in the personal injury case study at page 88. The notice of application is the county court equivalent of the summons in the High Court. Normally the court will complete the lower section and serve notice of the application on the opponent. However, the solicitor can request the return of two completed copies and serve one copy on the other side. This may occur where the solicitor wishes to effect personal service or if the solicitor does not wish to effect service immediately as a matter of tactics.

STEP 8

Tom prepares and serves the affidavit in support of the application for security for costs on Nixons.

He also files the original affidavit at court.

RENT-A-TENT LTD v HAWTHORN LTD

Document 22

Watkins & O'Dwyer
Solicitors

17 Sycamore Avenue
Oldcastle OL10 1BR
Tel. 011-111-1111
Fax 011-111-1111
DX Oldcastle 1000

Partners: J. Watkins
A. O'Dwyer

3 July 1997

Your ref: PT/4/101
Our ref: TW/DR/623

Nixons
16 High Street
Oldcastle
OL1 2XL

Dear Sirs

<u>Re: Rent-A-Tent Limited v Hawthorn Limited</u>

We enclose a copy of the sealed notice of application we have now received back from the Court office and you should have received a sealed copy by way of service directly from the Court, returnable on 21 July 1997.

We additionally enclose by way of service, a copy affidavit and two exhibits sworn in support of the application. Kindly acknowledge receipt.

Yours faithfully

Watkins & O'Dwyer

Document 23

Watkins & O'Dwyer
Solicitors

17 Sycamore Avenue
Oldcastle OL10 1BR
Tel. 011-111-1111
Fax 011-111-1111
DX Oldcastle 1000

Partners: J. Watkins
A. O'Dwyer

3 July 1997

Our ref: TW/DR/623

The Chief Clerk
Oldcastle County Court
The Courthouse
Priory Street
Oldcastle
OL2 4TP

Dear Sir

Re: Rent-A-Tent Limited v Hawthorn Limited — Case No. OL794762

We enclose an affidavit and two exhibits sworn by Mr T. A. Wood in support of the Defendant's application for hearing on 21 July 1997. Kindly place these on the court file.

Yours faithfully

Watkins & O'Dwyer

RENT-A-TENT LTD v HAWTHORN LTD

Document 24

> Defendant: T. A. Wood: 1st
> Sworn: 27th June 1997
> Filed: 3rd July 1997
> Exhibits 'TAW' 1 and 2

IN THE OLDCASTLE COUNTY COURT   Case No. OL794762

BETWEEN

RENT-A-TENT LIMITED   <u>Plaintiff</u>

and

HAWTHORN LIMITED   Defendant

AFFIDAVIT

I Thomas Arthur Wood of 17 Sycamore Avenue, Oldcastle, OL10 1BR Solicitor make oath and say as follows:

1. I am an assistant solicitor with Messrs Watkins & O'Dwyer, Solicitors for the Defendant and I have the conduct of this action and am duly authorised to make this Affidavit on behalf of the Defendant. The matters to which I hereinafter depose are within my own personal knowledge or otherwise come into my knowledge in the manner and from the source as stated. I make this Affidavit in support of the Defendant's application for an order that the Plaintiff do provide security for the Defendant's costs of this action.[1]

2. The details of the Plaintiff's claim and the Defendant's Defence and Counterclaim appear in the pleadings to this action. I would submit that it is readily apparent that the Plaintiff does not have a claim which is unarguable (and is most certainly not one for which it could seriously consider making an application for summary judgment) but, on the contrary, the Defendant's pleaded Defence and Counterclaim answers in full the allegations made by the Plaintiff and certainly provides a solid foundation upon which the Defendant appears able to successfully resist the Plaintiff's claim.[2]

3. There is now produced and shown to me marked 'TAW 1' a true copy of a company search I caused to be made on the Plaintiff company which shows that it was incorporated on 1st October 1984 with an authorised share capital of 1,000 ordinary shares of £1 each. Of this authorised share capital only 100 have been issued, with 99 to Mr R. Dancer and the remaining one share to a Mrs Winifred Dancer whom I assume to be the wife of Mr R. Dancer. It is therefore immediately apparent that the Plaintiff was established as a small family owned and run company without any significant capital base.[3]

4. Included in the company search results are copies of the latest filed accounts for the Plaintiff, for the period to 31st December 1996 and these accounts provide the current year's figures and then, for comparison purposes, the relevant figures for the financial year to 31st December 1995 that the following indicators of the Plaintiff's failing business success are apparent:

(a) The Plaintiff's turnover has decreased by nearly 30%.

(b) The cost of sales has increased by nearly 20%.

(c) The trade creditors have increased by 15% to £140,000.

(d) The Plaintiff made a net loss for the year ending 31st December 1996 of £12,000.

5. I would now refer the Court to the copy charges register included in the company search result from which it can be seen that earlier this year, on 17th February, the Plaintiff granted a second fixed and floating charge (behind Royal National Bank plc) over its entire undertaking to Forcem Factors Limited. I would submit that this is indicative of the Plaintiff having very recently taken on new liabilities from this factoring company, perhaps as a result of cashflow problems.

6. Finally, in considering matters which would reflect on the Plaintiff's financial standing, there is now produced and shown to me marked 'TAW 2' at page 1 a true copy letter sent by Mr Dancer of the Plaintiff company to the Defendant dated 17th January 1997 wherein, in the final paragraph, Mr Dancer makes a point that the Plaintiff had arranged a facility with its bankers to pay for the dancefloor tiles. Given the Plaintiff's complaints and the intention not to pay for the dancefloor tiles, I readily assume that this facility is no longer available to the Plaintiff and, in consequence, in the event that the Defendant is successful in its defence, then there cannot be much doubt that the Plaintiff will then be liable to the Defendant on the Defendant's counterclaim together with the costs of the action and it appears unlikely the Plaintiff will have the resources available to it to satisfy the Defendant's contractual counterclaim, let alone the claim for costs.

7. As a result of the matters set out above I wrote to the Plaintiff's solicitors by letter dated 17 June 1997 requesting them to provide some assurance as to the Plaintiff's financial position or otherwise security for costs. A true copy of my letter is included at page 2 to 'TAW 2'. The Plaintiff, in response, has failed to provide the assurance requested or otherwise proposals for security to be given.[4]

8. It is in these circumstances that I respectfully submit to the Court that it appears distinctly likely that in the event of the Defendant successfully defending the Plaintiff's claim then the Plaintiff will not be in a position to abide by the inevitable costs order that will be made against it.

9. With regard to the extent of the Defendant's costs, I have included at page 3 to 'TAW 1' a schedule which, in Part 1, provides details of the costs which the Defendant has incurred to the date of preparation and swearing of this Affidavit, in Part 2 the costs estimate for further costs up to and including the discovery process and then, in Part 3, a further estimate of costs for discovery for steps up to and including trial (these costs do include a provision for an expert to become involved which is undoubtedly going to be necessary given the nature of the alleged defects by the Plaintiff). From this information it may be seen that the estimated total costs and disbursements to the Defendant proceeding to a 2 day trial will be £7,500.[5]

10. I would accordingly submit to the Court that this is a case where the Defendant's exposure to the prospect of being unable to enforce the costs order against the Plaintiff should be limited as far as possible by the Court ordering the Plaintiff to give security for the Defendant's costs in the sum of £7,500.

Sworn at 14 New Lane, Oldcastle
in the County of Oldshire
this 27th day of June 1997
Before me,

Thomas Wood (signed)

A. N. Other (signed)

Solicitor

RENT-A-TENT LTD v HAWTHORN LTD

NOTES: AFFIDAVIT

Generally, you should refer to the notes and commentary on affidavits in the personal injury case study at pages 102 *et seq*.

(1) Paragraph 1 simply sets out the status of the deponent and the nature of the application. Additionally, as the deponent in this case is Tom he states that the information is within his own personal knowledge unless otherwise stated, thereby enabling him to introduce hearsay evidence.

(2) This paragraph emphasises that there is a genuine dispute between the parties and no side has a strong enough case to either justify a claim for summary judgment (either for the plaintiff or the defendant on its counterclaim). Only if this situation existed would it be appropriate to go into the evidence of the case.

(3) Again, we do not reproduce the company search results but, as the purpose of this affidavit is to show that Rent-A-Tent may not be able to pay the defendant's costs, then as much information as possible about the financial standing of the company should be included. Paragraphs 3–6 describe the share capital of the company, details the company's accounts, and any charges over the company. Additionally, at paragraph 6 the affidavit implies the plaintiff was to pay for the tiles by way of a loan or an overdraft facility arranged with its bank which no longer exists. The defendant therefore alleges that without this facility the plaintiff will be unable to meet the defendant's claim.

(4) Paragraph 7 states that the defendant has already requested that the plaintiff provide some sort of security. This demonstrates that at all times the defendant has been reasonable and also that perhaps the plaintiff is unable to provide any security. Additionally had the defendant failed to make a written request of the plaintiff to provide security then the costs of a successful application would not necessarily be ordered against the plaintiff.

(5) Paragraph 9 details the defendant's costs. This will be necessary to assist the court in deciding an appropriate amount for which security should be given.

Commentary: Application for Security for Costs

1. The application for security for costs is made pursuant to CCR Ord. 13, r. 8; (RSC Ord. 23) and the Companies Act 1985, s. 726(1). The basis upon which the court may grant an order is if it appears on the evidence that the plaintiff company will not be able to comply with the adverse costs order if the defendant is successful in the defence of the claim.

2. The defendant may make the application where the plaintiff is resident abroad (but note position of EU citizen in *Fitzgerald* v *Williams* [1996] 2 WLR 447) or has deliberately misstated his address in a summons or has changed his address or, as in this case, is a limited company and there are grounds to believe it may not be able to pay the defendant's costs. The court, however, will not always order a company to give security, even if it appears that the company cannot pay, if it would stifle the plaintiff's claim. There is no general jurisdiction to award security for costs simply because the plaintiff is impecunious. Note that the application should be made as early as possible as the court will take into account the extent to which the plaintiff has already incurred costs without an order for security.

3. In considering the application, the court will not consider in detail the merits to each party's case and it is inappropriate in the evidence to go into the detail of the case *unless* it is to demonstrate that there is a significant disparity between the relevant strengths and weaknesses of each party's case such as, in the case of the plaintiff, may justify an application for summary judgment or, in the case of the defendant, leads to a strong belief that the plaintiff's claim lacks any merit.

4. If security is ordered, an amount will usually be paid into court but the court can order some other form of security, e.g., a bank guarantee. Until security is provided, further proceedings will be stayed.

STEP 9

The application for security for costs is heard. Whilst we have not reproduced it here, Tom will prepare an attendance note of the hearing which should record, briefly, the arguments of the other side and the judgment and reasoning of the district judge, together with time involved (including travel and waiting). Tom is unsuccessful.

The hearing took place at which each party was represented by their respective solicitors with the only evidence before the court being Tom's affidavit and exhibits. Mr Nixon, appearing for Rent-A-Tent, did not seek to take issue with Tom's points on Rent-A-Tent's lack of financial stability, but rather simply relied upon the points he had made in correspondence with Tom (which Tom had purposely not included in the evidence which he had filed). He successfully argued that if a costs order were made against Rent-A-Tent, then Rent-A-Tent would not be able to comply with that costs order. Consequently either (a) the proceedings as a whole would be stayed, thus depriving the defendant of the ability in pursuing in these proceedings its counterclaim, or (b) if the court attempted to simply stay the plaintiff's claim but allowed the defendant to continue with its counterclaim, the plaintiff's defence to that counterclaim would be on the basis of the breaches complained of in the Particulars of Claim, those matters would in any event have to be aired and the consequent costs incurred. Therefore, if the defendant wished to pursue its counterclaim, then the costs would be incurred in any event and it would be unfairly prejudicial in those circumstances to deprive the plaintiff of the ability to seek damages on the basis of the breaches complained of.

This argument found favour with the district judge and consequently the application for security for costs was dismissed and costs were ordered to be paid by the defendant to the plaintiff in any event.

RENT-A-TENT LTD v HAWTHORN LTD

Document 25

IN THE OLDCASTLE COUNTY COURT   Case No. OL794762

BETWEEN

RENT-A-TENT LIMITED   Plaintiff

and

HAWTHORN LIMITED   Defendant

———————

ORDER

———————

UPON READING the Affidavit of Thomas Arthur Wood sworn on 27th June 1997

AND UPON HEARING solicitors for both parties

IT IS ORDERED that:

1. The Defendant's application for security for costs be and is hereby dismissed.

2. The costs of and occasioned by the application be paid by the Defendant to the Plaintiff in any event.

3. The Plaintiff do file and serve a Reply and Defence to Counterclaim within 21 days.

4. Automatic directions to apply thereafter with time to run from today.

Dated this 21st day of July 1997

Commentary: The Order

1. In the county court the court will draw up and serve the order, unlike the High Court (see the personal injury case study at page 112).

2. The costs of this application are to be paid by the defendant but will not become payable until the conclusion of the action at which time there will be an order for taxation. It is possible, on an interlocutory order for costs, to ask the court to include an order for taxation in which case the successful party would then be able to seek payment of his costs by either agreement or proceeding to taxation without awaiting the conclusion of the proceedings. Such an order is rarely asked for and more rarely granted.

STEP 10

Tom receives a request for further and better particulars from the other side, and subsequently also their reply to defence to counterclaim. Tom also sends an interim bill to Hawthorn at this stage for the costs incurred to date (not reproduced).

Document 26

Nixons

16 High Street
Oldcastle
OL1 2XL

28 July 1997

Your ref: TW/DR/623
Our ref: PD/4/101

Watkins & O'Dwyer
17 Sycamore Avenue
Oldcastle
OL10 1BR

Dear Sirs

Re: Rent-A-Tent Limited v Hawthorn Limited

We enclose by way of service a Request for Further and Better Particulars of the Defence and Counterclaim. Kindly confirm we can extend time for service of our Reply and Defence to Counterclaim until you have supplied these Particulars.

Yours faithfully

Nixons

Partners: J. D. Nixon, P. T. Turner, H. A. Tubby

RENT-A-TENT LTD v HAWTHORN LTD

Document 27

IN THE OLDCASTLE COUNTY COURT   Case No. OL794762

BETWEEN

RENT-A-TENT LIMITED   <u>Plaintiff</u>

and

HAWTHORN LIMITED   <u>Defendant</u>

REQUEST FOR FURTHER AND BETTER PARTICULARS
OF THE DEFENCE AND COUNTERCLAIM

1. Under paragraph 3

Of 'such late delivery was solely caused by the late delivery by Metal Limited of the aluminium extrusions'

State:

(1) The actual date of delivery of the aluminium extrusions.

(2) The date upon which the Defendant originally expected delivery.

(3) Whether the Defendant agreed with Metal Limited the date for delivery and, if so, fully particularise how the agreement was reached, identifying as precisely as possible the individuals involved, dates, words spoken and, if in writing, supply a copy of the same.

2. Under paragraph 4

Of the agreement alleged under each particular sub-paragraphs (a)–(f)
State for each particular sub-paragraph:

(1) When and where the agreement was made.

(2) Identify the individuals involved in reaching the agreement.

(3) If the agreement was made verbally, identify as precisely as possible the words spoken.

(4) If the agreement was made in or otherwise evidenced by writing supply copies of the same.

3. Under paragraph 12

Of 'caused the Defendant loss of profit on these 700 tiles equating to £7,700'

State precisely how the Defendant has calculated this loss of profit providing full particulars of the calculations involved in doing so and supply copies of all relevant accounting documentation.

Dated this 28th day of July 1997

(signed)

....

To: Watkins & O'Dwyer
17 Sycamore Avenue
Oldcastle OL10 1BR

Messrs Nixons
16 High Street
Oldcastle OL1 2XL

Defendant's Solicitors

Plaintiff's Solicitors

Commentary: Request for Further and Better Particulars

1. Under the County Court Rules, the ability to seek further and better particulars is found in Ord. 6, r. 7 (Particulars of Claim) and Ord. 9, r. 11 (Defence). For a fuller note as to when such a request is appropriate, see RSC Ord. 18, r. 12(3) *et seq.* and the ensuing notes in *The White Book* at 18/12/29 *et seq.* Generally you would use this request when you want your opponent's pleading to be more specific or if you need to know something which the pleading does not tell you.

In this example the plaintiff has served a request to:

(a) find out if the extrusions were really delivered late, by questioning if any delivery date had been agreed between Metal Ltd and the defendant;

(b) find out if the terms of the agreement were really as specified by the defendant, by asking that they provide information as to how the agreement was reached;

(c) find out if the defendant has really sustained a loss of profit by requesting that the defendant prove this loss.

2. The practice is to serve a request in the form illustrated here and, as you will see in the reply provided by the defendant, the request would then be incorporated into the further and better particulars provided in response (see pages 209 *et seq.*). However, you should note that it is no objection to a request that it is not in this form but is simply, perhaps, contained in a letter. If the request is validly made then the party to whom it is made should respond albeit incorporating the request into a formal reply which can then be included and read with the pleadings.

3. In the county court you must file the particulars in addition to serving them on your opponent.

4. If the other side do not comply with the request then you can apply to the court. The application will be made by summons in the High Court and by notice of application in the county court, there is no need for a supporting affidavit. The application should annex the request.

5. If an order is obtained, it will specify the particulars that must be given and the time limit in which they must be given. If the party fails to comply with the order then you can apply for an unless order (again by a summons/notice of application). An unless order provides for non-compliance, i.e., striking out the statement/particulars of claim or the defence, if the defaulting party persistently fails to comply with an order. Following the decision in *Hytec Information Systems* v *Coventry County Council* (1996) *The Times*, 27 December it now seems that a breach of an unless order will have severe consequences (in this case the defence was struck out) unless the defaulting party can convince the court that his failure to comply has been caused by something outside his control. *Hytec*, however, emphasised that each case would be treated on its own facts.

RENT-A-TENT LTD v HAWTHORN LTD

Document 28

Watkins & O'Dwyer
Solicitors

17 Sycamore Avenue
Oldcastle OL10 1BR
Tel. 011-111-1111
Fax 011-111-1111
DX Oldcastle 1000

Partners: J. Watkins
A. O'Dwyer

31 July 1997

Your ref: PT/4/101
Our ref: TW/DR/623

Nixons
16 High Street
Oldcastle OL1 2XL

Dear Sirs

Re: Rent-A-Tent Limited v Hawthorn Limited

Thank you for your letter of 28 July.

Whilst we are prepared to provide you with the particulars sought, we do not accept that this should delay you in serving your Reply and Defence to Counterclaim and we do require service in accordance with the Order of 21 July by 11 August otherwise we will apply for judgment on our Counterclaim.

Yours faithfully

Watkins & O'Dwyer

Commentary: Reply and Defence to Counterclaim

Generally in the county court there is no requirement for the plaintiff to serve a reply and defence to counterclaim and therefore judgment in default cannot be entered on the counterclaim. However, in our case, the plaintiff has been ordered to file this pleading and Tom can apply for judgment in default although this should be by way of ordinary notice of application with a hearing date, as with his application for security.

Document 29

Nixons

16 High Street
Oldcastle
OL1 2XL

11 August 1997

Your ref: TW/DR/623
Our ref: PD/4/101

Watkins & O'Dwyer
17 Sycamore Avenue
Oldcastle
OL10 1BR

Dear Sirs

Re: Rent-A-Tent Limited v Hawthorn Limited

As requested we enclose by way of service our Reply and Defence Counterclaim.

In the event that we do not receive the Further and Better Particulars pursuant to the Request dated 28 July 1997 within the next seven days we will issue an application for an appropriate Order.

Yours faithfully

Nixons

Partners: J. D. Nixon, P. T. Turner, H. A. Tubby

RENT-A-TENT LTD v HAWTHORN LTD

Document 30

IN THE OLDCASTLE COUNTY COURT Case No. OL794762

BETWEEN

RENT-A-TENT LIMITED Plaintiff

and

HAWTHORN LIMITED Defendant

REPLY AND DEFENCE TO COUNTERCLAIM

REPLY

1. Save insofar as the same consists of admissions the Plaintiff joins issue with the Defendant upon its defence.

2. As to paragraphs 3 and 4, the Plaintiff repeats paragraph 4 of its Particulars of Claim. Further it is averred that if any modifications were agreed (which is in any event denied) then in agreeing such modifications the Plaintiff at all times relied upon the expertise of the Defendant as Joiners and Shopfitters and in reliance upon representations that such modifications would not detract from the appearance and integrity of the tiles when compared to the sample tiles.[1]

3. Further insofar as it is alleged by the Defendant that the defects complained of arise due to the default of Metal Limited, it is averred that as part of the agreement between the Plaintiff and the Defendant, the Defendant agreed to source all materials for the manufacture and supply of the tiles and pursuant to this the Defendant introduced the Plaintiff to Metal Limited as a reliable source for the aluminium extrusions. In reliance upon that introduction, the Plaintiff agreed that Metal Limited should provide the aluminium extrusions and at all material times the Defendant was in contact with Metal Limited to arrange for the manufacture and supply of the aluminium extrusions.[2]

DEFENCE TO COUNTERCLAIM

4. The Plaintiff repeats its Particulars of Claim herein and by reason thereof denies it is indebted to the Defendant in the amount claimed or any other sum.[3]

DATED this 11th day of August 1997

(signed)

TO: The Court and
Watkins & O'Dwyer
17 Sycamore Avenue
Oldcastle OL10 1BR

....
Nixons
16 High Street
Oldcastle OL1 2XL

Defendant's Solicitors

Plaintiff's Solicitors

NOTES: REPLY AND DEFENCE TO COUNTERCLAIM

(1)   At paragraph 2 the plaintiff pleads in the alternative. It is denied that any agreement was reached referring to the modifications. However, the pleading then continues by stating that even if the agreement was as the defendant alleges, the plaintiff relied on the defendant's expertise that the tiles would be as good as the sample tiles, and as the tiles were defective the defendant is still in breach.

(2)   At paragraph 3 the plaintiff alleges that the defendant had agreed to source the aluminium extrusions from Metal Limited. Therefore the defendant cannot exculpate itself by relying on the late delivery of the aluminium extrusions by Metal Limited as the defendant has agreed to be responsible for the supply of the aluminium.

(3)   The defence to counterclaim simply relies on the particulars of claim, in much the same way as the counterclaim relied on the defence (see page 186).

Commentary: Reply and Defence to Counterclaim

Only serve a reply if you wish to plead to the matters raised in the defence, whereas whilst a defence to counterclaim is not a strict requirement it is desirable. In the absence of a reply there is an implied joinder of issue (see RSC Ord. 18, r. 14). The reply should not plead any matters inconsistent with the particulars of claim.

STEP 11

Tom serves the reply to the request for further and better particulars on the plaintiff's solicitors. Additionally, the reply reinforces Tom's concern to join Metal Ltd and so, by agreement with Anne Francis, he drafts the third party notice and application for leave to issue. The application is not opposed and leave is given with third party directions.

Document 31

IN THE OLDCASTLE COUNTY COURT   Case No. OL794762

BETWEEN

RENT-A-TENT LIMITED   <u>Plaintiff</u>

and

HAWTHORN LIMITED   <u>Defendant</u>

FURTHER AND BETTER PARTICULARS OF THE DEFENCE
AND COUNTERCLAIM PURSUANT TO A REQUEST
DATED 28TH JULY 1997

1.   Under paragraph 3

Of 'such late delivery solely caused by the late delivery by Metal Limited of the aluminium extrusions'

State:

  (1)   The actual date of delivery of the aluminium extrusions.

  (2)   The date upon which the Defendant originally expected delivery.

RENT-A-TENT LTD v HAWTHORN LTD

(3) Whether the Defendant agreed with Metal Limited the date for delivery and, if so, fully particularise how the agreement was reached, identifying as precisely as possible the individuals involved, dates, words spoken and, if in writing, supply a copy of the same.

REPLY

(1) The extrusions for completion of the 300 tiles were delivered in two batches. The first batch for the first 120 tiles supplied were delivered on or about 27th January 1997 and the remaining extrusions for the balance of the 180 tiles were delivered on or about 24th February 1997.

(2) Delivery of sufficient of the aluminium extrusions for completion of 300 tiles was expected by the end of January 1997.

(3) On or about 17th January 1997 John Irons of Metal Limited telephoned Anne Francis of the Defendant company when he confirmed he had made an agreement with Mr Dancer of the Plaintiff company for the supply of the aluminium extrusions and Mr Irons enquired of Ms Francis when the extrusions for the first 300 tiles would be needed. Ms Francis responded that in order to complete the first 300 tiles for the end of February, the Defendant would require the extrusions by the end of January. Mr Irons stated that this 'might be a bit tight' but he thought it should be possible to meet that date.

2. Under paragraph 4

Of the agreement alleged under each particular sub-paragraphs (a)–(f)
State for each particular sub-paragraph:

(1) When and where the agreement was made.

(2) Identify the individuals involved in reaching the agreement.

(3) If the agreement was made verbally, identify as precisely as possible the words spoken.

(4) If the agreement was made in or otherwise evidenced by writing supply copies of the same.

REPLY

With regard to the agreement on every point mentioned in sub-paragraphs (a)–(f), these matters were agreed at a meeting which took place on the 13th January when Mr Dancer of the Plaintiff company attended at the Defendant's premises and met with Ms Francis and George Best, the Defendant's production manager. This meeting took place in the context that, over the previous 4 weeks the Defendant had disassembled one of the sample tiles provided by the Plaintiff in order to see what modifications could be made to achieve an overall costs saving. At the meeting George Best, by reference to the disassembled tile and a complete tile, explained to Mr Dancer each and every modification specifically referred to in sub-paragraphs (a)–(f) and Mr Dancer specifically agreed to these modifications being made for the purposes of achieving a costs saving on the production costs of the tiles. The agreement is evidenced by a letter from Ms Francis to Mr Dancer dated 15th January 1997 a copy of which is served herewith.

3. Under paragraph 12

Of 'caused the Defendant loss of profit on these 700 tiles equating to £7,700'

State precisely how the Defendant has calculated this loss of profit providing full particulars of the calculations involved in doing so and supply copies of all relevant accounting documentation.

REPLY

The total manufacturing cost for each tile was £24.00, comprising £16.00 labour costs, £6.00 materials and £2.00 contribution to overhead. This gave a gross profit on each tile of £11.00 which, for 700 tiles totals £7,700. The evidence in support of the costings will be by way of the Defendant's management accounts and costings to be provided on discovery.

Dated this 18th day of August 1997

(signed)

....

To: Nixons
16 High Street
Oldcastle OL1 2XL

Plaintiff's Solicitors

Watkins & O'Dwyer
17 Sycamore Avenue
Oldcastle OL10 1BR

Defendant's Solicitors

Commentary: Reply to Further and Better Particulars

See commentary at page 205.

Document 32

¹

IN THE OLDCASTLE COUNTY COURT

Case No. OL794762

BETWEEN

RENT-A-TENT LIMITED

Plaintiff

and

HAWTHORN LIMITED

Defendant

and

METAL LIMITED

Third Party

To (the third party) Metal Limited

TAKE NOTICE that this action has been brought by the Plaintiff against the Defendant and that the Defendant, claims against you that it is entitled to be indemnified [2] by you against liability in respect of:

    (a)   the failure to deliver 300 tiles to the Plaintiff by 28th February 1997 as alleged at paragraph 4 of the Particulars of Claim;

    (b)   the defects complained of by the Plaintiff at sub-paragraphs 4(c), (e), (f)(iii) and (f)(iv) of the Particulars of Claim.

The grounds of the Defendant's claim are—

    (1) On or about 15th January 1997 you agreed with the Plaintiff to manufacture and supply aluminium extrusions ('the extrusions') for 300 dancefloor tiles

(2)   The extrusions would in all respects be manufactured and supplied by you in accordance with a sample provided to you by the Defendant for inspection prior to the said agreement and be of satisfactory quality

(3)   The extrusions would be supplied by you and delivered directly to the Defendant by no later than 31st January 1997

(4)   In breach of the matters aforesaid you:

(a)   failed to supply the extrusions by 31st January 1997 and did not do so until 24 February 1997 with this delay causing the delay complained of by the Plaintiff at paragraph 4 of the Particulars of Claim; and

(b)   in respect of the defects complained of by the Plaintiff at sub-paragraphs 4(a), (e), (f)(iii) and (f)(iv) of the Particulars of Claim, if such defects exist they are defects in your manufacture of the extrusions and consequently the extrusions supplied by you are defective and/or do not accord with the sample supplied to you and/or are not of satisfactory quality.

If you dispute the Plaintiff's claim against the Defendant or the Defendant's claim against you, you must within 14 days after the service of this notice upon you take or send to the court two copies of your defence.

If you fail to do so you may be deemed to admit—

(1)   the Plaintiff's claim against the Defendant; and

(2)   the Defendant's claim against you; and

(3)   your liability to indemnify the Defendant; or

(4)   the validity of any judgment in the action;

And you will be bound by the judgment in the action.

DATED

Address all communications to the Chief Clerk AND QUOTE THE ABOVE CASE NUMBER

THE COURT OFFICE AT THE COURTHOUSE, PRIORY STREET, OLDCASTLE, OL2 4TP

is open from 10 a.m. to 4 p.m. Monday to Friday

NOTES: THIRD PARTY NOTICE

(1)   The form of the notice is in keeping with the Practice Form found in *The Green Book*, form N15.

(2)   Form N15 has four options as to alternative claims against the third party, i.e., a contribution, an indemnity, some other relief or remedy, or the determination of a common question or issue. In this case Hawthorn are only seeking an indemnity from the third party for those particular complaints brought about by the default of the third party.

Commentary: Third Party Notice

The rules governing third party proceedings are found in CCR Ord. 12 (RSC Ord. 16) and are designed to allow all claims between various parties arising from the same set of circumstances to be decided in the same action. The nature of the claim which can be made in the third party notice is set out in CCR Ord. 12, r. 1(1).

The notice can be issued *without* leave if no date for the initial hearing (pre-trial review) has yet been fixed or before pleadings are deemed closed in a case to which automatic directions apply. In this case, as pleadings are deemed closed, Tom needs to apply for leave.

The application for leave is on notice to the plaintiff (but not the third party) and the notice of application should have a copy of the third party notice attached to it. There is also a fee payable of £50. At the hearing, if the district judge grants leave, directions will also be given 'as to the service of the third party notice and as to the future conduct of the proceedings' (CCR Ord. 12, r. 1(3)).

Once leave is granted ordinarily the third party notice will be served by the court in the same way as a summons and be accompanied by a copy of the summons, particulars of claim, defence, any other pleading in the action together with the order giving leave which should additionally contain directions given by the court on hearing that application (see Document 34).

In cases where leave is not required (see above) the defendant should file at court three copies of the third party notice (a copy for the court, plaintiff and third party) and a full set of pleadings for service on the third party (see further *The Green Book*, Procedural Table No. 7). The court will then fix a date for the pre-trial review and specify it in the third party notice which is then served together with the summons and any pleadings on the third party usually not less than 21 days before the return day. In addition a copy of the third party notice is served on the plaintiff. The third party must then file a defence within 14 days of the service of the third party notice and should he default in this he may be ordered to do so on penalty of being debarred altogether (see CCR Ord. 13, r. 2).

If the third party subsequently fails to appear at trial he may be deemed to admit any claim stated in the notice and will be bound by any judgment in the main action, notwithstanding the fact he may have filed a defence. Where he does appear he will be allowed to take such part as the court shall so direct, e.g., cross-examination of witnesses etc.

RENT-A-TENT LTD v HAWTHORN LTD

Document 33

IN THE OLDCASTLE COUNTY COURT

Case No. OL794762

BETWEEN

RENT-A-TENT LIMITED

Plaintiff

and

HAWTHORN LIMITED

Defendant

I WISH TO APPLY FOR leave to issue a third party notice to join Metal Limited as a third party pursuant to CCR Ord. 12 r. 1(1) and that the costs of this application be costs in the cause.

Dated 20th August 1997

Signed . . . .
Defendant's Solicitor

Address for service:

17 Sycamore Avenue
Oldcastle
OL10 1BR

THIS SECTION TO BE COMPLETED BY THE COURT

To the Plaintiff/Defendant

TAKE NOTICE that this application will be heard by the District Judge at
                        on   at   o'clock.

If you do not attend the Court will make such Order as it thinks fit.

Document 34

IN THE OLDCASTLE COUNTY COURT   Case No. OL794762

BETWEEN

RENT-A-TENT LIMITED Plaintiff

and

HAWTHORN LIMITED Defendant

Upon hearing solicitors for the Plaintiff and the Defendant

It is ordered that:

1.   The Defendant do have leave to issue a third party notice against Metal Limited in the form initialled by the District Judge.

2.   The Defendant shall file in court three copies of the third party notice together with one copy of each of the summons, particulars of claim, defence and counterclaim, further and better particulars of the defence and counterclaim and the reply and defence and counterclaim whereupon the proper officer shall issue and effect service of the third party notice accompanied by the other copy pleadings and a sealed copy of this order upon the Third Party, such service to be effected in accordance with Ord. 7, r. 10(a)(b).

3.   Within 14 days of service of the third party notice pursuant to paragraph 2 of this order, the Third Party shall file in court and serve upon the Plaintiff and Defendant its defence (if any) to the third party notice and in default the Defendant shall have liberty to apply for further order by reason thereof.

4.   In the event of the Third Party filing and serving its defence in accordance with paragraph 3 of this order then automatic directions under Ord. 17, r. 11 shall apply as between all parties to this action with time to run 28 days after service of the third party notice.

5.   Costs in the cause.

6.   Liberty to apply.

DATED this 22nd day of September 1997

Commentary: Order Giving Leave for Third Party Notice

When giving leave the court must also consider directions as to service and for the further conduct of the proceedings (CCR Ord. 12, r. 1(3)). If, however, the court makes no directions as to service then the third party notice should be served in the same way as a summons (see CCR Ord. 12, r. 1(6)) and additionally the court will usually then order a date to be fixed for attendance when the third party directions will be given, in which case this will effectively be the same procedure as issuing without leave (see commentary at page 213).

The example order we have included is all-embracing and, in practice, unusual although the authors' view is that there is no reason why this should not be more commonly adopted as opposed to fixing in

RENT-A-TENT LTD v HAWTHORN LTD

any event a pre-trial review date. There is no reason why directions cannot automatically follow once the third party files its defence. The liberty to apply provisions emphasises the ability of any of the parties to apply for any further directions they consider appropriate and, particularly the ability of the defendant to apply under Ord. 13, r. 2 for a debarring order to the effect that the third party shall be deemed to admit the claims of the plaintiff and defendant and be bound by the judgment if no defence to the third party notice is served. Additionally, paragraph 2 of this order is useful as an in house standard draft to remind you and the court staff of the procedure for service.

STEP 12

Tom instructs an expert to prepare a report.

Document 35

Watkins & O'Dwyer
Solicitors

17 Sycamore Avenue
Oldcastle OL10 1BR
Tel. 011-111-1111
Fax 011-111-1111
DX Oldcastle 1000

Partners: J. Watkins
A. O'Dwyer

23 September 1997

Our ref: TW/DR/623

Professor E. A. Cleaver
Department of Mechanical &
   Structural Engineering
Newtown University
East Road
Newtown
NE15 6FZ

Dear Professor Cleaver

<u>Re Portable Dancefloor System</u>

Further to our recent telephone conversation when you kindly agreed to consider a number of dancefloor tiles with a view to preparing a report on the design and manufacture, I am arranging for this letter to be hand delivered to you together with four tiles being two which I refer to as sample tiles and two of the tiles subsequently manufactured by my client, Hawthorn Limited.

To expand on our telephone conversation as to the reason why I require this report, I act for Hawthorn Limited who is the Defendant to an action commenced against it by Rent-A-Tent Limited for damages as a result of alleged defects which exist in the tiles manufactured by my client over and above those in the sample tiles.

Hawthorn were approached by Rent-A-Tent in December of last year with an enquiry as to whether they could manufacture dancefloor tiles for Rent-A-Tent at a cheaper cost than those Rent-A-Tent already had manufactured by a third party company, Regal Oak Limited.

Mr Dancer of Rent-A-Tent met with my client and brought with him a number of the dancefloor tiles manufactured by Regal Oak Limited. These are the sample tiles, two of which you have with this letter. The basic enquiry of my client was whether they could manufacture tiles to a similar specification to the sample tiles but at a cheaper cost than the £70 plus VAT which Regal Oak had charged. My client's case is that certain modifications were agreed to the manufacture as against the sample tiles and as a result of these modifications it proved possible for them to manufacture these modified tiles at £35.00 plus VAT for each tile.

The complaints Rent-A-Tent now make are as follows:

(a) Locking latches — these have been manufactured without adequate pre-load. Furthermore the length of the latch member is 165mm as opposed to 300mm on the specimen tiles.

(b) Location strip — these have not been grub-screwed to the body of the tile and are therefore prone to become mis-aligned.

(c) Edge trims — these fail to interlock satisfactorily making assembly and disassembly difficult.

(d) Release access hole — brass ferrules have been omitted and with repeated usage the hole edges will fray.

(e) Cutting burrs — the cuts have been inadequately machined and finished and cause and/or contribute to malfunction.

(f) Cosmetically — the appearance of the tiles is inferior to the sample tiles in the following areas:

 (i) texture of quality of wood finish;

 (ii) the finishing lacquer is rough affecting the frictional qualities of the dancefloor;

 (iii) the surface quality of the aluminium extrusions;

 (iv) the depth and colour of the anodising and dyeing of the aluminium extruded strips.

The response my client has given to each of these alleged defects is as follows:

(a) Locking latches — the pre-load is dependent upon the spring. The springs used by the Defendants are the same springs as used in the sample tile and provide adequate pre-load in comparison to the sample tile. The reduction in length is a modification agreed between the parties and in any event does not affect the function of the tile in comparison to the sample.

(b) Location strips — it was agreed that these would not be grub-screwed. They are secure and it is denied they are prone to become mis-aligned.

(c) Edge trims — it is denied that they fail to interlock satisfactorily, or, if there is such a fault that it is due to any default by the Defendant. The edge trims were manufactured by Metal Limited, being part of the aluminium extrusions supplied by them and if, which is denied, there are any defects these are due to a fault in manufacture by Metal Limited.

(d) Release access hole — it was agreed that the brass ferrules would be omitted and it is denied that with proper use the hole edges will fray.

(e) Cutting burrs — this is denied and in any event, insofar as the alleged defect relates to the aluminium extrusions supplied by Metal Limited, it is denied the Defendant is at fault.

RENT-A-TENT LTD v HAWTHORN LTD

   (f)   Cosmetically:

      (i)   Texture of quality of wood finish — it was agreed the Defendant could use any hardwood in manufacturing the tiles provided the overall appearance was uniform. The Defendant has used teak, as opposed to oak in the sample tile, and whilst the appearance and texture is different to oak, it is not admitted it is inferior to the sample tile or a breach by the Defendant.

      (ii)   Finishing lacquer — two coats of finishing lacquer have been applied (as opposed to four coats on the sample tile) as agreed and this provides a smooth finish.

      (iii) Surface quality of aluminium — this is denied but any defect which does exist is due to manufacture by Metal Limited.

      (iv) Depth and colour — this is denied but any defect which does exist is due to manufacture by Metal Limited.

With regard to the complaints involving Metal Limited, I have now joined Metal as a party to seek an indemnity if the allegations are proved.

I now require an expert's report prepared with a view to exchanging this with the other parties (they should also similarly be instructing their experts to prepare a report) and thereafter we may arrange a joint meeting of the experts in an attempt to agree as much common ground as possible and, consequently, a joint report. If the expert evidence cannot be agreed then it will be necessary for you along with the other experts to give evidence at the trial.

In the circumstances, I would like you to prepare a report which, subject to your own views, I think should speak as to the method of manufacture of each tile, the materials used, the differences between the two tiles and address the particular defects alleged by Rent-A-Tent and the answer to each of these defects given by my client.

In addition, if you are able to comment on the overall integrity of both the sample and modified tiles this would be useful, particularly in the context of how they would perform when assembled into a complete dancefloor. Both my client and I consider that the design of the sample tiles is defective in the sense that when assembled they would not provide a safe and secure dancefloor. You may require a greater number of tiles to consider this, if so please contact me and I will arrange with my client to have the additional tiles delivered to you.

In the meantime I would like to have an indication as to the extent of your fees, first for preparing this report, and second an indication as to your likely fees in responding to the other side's report and appearing as a witness. I will need to ensure that I have the authority of my client to incur those fees and a payment on account for them. Perhaps you can telephone me with this information and then confirm it in writing.

Finally, I do need your express agreement that any report you prepare is understood to be solely for the purposes of this litigation and should not be disclosed to any other parties without my agreement.

I look forward to hearing from you.

Yours sincerely

Tom Wood

Commentary: Letter to Expert

1. As for the letter instructing the expert in the personal injury case study (see page 55) the letter outlines the facts of the case and then continues by detailing the complaints made by Rent-A-Tent and the response given by Hawthorn. As you will note, this section of the letter is simply lifted from the particulars of claim and defence respectively.

2. The letter continues by asking that the expert comment on whether the prototype was defective in any event. There may be a temptation when instructing an expert to limit the instructions just to cover the allegations made. However, always explore all aspects of the claim. Do not forget of course to send the article/object which is the subject of the dispute to the expert. If for some reason this is not possible, e.g., the object is some machinery in a factory, then you should send clear, colour photographs and the expert should go and see it.

3. It is quite common, either by way of an informal enquiry at the telephone from the other side or otherwise by simply volunteering the information, for one party to reveal the identity of the expert they have instructed to the other side. However, you may consider not divulging this information until you have ascertained that the report of your chosen expert is favourable. In the event that you receive an unfavourable report which you do not intend to rely upon, then your failure to produce a report from that expert may alert the other side to your difficulties and confirm their belief in the merits of their case.

STEP 13

Tom receives a call from Professor Cleaver who indicates a fee of £300 for the report plus VAT and any further involvement to be charged at £75 plus VAT per hour. Anne Francis agrees to that fee and forwards to Tom a payment on account of £500. Tom then instructs Professor Cleaver to proceed.

STEP 14

Metal Limited have now instructed solicitors and a defence is served.

Document 36

IN THE OLDCASTLE COUNTY COURT

Case No. OL794762

BETWEEN

RENT-A-TENT LIMITED

Plaintiff

and

HAWTHORN LIMITED

Defendant

and

METAL LIMITED

Third Party

DEFENCE TO THIRD PARTY NOTICE

1. The Third Party denies any and all liability as alleged in the third party notice and makes no admission as to the Plaintiff's claim against the Defendant

2. It is admitted that:

RENT-A-TENT LTD v HAWTHORN LTD

(a)   the Defendant supplied a sample tile to obtain comment from the Third Party as to the Third Party's ability to manufacture and supply extrusions in accordance with the sample

(b)   the Third Party confirmed its ability to manufacture the extrusions in accordance with that sample

(c)   the Third Party was subsequently approached by and agreed with the Plaintiff on or about 15 January 1997 for the manufacture and supply of extrusions sufficient for 300 tiles at a cost of £3,000 plus VAT

(d)   the extrusions were, pursuant to the Plaintiff's request, to be delivered to the Defendant

(e)   the extrusions were not delivered until 24 February 1997

3.   It is denied that:

(a)   at the time of the agreement between the Plaintiff and the Third Party any time for delivery was discussed or otherwise date agreed

(b)   the Third Party had any obligation to supply the extrusions by 31 January 1997 or otherwise the Third Party was in breach by not supplying the extrusions until 24 February 1997

(c)   the extrusions supplied were defective as alleged and/or did not comply with the sample supplied by the Defendant and/or were not of satisfactory quality

DATED this 13th day of October 1997

To: (1) The Court
(2) Nixons
16 High Street
Oldcastle OL1 2XL
Plaintiff's Solicitors

(3) Watkins & O'Dwyer
17 Sycamore Avenue
Oldcastle OL10 1BR
Defendant's Solicitors

....
Bowman & Co
42 Down Street
Oldcastle OL8 2JE
Third Party's Solicitors
Tel: 011-666-999
ref: CM/123

Commentary: Defence to Third Party Notice

In its defence, Metal Ltd has addressed the particular complaints made against it by admission and denial. This is sufficient and there is no need for any averments to be made with particular regard to what was or was not agreed on date of delivery. The witness statement which John Irons later gives elaborates on the lack of time limits being expressly or strictly agreed (see page 234).

Also note the agreement pleaded at paragraph 2(c) as to the agreed price of £3,000 + VAT. It is apparent Metal has not been paid and in practice it is likely Metal will include a counterclaim against Rent-A-Tent for this money (see CCR Ord. 12, r. 5). However for the purposes of this illustration this counterclaim has not been included.

STEP 15

The parties then serve their respective lists of documents. The plaintiff's list is not reproduced but it does not disclose anything which appears to support the claim as to the lost sales. This increases Tom's belief as to Rent-A-Tent's lack of any firm orders and Tom considers interrogatories (see page 239 where he raises this with Anne). Metal's list simply discloses the delivery notes for the titles and is not reproduced.

Document 37

IN THE OLDCASTLE COUNTY COURT   Case No. OL794762

BETWEEN

RENT-A-TENT LIMITED   Plaintiff

and

HAWTHORN LIMITED   Defendant

and

METAL LIMITED

LIST OF DOCUMENTS

Third Party

The following is a list of documents which contain information about matters in dispute in this case which are or have been in my possession.

SCHEDULE 1, PART I[1]

I have in my possession the documents numbered and listed here. I do not object to you inspecting them.

No.	Document	Date
1.	Fax Plaintiff to Defendant.	03.01.97
2.	Order Defendant to Plaintiff.	13.01.97
3.	Copy letter Defendant to Plaintiff.	15.01.97
4.	Letter Plaintiff to Defendant.	17.01.97
5.	Delivery note High Tension Limited to Defendant.	18.01.97
6.	Invoice High Tension Limited to Defendant.	18.01.97
7.	Copy letter Defendant to Plaintiff.	20.01.97
8.	Letter Plaintiff to Defendant.	22.01.97

9.	Delivery note Third Party to Defendant.	27.01.97
10.	Copy letter Defendant to Plaintiff.	06.02.97
11.	Copy letter Plaintiff to Defendant.	15.02.97
12.	Duplicate delivery note Defendant to Plaintiff.	21.02.97
13.	Delivery note Third Party to Defendant.	26.02.97
14.	Duplicate delivery note Third Party to Defendant.	21.03.97
15.	Copy letter Defendant to Plaintiff.	15.04.97
16.	Duplicate invoice Defendant to Plaintiff.	15.04.97
17.	Letter Nixons to Defendant.	13.05.97
18.	Defendant's management accounts.	Sept to Dec 1996
19.	Defendant's manuscript costing sheets (4).	Undated
20.	Defendant's manuscript diagram and other jottings	Undated
21.	Correspondence common to the parties' solicitors.	Various dates
22.	Pleadings, applications and orders.	

SCHEDULE 1, PART II[2]

I have in my possession the documents numbered and listed here but I object to you inspecting them.

All notes, correspondence, memoranda, and other documentation brought into being by the Defendant and their legal advisers in contemplation and for the purpose of these proceedings.

I object to you inspecting these documents because:

They are by their nature protected by legal professional privilege.

SCHEDULE 2[3]

I have had the documents numbered and listed below, but they are no longer in my possession.

Such originals of these documents as listed in Schedule 1, Part I, as forwarded to their respective addressees on their respective dates.

---

[4]

All the documents which are or have been in my possession and which contain information about the matters in dispute in this case are listed in Schedules 1 and 2.

Signed ....
Solicitors for the Defendant

Dated 20th October 1997

RENT-A-TENT LTD v HAWTHORN LTD

Case No. OL794762

IN THE OLDCASTLE COUNTY COURT

BETWEEN

RENT-A-TENT LIMITED   Plaintiff

and

HAWTHORN LIMITED   Defendant

and

METAL LIMITED   Third Party

LIST OF DOCUMENTS

Watkins & O'Dwyer
17 Sycamore Avenue
Oldcastle
OL10 1BR

Solicitors for the Defendant

RENT-A-TENT LTD v HAWTHORN LTD

NOTES: LIST OF DOCUMENTS

(1) Schedule 1 Part 1 lists the documents which Hawthorn have in its possession, custody or power and which it will allow the other parties to inspect. Correspondence between the parties' solicitors is referred to as 'correspondence passing between the parties' solicitors' and need not be individually listed.

(2) Schedule 1 Part 2 lists the documents which Hawthorn has in its possession, custody or power and it objects to producing. For example, Hawthorn objects to disclosing its correspondence with Tom on the grounds of legal professional privilege. As Tom does not want to reveal anything about the nature of these documents then just a general description of the documents is given, e.g., 'letters passing between solicitor and plaintiff for the purposes of obtaining legal advice'.

For a detailed discussion of privilege see the personal injury case study at page 107.

(3) Schedule 2 lists those documents which have been but are no longer in Hawthorn's possession, custody or power. Usually this is just the original letters listed in Schedule 1 Part 1. Additionally, Hawthorn must state when these documents were last in its possession and, if known, where the documents are now.

(4) Note that there is no notice to inspect at the end of the list, unlike the High Court list of documents. However, inspection must be provided if requested by the other side (see CCR Ord. 14, r. 3). Usually inspection takes place at the office of solicitors serving the list. However, in cases where the documents are probably uncontroversial physical inspection is rare; usually the documents will simply be photocopied on the request of the other side's solicitors and on their undertaking to pay the reasonable photocopying charges of the disclosing party's solicitor.

Commentary: Discovery

Generally for the meaning and ethics of discovery see the personal injury case study at page 107. However, we consider two further points, (1) when privilege is lost and (2) orders for discovery.

1. What if Tom mistakenly disclosed a document which is privileged? Generally the privilege is lost, although Tom could apply to the court for an injunction to try and prevent the other side using the document. The decision as to whether the document may be used will be at the discretion of the court. In *Derby v Weldon* [1990] 3 All ER 762 the plaintiff's solicitor included 14 documents for which they claimed legal professional privilege. The defendant's solicitor realising the plaintiff's mistake asked for copies of those documents. The plaintiff's solicitors then realised their mistake and sought delivery up of those documents from the defendant's solicitors. The case eventually went to appeal and the court ruled that where privileged documents belonging to a party were inadvertently disclosed in circumstances where the other side knew there had been a mistake but sought to take advantage of it, the court had the power to order that the documents should be returned where it was plain that the defendant was planning to take advantage from an obvious mistake.

Derby v Weldon followed the principles first canvassed in *Guinness Peat Properties v Fitzroy Robinson Partnership* [1987] 2 All ER 716, a case concerning waiver of privilege. In this case the court said the relevant principles to be adopted were:

(a) Where solicitors have mistakenly included a document for which they could claim privilege in Schedule 1 Part 1 the court will allow them to amend the list pursuant to RSC Ord. 20, r. 8 if inspection had not yet taken place.

(b) Once the other side has inspected the document then generally it is too late for the court to grant the disclosing party injunctive relief.

(c) However, the court can and should grant injunctive relief to the disclosing party where it appears that the other party has procured the inspection of the document by fraud or realised on inspection that the document had been mistakenly disclosed. Only in very limited circumstances, e.g., where there has been inordinate delay, would the court not intervene.

This is to be compared with the more recent decision of the Court of Appeal in *Pizzey v Ford Motor Co. Ltd* (1993) *The Times*, 8 March 1993 where the plaintiff's solicitor had mistakenly disclosed an unfavourable medical report. The court held that if the other party's solicitor honestly and reasonably believed that privilege had been waived then the court would not prevent its use by that party at trial. Note that the court held the onus was on the plaintiff to satisfy the court that a hypothetical reasonable solicitor receiving the reports ought to have realised that there had been a mistake.

However, note Principle 16.07 in the *Solicitors' Practice Rules* which places an obligation on a solicitor not to read a privileged document but to return it to the other side if it is obvious that it has been mistakenly disclosed.

The moral of this tale appears to be that the court will endeavour to prevent solicitors gaining advantage of obvious mistakes made in the discovery process but if the other side use the documents disclosed honestly believing that privilege has been waived then the court will not intervene.

See also *G. E. Capital Corporate Finance Group Ltd* v *Bankers Trust Co.* [1995] 1 WLR 172. The issue in this case was whether the plaintiff's solicitors were entitled to cover up parts of documents which they had disclosed on discovery. Sections of the documents had been covered up on the grounds of privilege or that the section was of no relevance to the action. The court held that solicitors were entitled to edit the documents in this way.

2. What if one party failed to give discovery pursuant to automatic discovery? If Rent-A-Tent had failed to give discovery then Tom should first write to Nixons requesting they comply with the rules within a specified time limit. If this is not successful then Tom should apply to the court by a notice of application (see page 194) for an order that Rent-A-Tent make discovery within a specified period. Tom should ask for an 'unless order'. Unless Rent-A-Tent comply with such an order then its claim may be dismissed (in the case of a defendant, then the defence would be struck out).

STEP 16

Tom meets with Anne Francis and George Best to prepare the witness statements.

RENT-A-TENT LTD v HAWTHORN LTD

Document 38

IN THE OLDCASTLE COUNTY COURT   Case No. OL794762

BETWEEN

RENT-A-TENT LIMITED   Plaintiff

and

HAWTHORN LIMITED   Defendant

and

METAL LIMITED   Third Party

WITNESS STATEMENT OF ANNE FRANCIS

I Anne Francis of 7 Burlington Mews, Oldcastle, OL3 4JW Company Director will say as follows:

1.   I am the Managing Director of Hawthorn Limited, a company I established with my husband 6 years ago as a small specialist joinery company but which has now grown to be a successful joinery and shopfitting company with 25 employees, including myself. I am responsible for the administration and marketing of the company.

2.   In early December 1996 I took a telephone call from Robert Dancer who informed me that he had a company, Rent-A-Tent Limited, and he wanted to know if we would be interested in manufacturing for him some portable dancefloor tiles. He briefly explained on the telephone what these were and that he had a number of prototypes manufactured but they were proving to be too expensive. What he wanted was to bring some of his prototypes to us and basically get a quote from us to manufacture them for him.

3.   I agreed to a meeting with Mr Dancer and this was arranged for 18th December at my office.

4.   At that meeting, which took place in the morning, I met with Mr Dancer and additionally my Production Manager, George Best, was present. Mr Dancer brought with him 4 of his prototype tiles which I understood had been manufactured by Regal Oak Limited, a company based in Edinburgh known to me as a high class joinery company particularly specialising in quality reproduction and modern furniture.

5.   Mr Dancer had explained on the telephone that he had designed these tiles which he regarded as better than anything else available, principally due to the ease of assembly and secure locking system. Neither I nor George Best had any experience of such a portable dancefloor system and at the meeting Mr Dancer elaborated and, by reference to the prototypes, explained how each tile had, on two adjacent edges, a 'male' locking mechanism and on the other two adjacent edges a 'female' locking mechanism. When the tiles were assembled into a complete dancefloor, the male sides would slot into the female sides on adjoining tiles and the complete floor would then be surrounded by aluminium edges which would add to the strength of the floor.

226

RENT-A-TENT LTD v HAWTHORN LTD

6. The tiles were made up of wooden strips approximately 2 inches wide and 2 feet long. Twelve of these strips would be bound together by glue with a rubber backing and then this would be surrounded by aluminium edging which would be cut from extruded aluminium and assembled on the tile, being secured in place by glue and grub-screwed, to form the male and female locking system. Each female edge had a drill hole into which was affixed a brass ferrule and this hole was used to release the tiles by inserting a simple release tool which would push down the inserted male mechanism and allow the tiles to be pulled away from each other.

7. The quality of manufacture of these prototype tiles was very high — the wood was good quality oak, there was a high quality lacquer finish which had obviously been achieved with perhaps 4 or 5 separate coats, the aluminium was clearly very well machined and the overall impression was one of great quality which could only be achieved by the use of top quality materials and craftsmanship. I was not surprised when Mr Dancer told us that Regal Oak Limited wanted to charge £70 per tile to manufacture these. He wanted to know if we could manufacture them at a cheaper price and he said he was thinking of something around £40 per tile.

8. George Best said that he was sure we could manufacture the tiles although the aluminium extrusions would have to be supplied from an outside contractor and if we were to do it at the price Mr Dancer was talking about then he couldn't expect them to be of the same quality as the prototypes. Mr Dancer accepted this and said that provided that the tiles would do the job and looked OK then he did not mind if they were not exact replicas of the prototype. It was agreed that he would leave the 4 prototype tiles with us for 2 weeks during which time George would disassemble one and we would see what we could do to keep the costs down. We agreed to contact him again in 2 weeks' time.

9. During the next 2 weeks George disassembled one of the prototypes, although this only meant taking the aluminium edges off and disassembling these into their component parts to see how they were made up. I discussed the project with George and we agreed that we could manufacture the tiles and make cost savings as follows:

(a) use a cheaper wood;

(b) only apply two coats of lacquer finish;

(c) dispense with the grub screws;

(d) shorten the male interlocking latches;

(e) dispense with the brass ferrules.

10. With regard to the aluminium extrusions George suggested that we put Mr Dancer in touch with Metal Limited, a metal furnishing company who we had used before to supply us with aluminium frames for shopfitting projects. The other parts, being screws and the springs for the assembly of the interlocking system, we would obtain ourselves, although we would need to obtain the springs from an outside source, ideally the same source as had supplied them for the prototype.

11. I telephoned Mr Dancer about the springs and he said he would have to find out who supplied them, discreetly, from Regal Oak. That same day he sent me a fax to confirm the supplier of the springs was a company in Bristol, High Tension Limited, and he gave me their telephone number. I telephoned and spoke to their Sales Director, a Mr Jarvis, and he recalled the supply to Regal Oak and confirmed he could supply us with as many of the springs as we wanted at a cost of £200 per 1,000. I told Mr Jarvis that we would probably want 4,200 but I would get back to him during the course of the next week.

RENT-A-TENT LTD v HAWTHORN LTD

12.   George contacted John Irons at Metal Limited and, one afternoon, went over to see him, taking one complete prototype tile with him and the aluminium edge parts from the disassembled one. When George came back he told me that Metal Limited could supply the aluminium extrusions and it would probably work out at a cost of £10 per tile.

13.   On the basis of all this information, George and I then worked out a costing for each tile. Taking into account the material and labour cost and contribution to overhead we came out with a figure of £6.00 for the materials, £16.00 labour cost and £2.00 contribution to overhead, giving a total manufacturing cost of £24.00 per tile, but this did exclude the aluminium supply, which would have to be dealt with as a separate matter between Rent-A-Tent Limited and Metal Limited.

14.   We generally have a profit mark up on most items of around 50%. In this case and bearing in mind the figure mentioned by Mr Dancer of 'around £40' we decided to mark the price up to £35.00 per tile on the basis of the additional cost of the aluminium of £10.00 per tile. We did say that we would be prepared to come down on this price by up to £2.00 per tile if Mr Dancer was unhappy, but as it was he didn't try and negotiate this price down.

15.   I telephoned Mr Dancer and an appointment was made for him to come and see us on 13th January. I told him on the telephone that we could manufacture the tiles at £35.00 plus VAT but this would be on the basis of the aluminium being supplied under a separate contract at a cost of about £10.00 per tile, and modifications for the prototype, which I felt George would need to explain to him at the meeting.

16.   The meeting took place when George and I met Mr Dancer and George explained the modifications to him. I can specifically recall George mentioning the following:

  (a)   we would not use oak but whatever hardwood was generally available to us at a competitive price. Teak was mentioned but George did not say we would definitely use teak. It was left open to us to use whatever hardwood we liked, although on the understanding that it would be uniform in final appearance;

  (b)   the prototype tiles appeared to have about five coats of lacquer finish. We would only apply two and this would be sufficient;

  (c)   we would not use grub screws — they were superfluous. Modern glues are very secure;

  (d)   the brass ferrules would be dispensed with;

  (e)   the length of the locking latches would be shortened.

17.   I told Mr Dancer that we had spoken to Metal Limited about the supply of the aluminium extrusions and George told him of his visit to see John Irons with a tile and the aluminium edging. He said that John Irons had confirmed Metal Limited could produce the extrusions and the additional cost would be about £10.00 per tile.

18.   Mr Dancer asked us whether we would sort out the supply of the extrusions directly with Metal Limited. I responded by saying that whilst we would of course liaise with them on the question of delivery and quantities, he would have to contract with Metal Limited directly given the volume and money involved. He agreed and I provided him with Metal Limited's address and telephone number on the basis that George was to immediately telephone John Irons and tell him to expect a call from Mr Dancer and George would drop off with John Irons the tile and separate aluminium edging that he had previously seen so that they could work from it.

19.   I'm not sure at what point we had a definite agreement to manufacture the tiles but it was undoubtedly accepted by this stage that we would do so. Mr Dancer was happy with our proposals and certainly didn't argue about the price. In fact he said that this was about what he had been hoping for.

20. I told Mr Dancer that the minimum initial manufacturing run would be 1,000 but thereafter he could have them in multiples of 100. He said that was fine and we should start with that 1,000 minimum although he anticipated that he would need more.

21. It was at this point that he said he had a contract to supply 300 tiles to Oldcastle University, and would it be possible to have these 300 ready by the end of February. I told him that this should be possible and we'd better get started. At this, the meeting concluded with Mr Dancer saying he would contact John Irons straightaway.

22. We started manufacture straightaway, using teak hardwood we had in stock initially and ordering further amounts. The first thing we had to do was to cut the strips and then bind these together, gluing them together and onto the rubber backing sheet. Once this had been done then they awaited the aluminium edging to be added.

23. The edging was received in continuous lengths from Metal Limited being extruded by them in one continuous process. The lengths comprised the edging strips and the strips which, when cut to size, would be fitted into the edging strip to form the 'male' locking latch and location strips.

24. The edging strips were cut to the length required for each tile and these, as they were, formed the 'female' sides and could be affixed to the tile by slotting them along the length of the tile and secured by glue.

25. The 'male' side however had to be assembled by insertion into the outside edge of the strip of three separate pieces, being (in order) a location strip, the locking latch and then a further location strip. The first location strip was inserted, using glue and a single screw, to secure it. The locking latch mechanism then to be inserted. This was connected by first inserting two springs, compressing these and then inserting the locking latch strip and then releasing the springs. The second location would be inserted and secured as before. The effect of being between the two secure location strips and the effect of the two springs held the locking latch secure. The completed 'male' side was then affixed to the tile as before and the tile was then complete (the lacquer had been applied to the wood prior to the edging being affixed).

26. To complete 300 tiles by the end of February would have needed the aluminium being supplied by the end of January. I spoke to John Irons at Metal Limited who telephoned me, saying that he had briefly met with Mr Dancer and agreed a price with him and when did we want the aluminium for, mentioning that Mr Dancer had told him the first 300 tiles should be ready by the end of February. I told Mr Irons that we would need the aluminium for the end of January. He did say that might be a bit tight but he should be able to do it.

27. However, by the end of January, only sufficient metal had been received for us to complete 120 tiles. These were completed by the 19th February. I telephoned and spoke to John Irons on two occasions during February to find out when the rest of the metal would be available. He was evasive and simply said that it was more complicated than he first thought. I did not chase more than this because I considered it was up to Mr Dancer. I spoke to him on the telephone on two or three occasions, the first at the beginning of February when I told him that the tiles would not be ready for the end of February due to the delay in delivery by Metal Limited. His response was to the effect that I should sort the problem out. Following this I telephoned John Irons (this was the first time I had telephoned him — prior to this their Production Manager had originally told George Best that there would be a delay) and he told me of his problem.

RENT-A-TENT LTD v HAWTHORN LTD

28.   I telephoned back to Mr Dancer (not immediately, perhaps a day or so later) and told him of my conversation with John Irons. Mr Dancer said, effectively, that he was not happy and he had an agreement with us for delivery by the end of February. I told him it was not our fault and if the metal was available we could give him the tiles by then. I suggested he sort it out with John Irons.

29.   About a week later Mr Dancer telephoned me and said he had spoken to John Irons and had been promised the metal would be available at the beginning of next week. The metal did not arrive and I again telephoned John Irons who more or less told me the same thing as before but he said that he should be able to get the metal to us by next week.

30.   I telephoned Mr Dancer and told him of my conversation. He said he had been let down again. I told him he had not been let down by us and if the metal was supplied next week then we should be able to let him have the tiles for mid-March. He asked me whether we had any finished and I told him we had 120. He asked us to let him have those and I agreed, arranging delivery with him to his premises for 21st February.

31.   The metal finally arrived from Metal Limited on 24th February. We completed the remaining 180 tiles and delivered them to Mr Dancer on 21st March.

32.   With regard to payment, when we agreed to manufacture the tiles at the meeting on 13th January, unfortunately I overlooked agreeing payment terms. I therefore wrote to Mr Dancer on 15th January when I confirmed the agreement and also raised the question of payment, suggesting payment for the first 300 on delivery and the payment for the balance of 700 on completion and delivery of 350 lots. Mr Dancer wrote back on 17th January effectively saying he was not happy with my proposal and saying he wanted to pay on completion and delivery of the whole 1,000 tiles, as this had been his understanding. I was not happy with this but, as I considered it was my own fault in not dealing with payment at the meeting (which is very unlike me), I did not respond but simply accepted this.

33.   Having delivered the total 300 tiles, I received a telephone call from Mr Dancer on 25th March when he said we should not manufacture any more tiles for the time being as he was having problems in Oldcastle University taking the 300 he had. I obtained the impression that this was simply a temporary delay and he would telephone in the next few days to confirm we should continue. I did not ask him what the problem was but simply said OK, we would put a hold on it for a few days.

34.   However, nothing further was heard from Mr Dancer for about 3 weeks and so, on 15th April, I raised and sent out to Mr Dancer an invoice for the 300 tiles at £35.00 each, totalling £10,500 plus VAT.

35.   Again nothing was heard from Mr Dancer and so on 9th May I telephoned him to clarify the position and to ask for payment of our invoice. He was quite short on the telephone, saying that he would contact me shortly about the remaining tiles and he would deal with our invoice. I did not press but understood this to mean that he would be asking us to re-commence manufacture of the tiles in the next few days and he would be arranging for payment of our invoice.

36.   I went away on holiday on 17th May and on that date the letter from Mr Dancer's solicitors, Nixons, arrived at the office. Unfortunately, nobody had bothered to respond to it, deciding to leave it for me to deal with on my return. I came back to the office on 3rd June and on that same day the summons arrived in the post.

37.   With regard to the summons I would like the following points:

Para 1 — Agreed. We had not had dealings with the plaintiff before but we were aware of them and their business.

RENT-A-TENT LTD v HAWTHORN LTD

<u>Para 2</u>—Agreed save that the Plaintiff's letter suggested that this price included the aluminium which was being obtained from Metal Limited. This was not the case — the Plaintiff contracted directly with Metal Limited.

<u>Para 3</u>   (a)   Not correct — we were told by Dancer that provided the tiles could do the job they were not concerned with too much detail as to finish or method of manufacture.

(b)   Purpose — this may be the case but we were only asked to manufacture dancefloor tiles in accordance with the sample tile — we were not asked to design and manufacture a dancefloor, only to manufacture tiles which were comparable to the prototype and functional.

(c)   Agreed — we did.

(d)   Agreed — they were.

(e)   Agreed but I do not recall there being any firm emphasis on this date by Dancer — he had simply said he would like the first 300 by that date as he had a sale agreed for them to the University — no date was mentioned as to when he was to supply the tiles to the University.

<u>Para 4</u>—The first 120 tiles were delivered by us to the Plaintiff's premises at Fetter Street on 21st February. The balance of 180 were more or less finished apart from awaiting the aluminium extrusions which needed to be cut and fitted when received from Metal Limited. If the extrusions had all been delivered by the end of January I think that we would probably have had the whole 300 tiles ready for 7th March. As it was, because we did not receive the remaining extrusions until 24th February, we did not complete the tiles until 20th March (working flat out) and delivered them to the Plaintiff at Fetter Street on 21st March (the driver told me that the other 120 were just where he had unloaded them!).

(a)   The 'pre-load' refers to the 'springiness' of the latch and whether it has any play in it. There is some play in the latch but this does not affect its interlocking capability and we have used the same springs as on the prototype and therefore the difference must be due to different tolerances in the manufacture of the extrusions by Metal Limited.

The lengths mentioned are correct but the reduction does not adversely affect the interlocking capability. The reduction in length was a cost saving modification and was specifically mentioned by George Best as a modification we would make at the meeting with Dancer on 13th January — he did not object.

(b)   The prototype was grub-screwed, but this was unnecessary — the glue we used was secure.

(c)   The edge trims were manufactured by Metal Limited — all we did was cut them to size and fit them to the tiles.

(d)   The omission was part of the cost saving — a hardwood was used and the edges do not fray with normal use.

(e)   Denied in so far as the extrusions were cut to fit by us.

(f)(i)   The prototype used oak, we used teak — certainly a different wood in appearance, but it had been agreed that we could use whatever hardwood we wanted provided it was uniform.

(ii)   I do not understand this — a hard resin clear varnish has been used and it was fine.

RENT-A-TENT LTD v HAWTHORN LTD

(iii) Again I do not understand — the extrusions were in any event supplied by Metal Limited under the separate agreement with the Plaintiff.

(iv) Ditto.

This statement consisting of 7 pages signed by me is true to the best of my knowledge and belief and I make it knowing that if it is tendered in evidence I shall be liable to prosecution if I have wilfully stated in it anything which I know to be false or I do not believe to be true.

Dated this 4th day of November 1997

Signed   Anne Francis

Commentary: Witness Statements

See the personal injury case study at page 118 for commentary on the changes introduced by the Civil Evidence Act 1995.

1.   As you will note, Anne's witness statement repeats virtually verbatim all of the information contained in her proof of evidence. In practice this may well not be the case and you should consider carefully what information you have which may be detrimental to your case and whether you can properly leave it out. In more difficult cases you will probably liaise with counsel in preparing the witness statements. Note that George Best's witness statement is not reproduced but would in all respects confirm what Anne has said.

2.   Tom sends the draft witness statements to Anne and George for approval. If Anne and George are happy with their statements then they will each sign their own statement and return it to Tom ready for exchange.

STEP 17

Tom writes to the other parties to confirm whether they are in a position to exchange witness statements. Tom receives a telephone call from Mr Nixon who confirms that he is ready to exchange witness statements. He also indicates that he is ready to exchange expert reports as soon as Tom is able. Tom speaks to Metal's solicitors and they also confirm they are ready.

The parties then exchange witness statements.

Document 39

Watkins & O'Dwyer
Solicitors

17 Sycamore Avenue
Oldcastle OL10 1BR
Tel. 011-111-1111
Fax 011-111-1111
DX Oldcastle 1000

Partners: J. Watkins
A. O'Dwyer

7 November 1997

Your ref: PT/4/101
Our ref: TW/DR/623

Nixons
16 High Street
Oldcastle
OL1 2XL

Dear Sirs

<u>Re: Rent-A-Tent Limited v Hawthorn Limited</u>

We are now in a position to exchange witness statements and write to enquire whether you are in a similar position. Perhaps you could telephone us on receipt of this letter, assuming you are able to exchange. We can then agree to mutual exchange by posting our respective statements to each other.

With regard to expert evidence, we anticipate having our report available very shortly and will contact you with a view to effecting exchange.

Yours faithfully

Watkins & O'Dwyer

[Similar letter to Bowmans (Solicitors for Metal Ltd) not reproduced]

RENT-A-TENT LTD v HAWTHORN LTD

Document 40

Watkins & O'Dwyer
Solicitors

17 Sycamore Avenue
Oldcastle OL10 1BR
Tel. 011-111-1111
Fax 011-111-1111
DX Oldcastle 1000

Partners: J. Watkins
A. O'Dwyer

17 November 1997

Your ref: PT/4/101
Our ref: TW/DR/623

Nixons
16 High Street
Oldcastle
OL1 2XL

Dear Sirs

Re: Rent-A-Tent Limited v Hawthorn Limited

Further to our telephone conversation of today, as agreed we now enclose by way of service copies of the witness statements of Anne Francis and George Best.

We look forward to receiving your own witness statements which you will be placing in the DX post to us today.

Yours faithfully

Watkins & O'Dwyer

Commentary: Exchange of Witness Statements

Exchange is pursuant to the automatic directions and should be simultaneous (see page 176, note (c)). Hence Tom agrees with the other parties the day on which the statements will be posted.

STEP 18

Tom peruses the plaintiff's discovery and the witness statements of Robert Dancer and John Irons (copies not reproduced). He notes that there is no mention of the alleged contract with Oldcastle University. Therefore he proceeds to draft interrogatories for service on Bob Dancer (for interrogatories see page 239).

John Irons' statement says that he was simply telephoned by Mr Dancer who referred to his conversation with Hawthorn and confirmed he wanted Metal to manufacture the extrusions — Mr Dancer told him to contact Hawthorn to agree a supply date — no deadline was mentioned.

Document 41

Watkins & O'Dwyer
Solicitors

17 Sycamore Avenue
Oldcastle OL10 1BR
Tel. 011-111-1111
Fax 011-111-1111
DX Oldcastle 1000

Partners: J. Watkins
A. O'Dwyer

20 November 1997

Our ref: TW/DR/632

Ms Anne Francis
Hawthorn Limited
4 Willow Vale
Oldcastle
OL9 2WN

Dear Anne

Re: Rent-A-Tent Limited

I enclose a copy of the witness statements I have now received from the other parties for Bob Dancer and John Irons. They obviously do not intend to call any other witnesses (apart from their expert).[1]

Please read through the statement and if you consider there is any need for further comment over and above the information I already have please let me know.

I do not think there is anything new or surprising in this statement. However, considering the lack of information as to the supposed agreement for the tiles to the University it does indicate to me, as you yourself believe, that there was never a firm commitment with Oldcastle University for the supply of the tiles. For this reason I intend to prepare and serve interrogatories which are essentially a list of questions to which Mr Dancer must respond.[2] The questions themselves will be framed in such a way as to obtain far more detail on the alleged agreement. In particular I would like to know who Mr Dancer has been dealing with at the University so that we can then approach them to obtain a statement. If this is possible then we will need to obtain the leave of the court to introduce that statement and call that person as a witness, but considering Mr Dancer's statement is lacking in detailed information I do not think this will be unduly difficult.[3]

Yours sincerely

Tom Wood

RENT-A-TENT LTD v HAWTHORN LTD

NOTES: LETTER TO ANNE FRANCIS

(1) On receipt of the witness statements from the other parties it is important that you forward copies to your client for comment. Even at this late stage it may be that your client has omitted to tell you a vital piece of information, either by not considering it necessary or just simply due to forgetfulness. By sending the other side's statement this may jog the client's memory. In any event you will want the client's comments on the statement for the purposes of preparation for trial.

(2) For commentary on interrogatories see page 240.

(3) Remember that you cannot adduce any evidence other than that contained in the witness statements you have exchanged with the other side unless you have the leave of the court.

STEP 19

Tom receives the expert report. He goes through it and sends a copy to Anne along with his comments. He requests that she and George should consider it immediately and let him have any particular comments and, in any event, to telephone him so that, assuming the report is approved, he can ask Professor Cleaver to have the report engrossed and the original forwarded to him for exchange.

Tom receives a phone call from George Best the following day to confirm that they have read through the report and are in entire agreement with what it says. Tom then contacts Professor Cleaver who subsequently sends three engrossed copies of the report.

The parties then simultaneously exchange expert reports.

NOTES: EXPERT REPORT

The expert report has not been reproduced; however here is a brief summary.

The report is on the whole supportive of Hawthorn's claim in that, perhaps most importantly, it is very critical of the original design of the tiles and contends that the sample tiles themselves, when assembled, would not provide a safe and acceptable dancefloor. Accordingly, the design of the dancefloor system is fundamentally flawed. Over and above this, whilst Professor Cleaver agrees that the overall aesthetic appeal of the modified tiles (particularly in the quality of finish and colour of the aluminium extrusions) is not as good as the sample tiles, the modified tiles are not inferior in the way they lock together to the sample tiles. The only important difference which appears to exist, and which is adverse to our case, is the omission of the brass ferrules in the release access holes. Professor Cleaver says this is likely (if the tiles were used as a dancefloor system) to lead to fraying and potential splitting of the wood. However, this adverse effect is almost entirely mitigated by his overall conclusion that the dancefloor tiles, with or without brass ferrules or using the sample or modified tiles, could not provide a safe and secure dancefloor when assembled.

Document 42

Watkins & O'Dwyer
Solicitors

17 Sycamore Avenue
Oldcastle OL10 1BR
Tel. 011-111-1111
Fax 011-111-1111
DX Oldcastle 1000

Partners: J. Watkins
A. O'Dwyer

26 November 1997

Your ref: PT/4/101
Our ref: TW/DR/623

Nixons
16 High Street
Oldcastle
OL1 2XL

Dear Sirs

Re: Rent-A-Tent Limited v Hawthorn Limited

Further to our telephone conversation today, as agreed, we now enclose by way of exchange the report of Professor Cleaver of the Department of Mechanical & Structural Engineering at Newtown University. We look forward to receiving your own report which you are placing in the DX post to us today.

Yours faithfully

Watkins & O'Dwyer

[Similar letter to Bowmans (Solicitors for Metal Ltd) not reproduced]

Commentary: Exchange of Expert Evidence

1. A party wishing to adduce expert evidence at the trial must apply to the court for guidance as to disclosure of that evidence, and comply with any order made (see RSC Ord. 38, rr. 36–44 and CCR Ord. 20, rr. 27, 28).

Note that in this case the disclosure is pursuant to the automatic directions, therefore no further application to the court is required (see page 175).

2. The report will contain all opinions the expert is qualified to give as within his expertise.

3. Before the trial you should check that your expert evidence is up to date.

4. The court can also order that the parties convene a without prejudice meeting where the respective experts narrow down the issues in dispute (see the personal injury case study at page 120).

RENT-A-TENT LTD v HAWTHORN LTD

5.   Once the report has been disclosed then that report may be put in as evidence. If the expert is not present then the evidence cannot be adduced without the party first seeking the direction of the court.

6.   Tom sent the report to Anne for her approval. If Anne had not agreed with the expert evidence then Tom would not have disclosed the report and it would have remained privileged. Tom need only disclose that evidence upon which the defendant intends to rely at trial.

STEP 20

Tom receives the other parties expert reports, prepared by Dr J. Hawkins for the plaintiff and Mr P. Smot for the third party. Neither is as comprehensive as Professor Cleaver's report but Dr Hawkins does criticise the tiles manufactured by Hawthorn. Tom sends the report to both Anne and Professor Cleaver for comment. We have not reproduced that report or this correspondence but Professor Cleaver gives comment by a letter of 1 December which basically accepts the criticisms of Dr Hawkins. However, he points out that these can largely be applied to the sample tile as well and reinforces his conclusion that it is the design that is mainly flawed, not the manufacture.

Document 43

Watkins & O'Dwyer
Solicitors

17 Sycamore Avenue
Oldcastle OL10 1BR
Tel. 011-111-1111
Fax 011-111-1111
DX Oldcastle 1000

Partners: J. Watkins
A. O'Dwyer

1 December 1997

Your ref: PT/4/101
Our ref: TW/DR/623

Nixons
16 High Street
Oldcastle OL1 2XL

Dear Sirs

Re: Rent-A-Tent Limited v Hawthorn Limited

We enclose by way of service upon you Interrogatories directed to Mr Dancer for a response. You will appreciate that these Interrogatories arise by virtue of the lack of detailed evidence in your witness statement as to the alleged agreement with Oldcastle University.

Until we receive your response to these Interrogatories we do not consider this matter is ready to be listed for trial. In the event that we do not receive your response to these Interrogatories within the time specified we will apply to the Court for an unless order against your client.

Yours faithfully

Watkins & O'Dwyer

RENT-A-TENT LTD v HAWTHORN LTD

Document 44

IN THE OLDCASTLE COUNTY COURT	Case No. OL794762

BETWEEN

RENT-A-TENT LIMITED	Plaintiff
and	
HAWTHORN LIMITED	Defendant
and	
METAL LIMITED	Third Party

INTERROGATORIES

TAKE NOTICE that you are required to answer in writing by Affidavit the following Interrogatories:

Of the allegation under paragraph 5 of the Particulars of Claim that the Plaintiff had been unable to market the dancefloor system for hire or sale and in particular has lost the sale of 300 tiles to Oldcastle University state:

(1) whether, at the time of the agreement reached between the Plaintiff and the Defendant, the Plaintiff had any firm orders for the supply by way of hire or sale of the dancefloor tiles and, if so, provide full particulars identifying the party or parties to whom the tiles were to be supplied, the date of the agreement and the date of supply, the manner in which the agreement was concluded and identify the individuals involved, and supply copies of all relevant documents evidencing the agreement.

(2) insofar as the Plaintiff alleges it has lost any orders for the supply by way of hire or sale of the tiles due to the alleged defects give full details of those orders so lost and precisely identifying the circumstances in which those orders came to be lost or otherwise cancelled, identifying the individuals involved and provide copies of any documents evidencing such loss or cancellation.

(3) insofar as the Plaintiff alleges that it has lost the opportunity of marketing the dancefloor system for sale or hire, give full details of any market testing or other research carried out by or on behalf of the Plaintiff into the potential for the supply by sale or hire of the dancefloor system, to include the results of such market testing or other research and provide copies of all relevant documentation.

AND FURTHER TAKE NOTICE that the above Interrogatories are to be answered within 28 days from the date of service of this request upon you.

AND FURTHER TAKE NOTICE that the above mentioned Interrogatories are served upon Mr Robert Dancer, a Director of the Plaintiff Company.

NOTE: A party upon whom Interrogatories without order are served may, within 14 days of the service of Interrogatories, apply to the Court for the Interrogatories to be varied or withdrawn and upon such application the Court may make such order as it thinks fit including an order that the party who served the Interrogatories shall not serve further interrogatories without order.

DATED this 1st day of December 1997

(signed)

To: Robert Dancer and   . . . .
Messrs Nixons   Watkins & O'Dwyer
16 High Street   17 Sycamore Avenue
Oldcastle OL1 2XL   Oldcastle OL10 1BR

Defendant's Solicitors   Plaintiff's Solicitors

RENT-A-TENT LTD v HAWTHORN LTD

Commentary: Interrogatories — see RSC Ord. 26; CCR Ord. 14, r. 11

1.   Interrogatories are questions put to the other side to try and discover more about their case. In this instance Tom wants to know more about the alleged contract with Oldcastle University. The purpose of interrogatories is to secure an admission from the other side and to weaken their case. By asking for more information about the contract with Oldcastle University, Tom is hoping to establish that there was no such contract and therefore the plaintiff does not have a loss of profit claim. Additionally, Tom is requesting information about the alleged contracts that were lost and whether any market testing had been carried out by the plaintiff. He is trying to force the plaintiff to admit that they had no such contracts for the sale of the dancefloor tiles and had not carried out any research to establish whether or not there was a market for the tiles.

2.   The interrogatories must relate to a matter in question between the parties (in this case the contract with Oldcastle University and the alleged loss of profit) and must be necessary either to dispose fairly of the matter or for saving costs. Clearly the second requirement is also satisfied in this instance, if the plaintiff does not provide the information requested by Tom, then it may have to bear the costs of proving the same at trial.

3.   The interrogatories must have some bearing on the issue and form a step in proving liability. They cannot be used as a mere fishing expedition, i.e., to ask any question which does not relate to the cause or matter. (This rule does not apply where the interrogatories would secure an admission, e.g., where the defendant is asked whether or not it is his signature on the contract.) As for the suitable time to serve interrogatories (if at all) then generally speaking it will be when discovery and exchange of witness statements has taken place. This was the view in the recent cases of *Hall* v *Selvaco; Compton* v *Selvaco* (1996) *The Times*, 27 March where the court held that it was premature to serve interrogatories on the same day as a request for further and better particulars and before the exchange of witness statements. Interrogatories must always either save costs or assist in the conduct of the action. In *Hall* they would have added little or nothing to the information the plaintiff would have obtained from the witness statements and further and better particulars, and thus costs would be increased and not saved.

4.   As you can see from the example interrogatories they must be in plain language and capable of being answered by the recipient. Additionally note that:

(a)   the interrogatories must specify a period of time in which they are to be answered (not less than 28 days);

(b)   the interrogatories must be directed to a named individual;

(c)   as Tom is proceeding in the county court the interrogatories must specify that the plaintiff can apply within 14 days of service to the court to have the interrogatories varied or withdrawn.

5.   A party may only be served with interrogatories twice without order. Thereafter further interrogatories can only be served pursuant to a court order.

6.   Note that the plaintiff's reply should be on affidavit. The plaintiff could object to answering the interrogatories on the ground of privilege.

7.   If the plaintiff fails to reply to the interrogatories or have them varied or withdrawn then Tom should apply to the court for the claim to be struck out and for judgment to be entered on the defendant's counterclaim. The court may make any order it thinks just though practically the best Tom could hope for is an unless order (see page 205, paragraph 5).

STEP 21

Tom instructs counsel to advise on evidence.

Document 45

IN THE OLDCASTLE COUNTY COURT   Case No. OL794762

BETWEEN

RENT-A-TENT LIMITED <u>Plaintiff</u>

and

HAWTHORN LIMITED <u>Defendant</u>

and

METAL LIMITED <u>Third Party</u>

INSTRUCTIONS TO COUNSEL TO ADVISE
ON EVIDENCE

Counsel is sent herewith the following copy documents:

1. Pleadings and Orders.

2. Plaintiff's List of Documents, together with documents obtained on discovery.

3. Defendant's List of Documents, together with documents disclosed therein.

4. Third Party's List of Documents, together with documents discussed therein.

5. Proof of evidence of Anne Francis and George Best dated 19th June 1997.

6. Witness statements of Anne Francis and George Best dated 4th November 1997.

7. Witness statement of Robert Dancer dated 28th October 1997.

8. Witness statement of John Irons dated 31st October 1997.

9. Defendant's expert report of Professor E. A. Cleaver.

10. Plaintiff's expert report of Dr J. Hawkins.

11. Third Party's export report of Mr P. Smot dated 30th October 1997.

12. Defendant's interrogatories.

13. Solicitor correspondence.

Instructing Solicitors act for Hawthorn Limited, the Defendant, to a claim by Rent-A-Tent Limited and Counsel is referred to the pleadings for the details of the claim together with Hawthorn's defence and counterclaim. Counsel is then referred to the proofs of evidence of Anne Francis and George Best, the Director and Production Manager respectively of Hawthorn Limited for the comprehensive detail as to the circumstances in which the claim has arisen.

Counsel will see Instructing Solicitors have joined Metal Limited as the Third Party and that the pleadings have now been completed (albeit Counsel will note the Interrogatories which have been served on the Plaintiff and to which a response is awaited) and that witness statements and experts' reports have been exchanged.

Referring to the witness statement of Mr Dancer, Instructing Solicitors identify the matters in issue raised by that statement principally as follows:

1. The extent to which the modifications to the tiles were agreed at the meeting on 13th January.

2. The effect of the introduction of the Plaintiff to Metal Limited by the Defendant, the extent to which the Defendant was responsible for arranging the supply of the aluminium extrusions directly with Metal Limited and consequently the extent to which the Defendant can be liable for the defaults of Metal Limited.

3. The extent to which the Plaintiff had a firm order for the supply of tiles to Oldcastle University and otherwise the marketability of the dancefloor system.

Dealing with each of these points, Instructing Solicitors make the following observations:

1. Counsel will appreciate from the evidence of Anne Francis and George Best that they are adamant the modifications were specifically discussed and put to Mr Dancer at the meeting and Mr Dancer agreed to them. Mr Dancer's own recollection appears to be that all he was told at the meeting was that Hawthorn could manufacture the tile at a cost of £35 subject to modifications which were very minor and would not have an effect on the appearance or performance of the tiles for use as a dancefloor system. Instructing Solicitors take the view that if this was all that was said at the meeting then it was questionable whether such a meeting was necessary and the agreement on this basis could quite easily be concluded on the telephone. In any event Instructing Solicitors consider that the extent to which matters were or were not agreed at this meeting is not now as important as it may have been as a result of the expert evidence which has been produced, both in the Defendant's own report and that disclosed by the other side.

Counsel is referred to those reports and should initially consider the Defendant's report of Professor E. A. Cleaver from which he will see that Professor Cleaver concludes that the design of the tiles was in any event flawed and they could not be used, either in their original or modified form, to provide a fully safe and secure operational dancefloor. Professor Cleaver suggests that there is a distinct likelihood that the tiles would come adrift from each other from the pressures exerted by dancing feet. Leaving this fatal design flaw to one side, Professor Cleaver then concludes that the modifications made to the tiles do not adversely affect the performance and stability of the sample tiles provided, except the only particular criticism which has been identified as the omission of the brass ferrules which could result in the modified tiles fraying and splitting during the course of their lifetime if they were to be used as a dancefloor. This criticism does of course have to be taken against the background, as mentioned, that the tiles in any event (with or without brass ferrules) could not provide a secure dancefloor. Referring to the Plaintiff's report of Dr J. Hawkins, Counsel will see this is certainly not as comprehensive as Professor Cleaver's report and particularly leaves out any comment as to the capabilities of the sample tiles to perform as a safe and secure dancefloor. The criticisms of the modified tiles appear to be made in isolation and the views of both Instructing Solicitors, the Defendant and Professor Cleaver are that this report may well have been 'edited' by the Plaintiff's solicitors to simply reflect the criticisms of the modified tiles when considering their ability, when assembled, to provide a secure dancefloor. Counsel will see Professor Cleaver's comments on this report in his letter to Instructing Solicitors of 1st December.

2. Insofar as the role of Metal Limited is concerned, Counsel will readily appreciate that the delay in delivery of the first batch of 300 tiles was entirely due to the delay by Metal Limited in providing the extrusions and Counsel will further appreciate that to a great extent the defects complained of by the Plaintiff, if they do exist, should properly be laid at the door of Metal Limited. Instructing Solicitors have accordingly joined Metal Limited as a third party.

Counsel will see that on the whole John Irons' statement supports the Defendant's position that the Plaintiff contracted directly with the Third Party and therefore the Defendant cannot be held to blame for the delays and defects attributable to the Third Party.

Finally on this point, Instructing Solicitors find it a little surprising that the Plaintiff has not joined Metal Limited as a Second Defendant (from Hawthorn's enquiries of Metal Limited, no separate proceedings have been taken by the Plaintiff against Metal Limited).

3. With reference to the alleged loss of the contract for supply of 300 tiles to the University, Counsel will note the paucity in the discovery of evidence to support that claim and the evidence available from the witness statement of Mr Dancer. As a result, Counsel will see the Interrogatories which have now been prepared and served and, assuming the information is provided, this will be forwarded to Counsel as soon as possible. If, however, it appears that it is going to be necessary to apply for an order against the Plaintiff to supply this information, Counsel will let Instructing Solicitors know whether he considers this to be unnecessary in the sense that he would choose not to pursue this line of enquiry.

With a view to representing the Defendant at the trial, Counsel is accordingly instructed to advise Instructing Solicitors on the evidence and what steps he considers should now be taken by Instructing Solicitors to have the Defendant's case in good order for the trial.

Should Counsel require any further information, he should not hesitate to contact Mr Wood of Instructing Solicitors.

Dated this 5th day of December 1997

RENT-A-TENT LTD v HAWTHORN LTD

Case No. OL794762

IN THE OLDCASTLE COUNTY COURT

BETWEEN

RENT-A-TENT LIMITED   Plaintiff

and

HAWTHORN LIMITED   Defendant

and

METAL LIMITED   Third Party

INSTRUCTIONS TO COUNSEL TO
ADVISE ON EVIDENCE

TO: Mr Artimus Smythe
Holy Chambers
Riverside Walk
Oldcastle
OL3 7PQ

Watkins & O'Dywer
17 Sycamore Avenue
Oldcastle
OL10 1BR

Tel No. 011–111-1111
Ref: TW/DR/623

Solicitors for the Defendant

Commentary: Instructions to Counsel

See personal injury case study at page 83.

1.   Tom has instructed counsel at this stage of the action as pleadings are now closed and the directions stage is almost complete, and Tom wants counsel's opinion before the matter goes to trial. If counsel is of the opinion that there are any weaknesses in the case, Tom will want enough time to try and remedy the defects before trial.

2.   Note that Tom has highlighted to counsel the three areas of dispute and outlined his views on each. Although it is counsel's job to advise, the solicitor should take the opportunity to sound out his views on the case.

3.   Rent-A-Tent might have added Metal Limited as a second defendant. Should Metal Limited be found to be at fault, Rent-A-Tent will have no recourse against it in the action.

4.   See the personal injury case study at page 84 for commentary on the format of the backsheet.

STEP 22

Tom receives counsel's advice. Counsel is happy with the evidence so far and is particularly pleased with the robust nature of Professor Cleaver's report. However, he advises Tom to serve a notice to admit facts on the plaintiff to deal with the plaintiff's separate agreement with Metal Limited.

RENT-A-TENT LTD v HAWTHORN LTD

Document 46

IN THE OLDCASTLE COUNTY COURT   Case No. OL794762

BETWEEN

RENT-A-TENT LIMITED   <u>Plaintiff</u>

and

HAWTHORN LIMITED   <u>Defendant</u>

and

METAL LIMITED   <u>Third Party</u>

TAKE NOTICE that the Defendant in this action requires the Plaintiff to admit for the purposes of this action only the several facts respectively hereunder specified.

AND the Plaintiff is hereby required, within 7 days after receiving this notice to admit the said several facts saving all just exceptions to their admissibility, as evidence in this action.

Dated 9th January 1997

....
Watkins & O'Dwyer
17 Sycamore Avenue
Oldcastle
OL10 1BR

Solicitors for the Defendant

To: Nixons
16 High Street
Oldcastle
OL1 2XL

Solicitors for the Plaintiff

The facts the admission of which is required are:

1. By an agreement made in or about January the Plaintiff contracted with Metal Limited for the supply of the aluminium extrusions to be used in the manufacture of tiles.

2. Pursuant to the said agreement, the aluminium extrusions were supplied by Metal Limited to the Defendant in the quantities and on the dates as alleged by the Defendant by its witness Anne Francis in her witness statement dated 4th November 1997.

Commentary: Notice to Admit Facts

1. Counsel has advised Tom to serve a notice to admit facts. This procedure is available where the opponent refuses to make a reasonable admission in his pleading and therefore forces you to the extra expense of calling the witness at trial. Tom has already employed one other procedure to try and force the defendant to admit facts, namely interrogatories (see page 239). *But* note this notice to admit is slightly inappropriate and should be regarded as illustrative only — it has been retained from the earlier editions of this book when the third party claim was not included. If Metal Ltd had not been joined then if these facts were not admitted then Tom would have to consider serving a witness summons on John Irons to require his attendance at trial to prove the contract between Metal Ltd and Rent-A-Tent and the delays. However, as Metal Ltd are joined and John Irons is a witness then there will be no savings in time and cost to which the defendant can point which may persuade the plaintiff to give these admissions which will of course be detrimental to its claim (see the following notes).

2. In the county court:

A party ... may, not later than 14 days before the trial or hearing, serve on any other party a notice requiring him to admit ... such facts, or such part of his case as may be specified in the notice.

If the party refuses to admit the facts:

If the party served with a notice to admit facts ... does not deliver a written admission of the facts within seven days after service of the notice on him, the costs of proving the facts and the costs occasioned by and thrown away as a result of his failure to admit the facts shall ... be borne by him.

3. The notice can relate to any fact in issue. Here Tom is serving a notice to force Rent-A-Tent to admit that they were responsible for contracting with Metal Ltd and that there were delays in Metal Ltd supplying the aluminium. See further CCR Ord. 20, r. 2 (RSC Ord. 27, r. 2).

STEP 23

The plaintiff's solicitors write to Tom pointing out that as John Irons will be a witness his notice to admit facts is inappropriate. They also fail to reply to the interrogatories. Tom discusses this with counsel who advises that Tom should not take the matter any further but simply draw the court's attention to this at the trial.

The plaintiff's solicitors write to Tom and ask him whether he is ready for trial. Tom confirms that he is ready and Nixons apply for a hearing date.

Commentary: Hearing Date

1. The plaintiff's solicitors have requested that the court allot the matter a hearing date. The plaintiff's solicitors have filed the note which they have agreed with Tom, and the third party's solicitors, giving an estimate as to the length of the trial and stating the number of witnesses to be called.

RENT-A-TENT LTD v HAWTHORN LTD

2.   At this stage there is no need to file bundles of copy documents as the court file will contain copies of the pleadings. Any other documents are filed later in the action (see commentary below).

Note: As the automatic directions apply, the plaintiff's solicitors must, within six months of the close of pleadings, request the court to fix a day for the hearing (see page 177, paragraph 5(e)).

3.   On receipt of the request for a hearing date, the court will place the case into the 'Warned List' for a period usually of two weeks. This means that the case should be heard during that period, but the Court Listing Office may give short notice as to the date of trial. This system operates to try and ensure that court time is not wasted: thus if cases are settled just before trial there are always cases to call on. Obviously, this can prove inconvenient to the solicitors, counsel, witnesses and the parties themselves, but if there are a large number of witnesses and experts etc. an application can be made for a fixed date.

STEP 24

Tom is contacted by Mr Nixon of the defendant's solicitors. He asks Tom what documents he wishes to have in the court bundle.

Commentary: The Court Bundle

1.   Pursuant to CCR Ord. 17, r. 12 the plaintiff's solicitors must prepare and file at court copies of all the documents intended to be used at trial either by the plaintiff or the defendant. This documentation must be filed before the trial for the convenience of the judge.

2.   As there is also a counterclaim and the third party claim the obligation to file the court bundle will rest equally with the defendant's solicitor (Tom). Additionally, Tom must give the plaintiff's solicitors advance notice of the documents that he intends to rely on, and must try and agree certain documents if possible, e.g., witness statements and expert witnesses as must the third party's solicitors.

3.   In the county court this rule applies to all cases proceeding directly to trial except cases which are not subject to the automatic directions nor to directions made at the pre-trial review.

4.   At least 14 days before the trial date, Tom has to contact the plaintiff's solicitors and tell them which documents he wishes to have included in the trial bundle. The plaintiff must lodge the bundles at least seven days before the day fixed for hearing.

5.   The plaintiff must lodge one bundle (not two as in the High Court). The bundle should be properly paginated and indexed containing the documents which both sides intend to rely on or which either party wishes to have before the court at the hearing.

6.   Additionally, at the same time, the plaintiff must file two copies of:

(a)   the request and reply to further and better particulars (see pages 204 and 209) and the answer to interrogatories (see page 239);

(b)   witness statements (see pages 226 *et seq.*) and expert reports (page 238) and an indication of whether they have been agreed;

(c)   notice of issue of legal aid and any amendment (not applicable here).

Note: In High Court cases this documentation is filed just before setting down or in the bundles lodged just before trial.

STEP 25

Tom issues a witness summons to be served on Professor Cleaver in accordance with counsel's advice.

RENT-A-TENT LTD v HAWTHORN LTD

Document 47

IN THE OLDCASTLE COUNTY COURT

Case No. OL794762

BETWEEN

RENT-A-TENT LIMITED

Plaintiff

and

HAWTHORN LIMITED

Defendant

and

METAL LIMITED

Third Party

Date of hearing:

20th day of April 1998 at 10:00 a.m.

Witness's name in full:

Professor Edward Albert Cleaver

His or her residence and business
or occupation:

22 Larch Crescent, Newtown, NE1 1TP
Professor in mechanical and structural
engineering at Newtown University

If documents or books are required to be
produced here specify them:

Sum to be paid or offered to witness:

£28.50

State by whom to be served:

The Court

Application made by the Defendant
whose address for service is:

17 Sycamore Avenue, Oldcastle, OL10 1BR
(Ref. TW/DR/623)

Dated:

8th April 1998

I request that Professor Edward Albert Cleaver be served with a witness summons by post. I certify that I have reason to believe that the summons if sent to the witness at the address stated in the request will come to his knowledge in time for him to attend Court on the day fixed for the hearing.

RENT-A-TENT LTD v HAWTHORN LTD

The Plaintiff understands that the witness will not be fined for failing to appear at the hearing unless the Judge is satisfied that the summons came to his knowledge in sufficient time to enable him to appear and that he was sent a sum of money to compensate him for loss of time and his travelling expenses.

Dated 8th April 1998

Signed........................

Watkins & O'Dwyer
Solicitors for the Defendant

Commentary: The Witness Summons

1. Now that Tom has a hearing date he must ensure that his witnesses attend. He has issued a witness summons to be served on his expert (for commentary on this see the personal injury case study at page 124). He has filed a N286 and completed the certificate of postal service. The summons may be served personally or through the court by post (unlike a subpoena in the High Court: see page 128 of the personal injury case study). Note there is now a fee payable of £20.

2. It must be served not less than four days before the trial. It will not be issued less than seven days before that date.

3. The witness must be given travelling expenses etc. plus a first instalment towards his allowance.

4. A witness summons is used in much the same way as a subpoena in the High Court (see page 128 of the personal injury case study).

STEP 26

The trial takes place on 23 and 24 April 1998. Hawthorn successfully defends the action and also succeed with its counterclaim. The plaintiff is ordered to pay the defendant's costs together with an indemnity in respect of the costs the defendant is ordered to pay the third party.

Commentary: Trial

1. At the commencement of the trial the judge may give directions as to the order of the proceedings (see CCR Ord. 22, r. 5A). This will include directions as to the ability of the third party to cross-examine the plaintiff's witnesses.

2. The plaintiff's advocate will make an opening speech outlining the facts and indicating the areas in dispute. Plans, photographs and the pleadings and all agreed documents will be referred to.

3. The plaintiff's advocate will then call the plaintiff. He will take the oath (or affirmation). Bear in mind that before the trial the parties had exchanged witness statements. The opposing advocate should indicate whether he is content to accept the evidence of the plaintiff as per his witness statement or whether he requires the evidence (either some or all) to be examined in the usual way, i.e., by non-leading questions and then cross-examination. There are tactical advantages with both methods. Where the plaintiff gives oral evidence he may contradict the evidence in his witness statement, or not adduce all of the evidence in the statement. If there is a doubt as to the credibility of any witness, then the other side may call them to the witness box to highlight any doubt. However, where the witness is an expert, unless the advocate believes the expert's evidence is flawed, there is probably little to be

gained by insisting that the expert gives oral evidence-in-chief. Experts are unlikely to change their views, but you can attempt to undermine the report by cross-examination.

4.   After the plaintiff has given evidence, the defendant's advocate will cross-examine him. Only in the cross-examination can leading questions be asked. The purpose of the cross-examination is to discredit the plaintiff and attack the credibility of his evidence, e.g., by showing the oral evidence contradicts what he previously said in his statement. During the cross-examination the cross-examining advocate puts his party's case to the party he is cross-examining. Usually the third party will also be allowed to cross-examine the plaintiff's witnesses.

5.   The plaintiff's advocate then may re-examine the plaintiff if he so desires, though the re-examination is confined to the areas covered by the cross-examination.

6.   The plaintiff's witnesses then give their evidence in the same way as for the plaintiff.

7.   If a witness is hostile to the party who called him then that party can apply to the court and have the witness declared hostile. The witness can then be cross-examined on the facts of the case and any previous inconsistent statements. The witness's character cannot be attacked by the party who called him, nor can a witness's previous convictions be disclosed. The court can accept the previous inconsistent statement as evidence but it is more likely that the court will take the view that the witness is not to be relied on.

8.   The defendant's advocate then presents the opening speech for the defence. If the defendant's advocate elects to make an opening speech, then he cannot make a closing speech, except with leave of the court.

9.   The defendant's witnesses then give evidence as for the plaintiff's witnesses. Should the defendant's advocate make a submission of no case to answer, then the defendant will only be able to call evidence with the leave of the court.

10.   At this point the third party will usually give its evidence in the same way although it may happen that the court would require the defendant to close its case and decide straightaway that the plaintiff's claim has failed and therefore not require to hear the third party's case.

11.   The case between the plaintiff and the defendant would be closed by the defendant's advocate making a closing speech (if he did not make an opening speech), followed by the plaintiff's advocate's closing speech. In the closing speech the plaintiff's advocate will summarise his own case and answer his opponent's submissions.

12.   The solicitor should have taken a verbatim note of the evidence as it is given. In this case the proceedings have been tape-recorded pursuant to the court's direction (see CCR Ord. 50, r. 9B).

13.   Hawthorn has been successful. County court judgments are payable within 14 days unless the judge otherwise orders (CCR Ord. 22, r. 2). Note that in the High Court, judgments are usually payable forthwith.

14.   As the amount is over £5,000, the judgment will carry interest at the statutory rate (currently 8 per cent) under the Judgments Act 1838, s. 17. Interest runs from the date on which the amount of the judgment debt was finally assessed or agreed (but remember that interest under s. 35A of the Supreme Court Act 1981 can be claimed up to the date of final judgment as opposed to interlocutory judgment). As for costs, interest will run from the date costs were awarded. Note that Hawthorn has also been awarded interest pursuant to County Courts Act 1984, s. 69.

15.   In keeping with usual practice costs follow the event in this scenario. Costs in this instance are to be taxed, if not agreed. See the personal injury case study at pages 143 *et seq.* for a discussion of taxation. With regard to third party proceedings, the court has the power to order costs beween the plaintiff and

RENT-A-TENT LTD v HAWTHORN LTD

the third party. Where the plaintiff loses an action which rendered third party proceedings inevitable then usually the plaintiff will be ordered to pay all parties' costs (see *Thomas* v *Times Book Co. Ltd* [1966] 1 WLR 911).

16. The court has drawn up the judgment. Note that this differs from High Court procedure where the obligation to draw up the judgment rests with the successful party (see RSC Ord. 42, r. 5).

STEP 27

Three weeks have gone by and no payment is received from Rent-A-Tent. Anne instructs Tom to commence enforcement proceedings. Tom transfers the matter from the county court to the High Court for enforcement. Tom then issues a writ of *fieri facias*.

RENT-A-TENT LTD v HAWTHORN LTD

Document 48

Præcipe for
Writ of Fieri Facias
(District Registry)
(O. 46, r. 6)

IN THE HIGH COURT OF JUSTICE High Court 1998. — R. — **No.** 1054

QUEEN'S BENCH **Division** County Court Plaint No. OL794762

[OLDCASTLE **District Registry]**

[Transferred from the OLDCASTLE County Court

by certificate dated the 23 day of JULY 19 98]

Between

RENT-A-TENT LIMITED

Plaintiff

AND

HAWTHORN LIMITED

Defendant

SPECIMEN

Seal a Writ of Fieri Facias directed to the sheriff of OLDSHIRE

against RENT-A-TENT LIMITED

of 76 FETTER STREET, OLDCASTLE OL16 2SU

in the County of OLDSHIRE

(1) Or ''Order'' or
''Award''.

upon a Judgment (¹) [of the OLDCASTLE County Court]

dated the 24 day of APRIL 1998, for the sum

of £ 21,385.00 debt and £ 3743.26 costs and interest, etc.

(2) Insert the
appropriate rate of
interest at date of
entry of judgment.

Indorsed to levy £ 2518.26 and interest thereon at (²) 8 per

cent per annum, from the 30 day of JULY 1998,

and £ 66·50 costs of execution

(Solicitor's name)
(Address)

WATKINS & O'DWYER
17 SYCAMORE AVENUE
OLDCASTLE OL10 1BR

~~Agent for~~
~~of~~

REF TW/DR/623

Solicitor for the DEFENDANT

Dated this 24 day of JULY 1998

253

RENT-A-TENT LTD v HAWTHORN LTD

1998.— R.—No. 1054

IN THE HIGH COURT OF JUSTICE
QUEEN'S BENCH **Division**

OLDCASTLE District Registry

RENT-A-TENT LIMITED

V

HAWTHORN LIMITED

SPECIMEN

PRÆCIPE
For Writ of Fieri Facias

WATKINS & O'DWYER
17 SYCAMORE AVENUE
OLDCASTLE
OL10 1BR

DEFENDANT'S Solicitor

Tel. No. 011-111-1111

Solicitor's Reference TW/DR/623

OYEZ The Solicitors' Law Stationery Society Ltd.,
Oyez House, 7 Spa Road, London SE16 3QQ

1.95 F28871
5050026

High Court E1* (DR)

** **

NOTES: WRIT OF *FIERI FACIAS*

(1) The writ begins with a recital of the judgment and a command to the sheriff.

(2) The writ then states the sum of money to be levied to include interest at the judgment rate.

(3) The writ ends with the date of issue and is indorsed with the party's name and address.

(4) Note that on the writ Tom has given the sheriff as much information as possible. If you know that the debtor has more than one office, or the make and registration number of his car, then you forward this information to the sheriff. The more information the sheriff has, the easier his job and the greater the chances of success.

(5) The fixed costs of £66.50 are prescribed pursuant to RSC Ord. 47, r. 4.

Commentary: Enforcement

1. In the county court interest is governed by the County Court Interest on Judgments Order 1991, which states that interest will not run on judgments of less than £5,000. Furthermore, as soon as the judgment debtor commences any enforcement proceedings in the county court interest ceases to run unless those proceedings fail to elicit any payment from the debtor. Hence Tom has transferred the matter to the High Court pursuant to County Courts Act 1984, s. 42. Where a party has obtained judgment in the county court, and the amount to be enforced by execution is £5,000 or more, it must be enforced in the High Court unless the proceedings originated under the Consumer Credit Act 1974. Where the sum is less than £1,000 (previously the limit was £2,000 but it has recently been amended pursuant to the High Court and County Courts Jurisdiction (Amendment) Order 1996 (SI 1996 No. 3141)) it must be enforced in a county court. In every other case the judgment creditor may enforce in either court (see art. 8 of the High Court and County Courts Jurisdiction Order 1991).

2. Transfer is simply effected by writing to the county court for a certificate of judgment and stating that this is required for enforcement purposes. On issue of that certificate, the judgment is, for nearly all purposes, a judgment of the High Court (see CCR Ord. 25, r. 13 and the notes in *The White Book* at 45/1/38). Enforcement proceedings include an application for oral examination.

3. Tom has chosen to issue a writ of *fieri facias*. The writ is valid for 12 months from the date of issue.

The usual practice is to enforce against assets in the following sequence: moveables, money, land and equitable interest. This process allows the sheriff's officer (High Court), or court bailiff (county court), to seize and sell the debtor's goods to pay the judgment debt and costs and costs of enforcement. The goods are sold by public auction, then the expenses of sale, the judgment debt and costs and the executing officer's costs are deducted and any surplus returned to the debtor.

4. Tom has completed two copies of a writ of *fieri facias* and a *praecipe* for a writ of *fieri facias*. He will take these documents with the judgment and the fee to the court office.

5. The court will then seal the writ and return it to Tom. Tom will then forward the writ to the under-sheriff for the county where Rent-A-Tent's registered office is situated (in other words the county where Oldcastle is situated). The sheriff will acknowledge receipt and send the writ to his officer for execution.

See further RSC Ords 45 and 46.

RENT-A-TENT LTD v HAWTHORN LTD

STEP 28

Tom receives a call from the sheriff. He has taken walking possession of Rent-A-Tent's premises; however he thinks he will be unable to execute the writ as most of the items appear to be equipment or goods on HP. Tom instructs him to withdraw.

Commentary: Execution

1.   The sheriff will return the writ marked *nulla bona*, meaning that there are no available goods.

2.   The sheriff can only execute against goods belonging to the debtor and therefore any goods which are subject to a third party claim, such as goods on HP (where title is rested in the finance company) or other third party goods, are not available to the sheriff even if in the physical possession of the debtor. If there is any dispute on a third party's claim then the third party will need to give notice to the sheriff of the claim, the sheriff will then in turn inform the creditor who will then decide whether to admit or deny the third party claim. If the claim is disputed by the creditor then the sheriff will need to issue an interpleader summons and the claim will be dealt with by the court (see RSC Ord. 17).

In addition, the sheriff is not allowed to execute against the debtor's tools of the trade and goods satisfying the basic domestic needs of the debtor and his family (see the Supreme Court Act 1981, s. 138(3A)). Again, if there is any dispute as to whether any goods fall within these exempt categories the matter can be brought before the court, although in this case the procedure has recently been revised to provide an expedited determination (see RSC Ord. 17, r. 2A).

STEP 29

Tom advises Anne that before taking any further steps, he intends to carry out some further investigations into the financial standing of Rent-A-Tent. He proceeds with the application to examine Winifred Dancer and obtains the order.

Document 49

Defendant: T. A. Wood: 2nd
Sworn: 14th August 1998

IN THE HIGH COURT OF JUSTICE
QUEEN'S BENCH DIVISION
[OLDCASTLE DISTRICT REGISTRY]

1998–R–No. 1054
County Court Plaint No. OL794762

[Transferred from the Oldcastle County Court by certificate dated the 23rd day of July 1998]

BETWEEN

RENT-A-TENT LIMITED   <u>Plaintiff</u>

and

HAWTHORN LIMITED   <u>Defendant</u>

AFFIDAVIT

I Thomas Arthur Wood of 17 Sycamore Avenue, Oldcastle, OL10 1BR Solicitor make oath and say as follows:

1.   I am an assistant solicitor with Messrs Watkins & O'Dwyer, Solicitors for the Defendant and I have the conduct of this action on behalf of the Defendant. I am duly authorised to make this Affidavit.

2.   On the 24th day of April 1998 Judgment was entered in the Oldcastle County Court for the Defendant on its counterclaim against the Plaintiff for £25,128.26 together with the costs to be taxed. By a Certificate of Judgment granted on the 23rd day of July 1998 for the purposes of enforcing the Judgment in the High Court, the proceedings were transferred to this court. The said judgment remains wholly unsatisfied.

3.   In order to enable the plaintiff to decide upon the methods to enforce the Judgment, it is desired to examine the Judgment debtor through its proper officer Winifred Dancer on the question of what, if any, debts are owing to it and whether it has any property or means of satisfying the Judgment debt. The last known address for the person to be examined is 34 Poplar Avenue, Horden, Oldcastle, OL21 4JL within the district of Oldcastle County Court.

4.   In the circumstances I ask for an Order that the said Winifred Dancer do attend before an officer of the Oldcastle County Court to be examined on the said questions and to produce upon such examination all books or documents in her possession relevant to the said questions.

Sworn at 21 Front Street, Oldcastle
in the County of Oldshire
this 14th day of August 1998
Before me,

T. A. Wood (signed)

B. Phipps (signed)

. . . .

Solicitor/Commissioner of Oaths

Defendant: T. A. Wood 2nd
Sworn: 14th August 1998
1998–R–No. 1054
County Court Plaint No. OL794762

IN THE HIGH COURT OF JUSTICE

QUEEN'S BENCH DIVISION

[OLDCASTLE DISTRICT REGISTRY]

BETWEEN

RENT-A-TENT LIMITED   Plaintiff

and

HAWTHORN LIMITED   Defendant

———————

AFFIDAVIT

———————

Watkins & O'Dwyer
17 Sycamore Avenue
Oldcastle
OL10 1BR

REF TW/DR/623

Document 50

IN THE HIGH COURT OF JUSTICE
QUEEN'S BENCH DIVISION
[OLDCASTLE DISTRICT REGISTRY]
[Transferred from the Oldcastle County Court by certificate dated the 23rd day of July 1998]

1998–R–No. 1054
County Court Plaint No. OL794762

BETWEEN

RENT-A-TENT LIMITED   Plaintiff

and

HAWTHORN LIMITED   Defendant

––––––––––

ORDER

––––––––––

UPON READING the Affidavit of Thomas Arthur Wood sworn herein on the 14th day of August 1998

IT IS ORDERED that Winifred Dancer, an officer of the above named Plaintiff do attend and be orally examined as to what, if any, debts are owing to the Plaintiff and whether the Plaintiff has any property or means of satisfying the Judgment herein dated the 24th day of April 1998, before the District Judge sitting at Oldcastle County Court at such time and place as he may appoint and that the said Winifred Dancer produce any books or documents in her possession or power relating to the same before the District Judge at the time of the examination and that the costs of the examination thereunder be in the discretion of the District Judge where the examination has taken place.

DATED this 21st day of August 1998

RENT-A-TENT LTD v HAWTHORN LTD

Commentary: Oral Examination

Tom has already carried out a company search to check the company's financial position (see page 180).

1.   An order for an oral examination is a court order requiring the judgment debtor to attend before an officer of the court and be examined on oath as to his means. The judgment creditor obtains the order by making an *ex parte* application to the court. In this case the judgment debtor is a company, therefore the order is made against an officer of the company, namely Winifred Dancer. Why? You may often find, with a small family company, that a relation is an officer but who may have no control or say as to what the company has been doing. In applying for the examination of this person, it can sometimes lead to family persuasion behind the scenes to have the 'rogue' director make proposals to settle the debt.

2.   In the county court no affidavit is required, the application is simply made by filling in the prescribed form. However, as Tom has transferred to the High Court, he must follow the High Court procedure in RSC Ord. 48 and consequently an affidavit is required. The affidavit should confirm the amount due, that the judgment creditor is entitled to enforce it and identify the person to be examined in the case of a corporate judgment debtor, and provide the address and nearest county court for that person.

3.   The examination will be fixed to take place in the county court. In the High Court Tom will draft the order (in triplicate) and lodge it with the affidavit and the court fee of £30.00. The district judge will consider the affidavit and draft order, and assuming he/she accepts it, will note the backsheet to the affidavit. The court will then seal the order and return two sealed copies to Tom. Tom will then forward a sealed copy to the county court and the county court will then issue a date for the examination. The order and notice of appointment will be served personally and Tom should tender conduct money (especially if he wants to enforce non-attendance by applying for committal — in which case he should also indorse a penal notice on the order — see form N77 in *The Green Book* for the appropriate wording). Conduct money is simply the debtor's reasonable travelling costs to and from court. The order requires Winifred Dancer to produce all relevant books and documents belonging to the company (see CCR Ord. 25, r. 3; RSC Ord. 48, r. 1).

STEP 30

The hearing takes place. Nothing of assistance is revealed, in fact it appears the company has no net assets.

Commentary: Hearing

1.   The hearing takes place before an officer of the court. Tom asked Mrs Dancer a list of questions and at the end of the examination Mrs Dancer is asked to sign a form containing a note of the evidence she has given.

2.   Note that Tom also asked for the costs of the application. The court has simply added these to the judgment debt.

3.   If Mrs Dancer had failed to attend, rather than proceed straight to applying for committal, Tom would have obtained a further date and served Mrs Dancer as before. If she then failed to attend, the court would be inclined to entertain an application for her committal for contempt.

4.   The ultimate sanction for non-attendance is committal to prison. To rely on this sanction the order must be indorsed with a penal notice. The appropriate wording in the county court is as follows:

'If you do not obey this order you will be guilty of contempt of court and may be sent to prison.'

See RSC Ord. 47, r. 7(4) and CCR Ord. 29, r. 11(1) for enforcement by committal and see *The White Book*, 45/7/6 and *The Green Book*, form N77 for the appropriate wording.

STEP 31

Tom informs Anne of the outcome of the oral examination and discusses with her winding-up the company. Despite the lack of any indication that it will bring forth payment, Anne instructs Tom to issue a winding-up petition.

Commentary: Winding-up Proceedings

(Note: What follows is only a brief outline of winding-up proceedings. It is by no means authoritative and for further detail students should consult texts such as *Totty on Insolvency* (FT Law & Tax).)

1.   Pursuant to the Insolvency Act 1986, s. 123 a company may be wound up if it is unable to pay its debts. There are four ways by which the petitioner can establish this ground and the one which Tom relies on is that there remains an unsatisfied judgment debt which Tom has sought to enforce. In this case there is no need to serve a statutory demand, which is the usual way by which a debtor commences winding-up proceedings (see Insolvency Act 1986, s. 123).

2.   Tom has issued the petition in the High Court. Note that not many petitions are issued out of the county court as the jurisdiction is limited (the share capital of the company whether limited or paid up must not exceed £120,000 and the registered office of the company must be within the jurisdiction of the court: see Insolvency Act 1986, s. 117).

3.   On completion of the petition, Tom will file three copies at court. The court will keep one and seal and return the remaining two. Tom must also file an affidavit verifying the petition together with the court fee (£80), and the deposit in respect of the Official Receiver's costs (£500).

STEP 32

Tom obtains a hearing date. He effects service of the petition and files an affidavit of service.

Commentary: Service of the Petition

1.   Tom has effected personal service of the petition at Rent-A-Tent's registered office. He could have effected service on a director or other officer or employee of the company.

2.   An affidavit of service must be then filed immediately after service.

STEP 33

Tom proceeds to advertise the petition.

Commentary: Advertisement of Petition

1.   Tom must notify any other creditors of Rent-A-Tent of the hearing date. The advertisement is in a prescribed form in the London Gazette and must be made not less than seven business days after service on the company and not more than seven business days before the hearing.

2.   Rent-A-Tent's creditors may contact Tom. Tom must then draw up a list of the creditors and indicate whether they support the petition. Tom must hand the list to the court on the day of the hearing but before the actual hearing.

3.   Additionally, Tom must, at least five days before the hearing, file at court a prescribed form which certifies that he has complied with the rules of advertisement and service.

RENT-A-TENT LTD v HAWTHORN LTD

4. Rent-A-Tent could apply for an injunction restraining presentation or advertisement of the petition. The application will be granted if it appears that the company is solvent or has a chance of defeating the claim against it.

STEP 34

The hearing of the winding-up petition takes place. The application is unopposed and Tom is successful.

Commentary: The Hearing

1. The application is heard in open court in front of a district judge.

2. If Rent-A-Tent had intended to oppose the application it should have served an affidavit in reply and this should have been served not less than seven days before the hearing.

3. The winding-up order takes effect from the date of presentation of the petition (see Insolvency Act 1986, s. 129). Once the order is made, no further action may be commenced against the company without the leave of the court (see Insolvency Act 1986, s. 130).

STEP 35

Tom fails to recover any monies on Hawthorn's behalf. He writes to Hawthorn Ltd informing them and enclosing a note of his fees. Note Hawthorn has paid agreed costs to Metal Ltd of £5,000.

Document 51

Watkins & O'Dwyer
Solicitors

17 Sycamore Avenue
Oldcastle OL10 1BR
Tel. 011-111-1111
Fax 011-111-1111
DX Oldcastle 1000

Partners: J. Watkins
A. O'Dwyer

23 October 1998

Our ref: TW/DR/623

Hawthorn Limited
4 Willow Vale
Oldcastle
OL9 2WN

VAT No. 666123444   Bill No. 1234

	NET £	VAT £	TOTAL £
Re Rent-A-Tent Limited			
Fourth account Final account for work done from 20 April 1998 to 23 October 1998	2,500	437.50	2,937.50
Disbursements			
Counsel's fees (unpaid)	1,500	262.50	1,762.50
Sub Totals	4,000	700.00	4,700.00

Payment on account   (0.00)

Amount payable   £4,700.00

J. Watkins (signed)[1]

Note: see overleaf for notice of your rights

RENT-A-TENT LTD v HAWTHORN LTD

NOTICE OF YOUR RIGHTS

If the work for which this invoice relates was non-contentious

1. If you are not satisfied with the amount of our costs you have the right to ask us to obtain a remuneration certificate from the Law Society.[2]

2. That Certificate will either say that our fee is fair and reasonable, or it will substitute a lower fee.

3. If you wish us to obtain a Certificate you must ask us to do so within a month of receiving this notice.

4. We may charge interest on unpaid bills and we will do so at the rate payable on judgment debts from one month after delivery of the bill.

5. (a) If you ask us to obtain a Remuneration Certificate, then unless we already hold the money to cover these, you must first pay

    (i) half our fee shown in the bill;

    (ii) all the VAT shown in the bill;

    (iii) all the disbursements shown as paid in the bill.

  (b) However, you may ask the Law Society at 8 Dormer Place, Royal Leamington Spa, Warwickshire, CV32 5AE, to waive these requirements so that you do not have to pay anything for the time being. You will have to show that exceptional circumstances apply in your case.

6. Your rights are set out more fully in the Solicitors (Non-Contentious Business) Remuneration Order 1994.

If the work for which this invoice relates was contentious or non-continuous

You may be entitled to have your charges reviewed by the Court by the procedure known as 'taxation'. This procedure is different from the Remuneration Certificate procedure set out above and it is set out in sections 70, 71 and 72 of the Solicitors Act 1974.[3]

NOTES: BILL

Note: This bill is only for the period from the trial to date. Tom will have billed Hawthorn on an interim basis and therefore it is only the costs of the trial and enforcement proceedings which remain outstanding. All disbursements (excepting counsel's fees) have been paid for on account. The bill is very brief as Tom will send with it a printout from the time recording system. With the advent of such technology it is no longer necessary to reproduce the detailed cumbersome bill of old. However, a client is entitled to a detailed bill should he request it.

(1) The bill or the covering letter sending out the bill must be signed by a partner.

(2) Note that point 1 of the bill informs the client of its right to seek a remuneration certificate. This is not applicable in this case as the work is contentious.

(3) It is not necessary to tell the client of the right to taxation but it is good practice to do so.

In any event note the limitations on the right to a remuneration certificate or taxation in case of, respectively, a non-contentious and contentious business agreement (see page 165 and the Solicitors Act 1974, s. 57 *et seq.*).

Epilogue

Tom is successful to the extent that he has managed to defend the claim; however, he has failed to recover any monies from Rent-A-Tent. He also failed to recover any of the costs from Rent-A-Tent hence Hawthorn will have to bear all of the costs of the action. The file is then closed (after payment is received from Hawthorn). Be conscious at all times of this as a potential outcome — it is unlikely the client will be particularly pleased!

PRE-ACTION RELIEF —
AN APPLICATION FOR AN ANTON PILLER INJUNCTION:
HAWTHORN LTD v *SIDNEY DIAMOND AND PLANK LTD*

Introduction

This is a brief case study to illustrate the sometimes urgent action that a solicitor may be called upon to take and the effectiveness of the courts' powers to grant relief where circumstances dictate the immediacy and urgency of the situation.

The solicitor is a partner in Tom Wood's firm, Sam Smith, and the client is again Anne Francis of Hawthorn Ltd.

HAWTHORN LTD v SIDNEY DIAMOND AND PLANK LTD

STEP 1

Sam Smith takes a telephone call on the morning of Monday 7 April 1997 from Anne Francis who briefly explains a major problem which is causing extreme concern. Over the last few months Hawthorn Ltd have been working on a new laminating process which would revolutionise existing procedures and make cheap but extremely good quality and durable laminated wooden surfaces widely available. Because of the sensitivity of this project only three employees, Sid Diamond, Alan Brown and Joe Price had been involved and they were fully aware of both the secrecy needed and the potentially huge commercial market. However, one of these employees, Sid Diamond, on Friday 4 April gave four weeks' notice to quit. He had two weeks' holiday which he was going to take but on Monday morning he had telephoned to say he was not feeling very well and he did not think he would be in certainly for the next few days. This of itself immediately caused Anne some concern and she with two other colleagues went through all the documents they held relating to the process and the computerised records. They have found that certain of the documents, which are in their nature manuscript diagrams and notes, are apparently copies when they should in fact be originals; also, certain of the computer disks have had their security tags broken which would allow them to be copied. Anne immediately believed Sid had copied the documents intending to leave all the originals but had inadvertently taken some originals and left copies, and has also copied the information from the computer disks. From her further enquiries Hawthorn have found an empty diskette box in the wastebin next to Sid's desk and by reference to the computer log-on data it appears Sid was in the office over the weekend on the system from 9.51 a.m. to 10.36 a.m. on Sunday 6 April. The point about the empty computer diskette box is that the cleaners empty all wastebins on Friday night and therefore the box could only have been put in the wastebin over the weekend.

Immediately Anne put two and two together and as far as she is concerned made four. She telephoned to speak to Sid but obtained no reply. She therefore that morning jumped into her car with her personnel director John Gibb and drove to Sid's house. As they were approaching Sid's house Anne saw a man walking out of the drive who she recognised as Kevin Jones, the production manager of Plank Ltd (a subsidiary of a large American conglomerate which had recently established a small factory unit in Oldcastle). He was carrying a large brown envelope and whilst they couldn't see clearly Anne and John are certain the envelope had a Hawthorn logo (a picture of a hawthorn tree) on it. All Hawthorn corporate stationery and envelopes have this logo. Anne wanted immediately to follow and stop Kevin Jones but John said he didn't think that was a good idea and that they should go back to the office immediately and contact Sam.

Anne is clearly concerned that Sid has given information to Plank Ltd and that whilst Hawthorn had been intending to apply to patent the process, unfortunately they had not yet put this in hand because from the point of view of speeding up the patent they did not wish to apply until they had successfully finalised the process.

Sam explains that in the circumstances that Anne has outlined to him he considers it best that an application be made immediately for an Anton Piller order. Sam explains that this is an injunction given by the court which will allow Hawthorn and its solicitors to enter Sid's home and Plank's offices, carry out a search for the computer disks and other documents relating to the process, and then remove these and retain them safely pending the full trial or further order of the court. Sam explains that the court would need to be satisfied that on the evidence it was virtually certain that Sid had done what Anne believes he has done and that Plank has been given some or all of the material. Also the court would need to be convinced that unless Hawthorn get all of the material back without delay then there is a significant likelihood that Hawthorn will suffer loss which would be extremely difficult to compensate for at a later stage.

Commentary: Anton Piller Injunction

The High Court has an inherent jurisdiction to make orders requiring parties to do or abstain from doing certain acts — mandatory and prohibitive injunctions. This power can be invoked by a party at any stage of the proceedings as well as seeking a final order at trial. The procedure for applying for an interlocutory injunction (as opposed to a final order at trial) is governed by RSC Ord. 29 and any practitioner applying for an injunction must be familiar with the principles upon which the court will grant such an order and the procedure which will be strictly applied.

An Anton Piller injunction takes its name from the case of *Anton Piller KG v Manufacturing Process Ltd* [1976] Ch 155 where the Court of Appeal effectively summarised and categorised the nature of this form of injunction. It allows a party to enter and search premises and to remove specified items in instances (admittedly rather rare) where the party is able to satisfy the court that it is vital to the interests of justice that the material to be searched for and removed is taken out of the hands of the other party immediately, in order to be preserved for the purposes of the action or to prevent that other party from unlawfully using such material so as to cause harm to the applicant which could not properly be compensated for at a later stage.

An application for an Anton Piller injunction should be sought only in extreme circumstances. It is a mandatory injunction which allows the plaintiff's agents to search and remove documents or property from the defendant's premises. Note that the order does not permit forcible entry; this must be by consent. If the defendant however fails to comply with this order he may be committed for contempt.

Generally, subject to certain exceptions, the county court does not have jurisdiction to hear an application for an Anton Piller injunction and the application should therefore be made to a High Court judge. Where the action involves intellectual property then the proceedings should be brought in the Chancery Division. The application for this injunction will always be on an *ex parte* basis and heard by the judge in court sitting in camera to ensure that there is no possibility of the defendant becoming aware of the application and so taking steps to destroy or otherwise hide away material.

STEP 2

Sam has arranged for Anne, John and Joe Price to come round to his office straightaway, emphasising that they should bring with them the computer disks, the copy documents together with an example of the original documents, the empty diskette box and a printout showing Sid was logged on to the computer over the weekend. In addition, they should bring information as to the process they are developing and an example of the corporate envelope. In the meantime he has telephoned the court listing office at Oldcastle District Registry to tell them he has an extremely urgent matter for which he needs to see a judge. The listing officer, having briefly spoken with the judge's clerk, has told him that he should attend at 1.30 p.m. and he will be able to see Mrs Justice Reed.

It is now 11 a.m.

Commentary: Listing an Urgent Application

It is of course imperative that the application can be heard as soon as possible. In the Chancery Division the application is made by motion (*ex parte* or on notice) and there will need to be affidavit evidence in support. Sam has all this to attend to but the first thing to do is to make sure that there is a judge available. In extremely urgent cases where it has not been possible to prepare all the documents the court can proceed solely on the basis of an affidavit or, in one case, simply a telegram, although these circumstances will be extremely rare and must be accompanied by an undertaking to issue a writ (if not yet issued) and verify the facts by affidavit without delay.

STEP 3

Sam instructs his trainee to telephone the local law society and obtain details of three solicitors who have the necessary experience to act as supervising solicitor and then to contact those solicitors in turn until he finds one who is available all that afternoon and early evening to attend on the execution of an Anton Piller order.

HAWTHORN LTD v SIDNEY DIAMOND AND PLANK LTD

Sam telephones Church Chambers, a barristers' set in Oldcastle which Sam knows well. He speaks to Paul Rose, a barrister of 10 years' call, who specialises in commercial litigation. Sam explains Hawthorn's problem and what steps he has taken from the point of view of wanting Paul Rose to appear on the application that afternoon. Sam and Paul agree that Sam will prepare an affidavit for Anne Francis to swear setting out the facts as she has told Sam, giving detail of the process and exhibiting as much information as possible to demonstrate its innovative nature. Paul also emphasises that the affidavit should exhibit all of the items which Sam has already asked Anne to bring. Sam will also then prepare further short affidavits for John Gibb to confirm Anne's evidence on the information given by Anne as to the enquiries made that day, and particularly seeing Kevin Jones, and also for Joe Price to confirm the confidential nature of their work and the process involved. Paul will pull out the various authorities so these can be referred to and made available to the judge and will also prepare a draft order using the prescribed form in *Practice Direction (Mareva Injunctions and Anton Piller Orders: Forms)* [1996] 1 WLR 1552 (see below) and have this available both on disk and on paper for the hearing. Paul and Sam agree that both Sid and Plank should be joined as defendants.

Commentary: The Supervising Solicitor

Following several important recommendations by the Vice Chancellor, Mr Donald Nicholls VC, in *Universal Thermosensors Ltd v Hibben* [1992] 3 All ER 257, a requirement for an independent solicitor to supervise the execution of an Anton Piller order was introduced by *Practice Direction (Mareva Injunctions and Anton Piller Orders)* [1994] 1 WLR 1233. The supervising solicitor should be an experienced solicitor who is familiar with the Anton Piller process and not a member or employee of the firm acting for the applicant. Local law societies maintain a register of local solicitors who can act as supervising solicitor and the evidence in support of the application (in Anne's affidavit) must include the identity and experience of the proposed supervising solicitor. Therefore Sam needs to contact a suitably qualified solicitor as soon as possible to obtain his/her agreement to act and that he/she will be willing to give the undertaking to the court required in the standard form of order (see page 283).

In October 1996, *Practice Direction (Mareva Injunctions and Anton Piller Orders: Forms)* [1996] 1 WLR 1552 was issued which revised the 1994 *Practice Direction*, and introduced new forms of orders which should be used. In addition, under *Practice Direction (Interlocutory Orders for Injunctions)* [1996] 1 WLR 1551 issued at the same time, wherever possible a draft order should be provided and a computer disk containing the draft should be available so that any amendments at court can immediately be made and the order sealed.

STEP 4

Sam's trainee reports back that Hannah Tubby of Nixons is available and she has faxed through her details confirming she is happy to undertake to the court in the terms of the supervising solicitor's undertaking in the standard form order. Sam drafts the affidavits and has them immediately typed up and faxed to Paul Rose. By that time Anne, John Gibb and Joe Price have arrived and they read through and approve the affidavits. Sam additionally drafts a generally indorsed writ and notice of motion.

It is now 1 p.m.

Document 1

IN THE HIGH COURT OF JUSTICE
CHANCERY DIVISION
[OLDCASTLE DISTRICT REGISTRY]

Ch. 1997–H–No.

BETWEEN

HAWTHORN LIMITED

Plaintiff

and

(1) SIDNEY DIAMOND
(2) PLANK LIMITED

Defendants

To the Defendants (1) Sidney Diamond of 17 Long Street, Oldcastle, OL7 4LM and (2) Plank Limited whose registered office is situate at 46 Old Acres, Oldcastle, OL3 1QX.

This Writ of Summons has been issued against you by the above named Plaintiff in respect of the claim set out on the back.

Within 14 days after the service of this Writ on you, counting the day of service, you must either satisfy the claim or return to the Court Office mentioned below the accompanying Acknowledgment of Service stating therein whether you intend to contest these proceedings.

If you fail to satisfy the claim or to return the Acknowledgment within the time stated, or if you return the Acknowledgment without stating therein an intention to contest the proceedings, the Plaintiff may proceed with the action and judgment may be entered against you forthwith without further notice.

Issued from the Oldcastle District Registry of the High Court this 7th day of April 1997.

Note: This Writ may not be served later than 4 calendar months beginning with that date unless renewed by Order of the Court.

IMPORTANT

Directions of Acknowledgment of Service are given with the accompanying form.

HAWTHORN LTD v SIDNEY DIAMOND AND PLANK LTD

The Plaintiff's claim is for:

(1) An injunction to restrain the Defendants or either of them from using or disclosing to any other party confidential information belonging to the Plaintiff relating to the Plaintiff's design and manufacturing process for wood laminating, such information having been unlawfully and without the knowledge of the Plaintiff removed by the First Defendant from the Plaintiff's premises on or about 6th April 1997.

(2) An Order for delivery up by each of the Defendants of all documentation, computer disks and other records belonging to the Plaintiff unlawfully and without the knowledge of the Plaintiff removed by the First Defendant from the Plaintiff's premises and made available by the First Defendant to the Second Defendant.

(3) An Order for delivery up by the Defendants and each of them of all documents, computer disks and all other form of record, whether in writing, mechanical, retrievable form or howsoever, containing all or any part or parts of the said confidential information.

(4) Damages.

The cause of action in respect of which the Plaintiff claims relief in this action arose wholly or in part at Oldcastle in the district of the Registry named overleaf.

This Writ was issued by Watkins & O'Dwyer of 17 Sycamore Avenue, Oldcastle, OL10 1BR.

Solicitor for the said Plaintiff whose address is:

46 Old Acres
Oldcastle
OL3 1QX

Solicitor's reference: SS/01/45

Telephone number: 011–111-1111

Ch. 1997–H–No.

IN THE HIGH COURT OF JUSTICE

CHANCERY DIVISION

[OLDCASTLE DISTRICT REGISTRY]

BETWEEN

HAWTHORN LIMITED   Plaintiff

and

(1) SIDNEY DIAMOND
(2) PLANK LIMITED   Defendants

WRIT OF SUMMONS

Watkins & O'Dwyer
17 Sycamore Avenue
Oldcastle
OL10 1BR

Tel. 011–111-1111

HAWTHORN LTD v SIDNEY DIAMOND AND PLANK LTD

Document 2

IN THE HIGH COURT OF JUSTICE
CHANCERY DIVISION
[OLDCASTLE DISTRICT REGISTRY]

Ch. 1997–H–No.

BETWEEN

<table>
<tr><td></td><td>HAWTHORN LIMITED</td><td>Plaintiff</td></tr>
<tr><td></td><td>and</td><td></td></tr>
<tr><td></td><td>(1) SIDNEY DIAMOND
(2) PLANK LIMITED</td><td>Defendants</td></tr>
</table>

NOTICE OF MOTION

Take Notice that the Court will be moved on Friday the 11th day of April 1997 at 10.00 a.m. or as soon thereafter as Counsel can be heard at Oldcastle District Registry, Quay Walls, Oldcastle, by Mr Paul Rose of Church Chambers, Oldcastle, OL2 4QP, Counsel for the above named Plaintiff for an Order:

1. Requiring the First Defendant Sidney Diamond to grant the Plaintiff access to the property at 17 Long Street, Oldcastle, OL7 4LM and to permit the Plaintiff to carry out a search of such premises and to remove the items listed in the schedule below.

2. Requiring the Second Defendant Plank Limited to grant the Plaintiff access to the property at 46 Old Acres, Oldcastle, OL3 1QX and to permit the Plaintiff to carry out a search of such premises and to remove the items listed in the schedule below.

3. That the costs of this application be costs in the cause.

SCHEDULE

1. Original or photocopies of manuscript notes and diagrams belonging to the Plaintiff.

2. Computer disks belonging to the Plaintiff.

3. Any other form of physical record of information or any part of such information contained with items listed at 1 and 2 to this schedule.

Dated this 4th day of April 1997

....
Watkins & O'Dwyer
17 Sycamore Avenue
Oldcastle
OL10 1BR

Solicitor for the Plaintiff

To: (1) Sidney Diamond
        17 Long Street
        Oldcastle
        OL7 4LM
        First Defendant

    (2) Plank Limited
        46 Old Acres
        Oldcastle
        OL3 1QX (registered office)
        Second Defendant

Ch. 1997–H–No.

IN THE HIGH COURT OF JUSTICE

CHANCERY DIVISION

[OLDCASTLE DISTRICT REGISTRY]

BETWEEN

HAWTHORN LIMITED   Plaintiff

and

(1) SIDNEY DIAMOND
(2) PLANK LIMITED   Defendants

_____

NOTICE OF MOTION

_____

Watkins & O'Dwyer
17 Sycamore Avenue
Oldcastle
OL10 1BR

Commentary: Writ and Notice of Motion

A generally indorsed writ will be issued. The notice of motion can very quickly be prepared from Sam's precedents. We have not reproduced the affidavits — they depose to the information set out at Step 1 and exhibit all of the relevant documents and items. Detail is given as to the process and Hannah Tubby's fax confirming her willingness to act is exhibited.

STEP 5

It is now 1.15 p.m. and Sam along with Anne Francis, John Gibb and Joe Price arrive at court where they meet Paul Rose. Anne and Sam have a brief conference with Paul during which Anne explains in a little more detail how precisely their new process is so radically different from everybody else's, and emphasises the potential huge financial rewards they stand to make by manufacturing themselves and licensing the process to other manufacturers. She makes the point that Plank Ltd, being part of an American multi-national company, would undoubtedly have the worldwide resources and ruthlessness (by reputation) to ensure that whatever happened they would finalise the process very quickly, seek to patent it as their own and immediately start commercial production on a huge scale. Consequently, Anne is entirely satisfied that unless they stop Plank getting their hands on the information then no matter what subsequently transpires in the court proceedings Hawthorn will never effectively be able to compete with Plank in this area and will lose future financial rewards. Sam's trainee issues the writ and the notice of motion and these are then taken to the listing office along with the affidavits and the draft order prepared by Paul Rose (on paper and on disk) to be given to the judge's clerk, who then takes them straight to Mrs Justice Reed for her to read through.

Commentary: Lodging the Application

Where practicable the papers to be used in the application should be lodged at least two hours before the hearing. Obviously sometimes, as in this case, that will not be possible but nevertheless the court will expect steps to be taken to ensure as much time as possible is made available for the judge to see the documents before the hearing.

STEP 6

It is now 1.45 p.m. and all concerned attend before Mrs Justice Reed. She has read through the papers.

Paul Rose then makes submissions referring the judge to the authorities, submitting that:

1.   The evidence quite clearly established that Hawthorn had been developing over a period of time a unique and extremely clever industrial process for which there was no indication that it was known to any material degree by any other party and in particular Hawthorn's competitors.

2.   Hawthorn thereby had a legitimate proprietary interest in this process which they were entitled to safeguard against the whole world and whilst it was unfortunate that they had not yet embarked on any patent application, firstly such an application was imminent and secondly even if an application had been submitted, that of itself would not deter an organisation such as Plank Ltd from attempting to steal a march by completing the process and commencing worldwide manufacture if detail of the process fell into their hands.

3.   The evidence was compelling: somebody had copied the documentary and computerised records of the process and removed these from Hawthorn's premises. Firstly simply on presumption, given the fact of Sid Diamond's departure, but secondly and compellingly on the evidence, it was beyond any reasonable doubt who had copied and removed without any authority the material record of the process.

4.   The involvement of Plank Ltd by its senior employee, Kevin Jones, was also clearly established and whilst neither Anne Francis nor John Gibb could be absolutely certain it was Hawthorn's envelope which

they saw, it would in fact be extraordinary in these circumstances if Kevin Jones was not involved and had not been given the information by Sid Diamond.

5. Taking the judge to the authorities, this case was clearly one in which it was essential in Hawthorn's interests for the court to grant the order sought, and in respect of which it was inconceivable that this would cause any prejudice to the defendants appreciating the safeguards inbuilt into the execution of the order.

Mrs Justice Reed agreed that this was a case where the court should grant an Anton Piller order and therefore made the order in the terms of the draft.

Document 3

IN THE HIGH COURT OF JUSTICE   Ch. 1997–H–No.
CHANCERY DIVISION
[OLDCASTLE DISTRICT REGISTRY]
BEFORE MRS JUSTICE REED
THIS 7TH DAY OF APRIL 1997

BETWEEN

HAWTHORN LIMITED   Plaintiff

and

(1) SIDNEY DIAMOND
(2) PLANK LIMITED   Defendants

ORDER TO ALLOW ENTRY AND SEARCH OF PREMISES

IMPORTANT:

NOTICE TO THE DEFENDANT

(1) This Order orders you to allow the persons mentioned below to enter the premises described in the Order and to search for, examine and remove or copy the articles specified in the Order. The persons mentioned will have no right to enter the premises or, having entered, to remain at the premises, unless you give your consent to their doing so. If, however, you withhold your consent you will be in breach of this Order and may be held to be in Contempt of Court. The Order also requires you to hand over any of such articles which are under your control and to provide information to the Plaintiff's Solicitors, and prohibits you from doing certain acts. This part of the Order is subject to restrictions.

(2) You should read the terms of the Order very carefully. You are advised to consult a Solicitor as soon as possible.

(3) Before you the Defendant or the person appearing to be in control of the premises allow anybody on to the premises to carry out this Order you are entitled to have the solicitor who serves you with this Order explain to you what it means in everyday language.

HAWTHORN LTD v SIDNEY DIAMOND AND PLANK LTD

(4) You are entitled to insist that there is nobody except Ms Anne Francis, Mr John Gibbs and Mr Joe Price present who could gain commercially from anything he might read or see on your premises.

(5) You are entitled to refuse to permit entry before 9.30 a.m. or after 5.30 p.m. or at all on Saturday and Sunday.

(6) You are entitled to refuse to permit disclosure of any documents passing between you and your Solicitors or Patent or Trademark Agents for the purpose of obtaining advice ('privileged documents').

(7) You are entitled to seek legal advice, and to ask the Court to vary or discharge this Order, provided you do so at once, and provided that meanwhile you permit the Supervising Solicitor (who is a Solicitor acting independently of the Plaintiff) to enter, but not start to search: see paragraph 3.

(8) If you Sidney Diamond the First Defendant and you Plank Limited the Second Defendant disobey this Order you may be found guilty of Contempt of Court and you or any of your directors may be sent to prison or fined and you may be fined or your assets seized.[1]

(9) If any person with knowledge of this Order procures, encourages or assists in its breach, that person will also be guilty of Contempt of Court.

THE ORDER

An application was made today 7th April 1997 by Counsel for the Plaintiff to the Judge who heard the application supported by the affidavits listed in Schedule 6 at the end of this Order and accepted the undertakings by the Plaintiff, the Plaintiff's Solicitors and the Supervising Solicitor set forth in the Schedules at the end of this Order.

As a result of the application IT IS ORDERED that:

Entry and search of premises and vehicles on or around the premises

1.(1) The Defendant must allow Mrs Hannah Tubby ('the Supervising Solicitor'), together with Mr Samuel Smith a Solicitor of the Supreme Court, and a partner in the firm of the Plaintiff's Solicitors Watkins and O'Dwyer and up to four other persons being one trainee solicitor with Watkins and O'Dwyer and three employees of the Plaintiff company accompanying them, to enter the premises mentioned in Schedule 1 to this Order and any other premises of the Defendant disclosed pursuant to paragraph 5(1) hereof and any vehicles under the Defendant's control on or around the premises so that they can search for, inspect, photograph or photocopy, and deliver into the safekeeping of the Plaintiff's Solicitors all the documents and articles which are listed in Schedule 2 to this Order ('the listed items') or which Mr Samuel Smith believes to be listed items. The Defendant must allow those persons to remain on the premises until the search is complete, and to re-enter the premises on the same or the following day in order to complete the search.

(2) This Order must be complied with either by the Defendant himself or by an employee of the Defendant or other person appearing to be in control of the premises and having authority to permit the premises to be entered and the search to proceed.

---

[1] This notice is not a substitute for the indorsement of a penal notice.

(3)   This Order requires the Defendant or his employee or other person appearing to be in control of the premises and having such authority as aforesaid to permit entry to the premises immediately the Order is served upon him, except as stated in paragraph 3 below.

Restrictions on the service and carrying out of paragraph 1 of this Order

2.   Paragraph 1 of this Order is subject to the following restrictions:

(1)   This Order may only be served between 9.30 a.m. and 5.30 p.m. on a weekday.

(2)   This Order may not be carried out at the same time as any search warrant.

(3)   This Order must be served by the Supervising Solicitor, and paragraph 1 of the Order must be carried out in her presence and under her supervision.

(4)   This Order does not require the person served with the Order to allow anyone except Ms Anne Francis, Mr John Gibbs and Mr Joe Price to enter the premises who in the view of the Supervising Solicitor could gain commercially from anything he might read or see on the premises if the person served with the Order objects.

(5)   No item may be removed from the premises until a list of the items to be removed has been prepared, and a copy of the list has been supplied to the person served with the Order, and he has been given a reasonable opportunity to check the list.

(6)   The premises must not be searched, and items must not be removed from them, except in the presence of the Defendant or a person appearing to be a responsible employee of the Defendant or in control of the premises.

(7)   If the Supervising Solicitor is satisfied that full compliance with sub-paragraph (5) or (6) above is impracticable, she may permit the search to proceed and items to be removed without compliance with the impracticable requirements.

Obtaining legal advice and applying to the Court

3.   Before permitting entry to the premises by any person other than the Supervising Solicitor, the Defendant or other person appearing to be in control of the premises may:

(1)   seek legal advice, and apply to the Court to vary or discharge this Order, provided he does so at once; and

(2)   gather together any documents he believes may be privileged and hand them to the Supervising Solicitor for the Supervising Solicitor to assess whether they are privileged as claimed. If the Supervising Solicitor concludes that any of the said documents may be privileged documents or if there is any doubt as to their status the Supervising Solicitor shall exclude them from the search and shall retain the documents of doubtful status in her possession pending further order of the Court.

While this is being done, the Defendant may refuse entry to the premises by any other person, and may refuse to permit the search to begin, for a short time (not to exceed two hours, unless the Supervising Solicitor agrees to a longer period). If the Defendant wishes to take legal advice and gathers documents as permitted, he shall first inform the Supervising Solicitor and shall keep her informed of the steps being taken.

HAWTHORN LTD v SIDNEY DIAMOND AND PLANK LTD

Delivery of listed items and computer printouts

4.(1) The Defendant must immediately hand over to the Plaintiff's Solicitors any of the listed items which are in his possession or under his control save for any computer or hard disk integral to any computer.

(2) If any of the listed items exists only in computer readable form, the Defendant must immediately give the Plaintiff's Solicitors effective access to the computers, with all necessary passwords, to enable them to be searched, and cause the listed items to be printed out. A printout of the items must be given to the Plaintiff's Solicitors or displayed on the computer screen so that they can be read and copied. All reasonable steps shall be taken by the Plaintiff to ensure that no damage is done to any computer or data. The Plaintiff and his representatives may not themselves search the Defendant's computers unless they have sufficient expertise to do so without damaging the Defendant's system.

Disclosure of information by the Defendant

5.(1) The Defendant must immediately inform the Plaintiff's Solicitors:

  (a) where all the listed items are; and

  (b) so far as he is aware

    (i) the name and address of everyone who has supplied him, or offered to supply him, with listed items;

    (ii) the name and address of everyone to whom he has supplied, or offered to supply, listed items; and

    (iii) full details of the dates and quantities of every such supply and offer.

(2) Within four days after being served with this Order the Defendant must swear an affidavit setting out the above information.

Prohibited acts

6.(1) Except for the purpose of obtaining legal advice, the Defendant or anyone else with knowledge of this Order must not directly or indirectly inform anyone of these proceedings or of the contents of this Order, or warn anyone that proceedings have been or may be brought against him by the Plaintiff until Friday 11th April 1997.

(2) The Defendant must not destroy, tamper with, cancel or part with possession, power, custody or control of the listed items otherwise than in accordance with the terms of this Order.

(3) The Defendant must not divulge any information contained within the listed items to any other party except to his solicitor for the purpose of obtaining legal advice.

UNDERTAKINGS

The Plaintiff, the Plaintiff's Solicitors and the Supervising Solicitor gave to the Court the undertakings contained in Schedules 3, 4 and 5 respectively to this Order.

DURATION OF THIS ORDER

Paragraph 6(2) of this Order will remain in force up to and including 11th April 1997 (which is 'the Return Date'), unless before then it is varied or discharged by a further Order of the Court.[2] The application in which this Order is made shall come back to the Court for further hearing on the Return Date.

VARIATION OR DISCHARGE OF THIS ORDER

The Defendant (or anyone notified of this Order) may apply to the Court at any time to vary or discharge this Order (or so much of it as affects that person), but anyone wishing to do so must first inform the Plaintiff's solicitors.

NAME AND ADDRESS OF PLAINTIFF'S SOLICITORS

The Plaintiff's solicitors are: Watkins & O'Dwyer
17 Sycamore Avenue
Oldcastle OL10 1BR

Name, address, fax and telephone numbers both in and out of office hours.

Tel: 011–111-1111 (office hours)   011–111-1111 (out of office hours)
Fax: 011–111-1111

INTERPRETATION OF THIS ORDER

1) In this Order 'he', 'him' or 'his' include 'she' or 'her' and 'it' or 'its'.

2) Where there are two or more Defendants then (unless the context indicates differently):

   (a) References to 'the Defendant' mean both or all of them.

   (b) An Order requiring 'the Defendant' to do or not to do anything requires each Defendant to do or not to do it.

   (c) A requirement relating to service of this Order, or of any legal proceedings, on 'the Defendant' means on each of them. However, the Order is effective as against any Defendant on whom it is served.

   (d) Any other requirement that something shall be done to or in the presence of 'the Defendant' means to or in the presence of any one of them or in the case of a firm or company a director or a person appearing to the Supervising Solicitor to be a responsible employee.

EFFECT OF THIS ORDER

1) A Defendant who is an individual who is ordered not to do something must not do it himself or in any other way. He must not do it through others acting on his behalf or on his instructions or with his encouragement.

2) A defendant which is a corporation and which is ordered not to do something must not do it itself or by its directors officers employees or agents or in any other way.

---

[2] The date should be the earliest practicable Return Date.

HAWTHORN LTD v SIDNEY DIAMOND AND PLANK LTD

SCHEDULE 1

The premises

(1) 17 Long Street, Oldcastle, OL7 4LM.

(2) 46 Old Acres, Oldcastle, OL3 1QX.

SCHEDULE 2

The listed items

(1) Original or photocopies of manuscript notes and diagrams belonging to the Plaintiff.

(2) Computer disks belonging to the Plaintiff.

(3) Any other form of physical record of information contained within the items at (1) and (2) to this schedule.

SCHEDULE 3

Undertakings given by the Plaintiff

(1) If the Court later finds that this Order or carrying it out has caused loss to the Defendant, and decides that the Defendant should be compensated for that loss, the Plaintiff will comply with any Order the Court may make. Further, if the carrying out of this Order has been in breach of the terms of this Order or otherwise in a manner inconsistent with the Plaintiff's Solicitors' duties as Officers of the Court the Plaintiff will comply with any order for damages the Court may make.

(2) To serve on the Defendant at the same time as this Order is served upon him (i) the Writ, (ii) a Notice of Motion for 11th April 1997 and (iii) copies of the affidavits and copiable exhibits containing the evidence relied on by the Plaintiff. Copies of the confidential exhibits need not be served, but they must be made available for inspection by or on behalf of the Defendant in the presence of the Plaintiff's solicitors while the Order is carried out. Afterwards they must be provided to a Solicitor representing the Defendant who gives a written undertaking not to permit the Defendant to see them or copies of them except in his presence and not to permit the Defendant to make or take away any note or record of the exhibits.

(3) To serve on the Defendant a copy of the Supervising Solicitors' report on the carrying out of this Order as soon as it is received.

(4) Not, without the leave of the Court, to use any information or documents obtained as a result of carrying out this Order nor to inform anyone else of these proceedings except for the purposes of these proceedings (including adding further Defendants) or commencing civil proceedings in relation to the same or related subject matter to these proceedings until after the Return Date.

SCHEDULE 4

Undertakings given by the Plaintiff's Solicitors

(1) To answer at once to the best of their ablity any question whether a particular item is a listed item.

(2) To return the originals of all documents obtained as a result of this Order (except original documents which belong to the Plaintiff) as soon as possible and in any event within two working days of their removal.

HAWTHORN LTD v SIDNEY DIAMOND AND PLANK LTD

(3) *While ownership of any item obtained as a result of this Order is in dispute, to deliver the article into the keeping of Solicitors acting for the Defendant within two working days from receiving a written undertaking by them to retain the article in safe keeping and to produce it to the Court when required.*

(4) *To retain in their own safe keeping all other items obtained as a result of this Order until the Court directs otherwise.*

SCHEDULE 5

Undertakings given by the Supervising Solicitor

(1) *To offer to explain to the person served with the Order its meaning and effect fairly and in everyday language, and to inform him of his right to seek legal advice (such advice to include an explanation that the Defendant may be entitled to avail himself of legal professional privilege) and apply to vary or discharge the Order as mentioned in paragraph 3 of the Order.*

(2) *To make and provide to the Plaintiff's Solicitors and to the Judge who made this Order (for the purposes of the Court file) a written report on the carrying out of the Order.*

SCHEDULE 6

Affidavits

The Plaintiff relied on the following affidavits:

(1) *Anne Francis sworn 7th April 1997 together with Exhibits, AF1, 2, 3, 4 and 5.*

(2) *John Gibb sworn 7th April 1997.*

(3) *Joe Price sworn 7th April 1997.*

Commentary: The Order

This form of order is now prescribed by the standard forms set out in *Practice Direction (Mareva Injunctions and Anton Piller Orders: Forms)* [1996] 1 WLR 1552.

Virtually the entire wording of the order is already set out in the standard form and requires very little amendment.

With regard to the undertakings, as mentioned at page 270, the role of the supervising solicitor became a requirement following the case of *Universal Thermosensors Ltd v Hibben* [1992] 3 All ER 257 and the duties of the supervising solicitor are set out in the undertaking at schedule 5 and can be identified as follows:

(a) to explain the meaning and effect of the order to the defendant in everyday language;

(b) to inform the defendant of his right to seek legal advice and the privilege against self-incrimination (but note this privilege may be curtailed, as in our case, in cases involving intellectual property);

(c) to inform the defendant of his right to vary or discharge the order provided he does so at once;

(d) to prepare a written report on the execution of the order and to provide it to the plaintiff's solicitor and the court.

HAWTHORN LTD v SIDNEY DIAMOND AND PLANK LTD

The plaintiff's undertakings are set out in schedule 3 to the order and those of the plaintiff's solicitor at schedule 4.

Also note the restriction on the times when the order can be executed, at item (5) to the notice to the defendant on the second page and in clause 2(i) of the order.

STEP 7

It is now 2.45 p.m. Sam telephones Hannah Tubby and arranges to meet with her in 10 minutes' time outside Plank's offices for the purposes of execution. Sam along with his trainee and Anne Francis, John Gibb and Joe Price arrive outside Plank's offices and meet with Hannah Tubby. Hannah is given a copy of the order which she reads through. They then enter Plank's offices and ask to speak to the managing director, James Logan. Mr Logan comes to the reception and Hannah Tubby serves the order on him explaining its effect. Mr Logan calls for Kevin Jones to come to reception. He arrives and is immediately told what is going on. At that point he readily admits he has computer disks in his desk and is then accompanied by all present into his office and he hands the disks to Sam. A thorough search is carried out of his office to include his desk, briefcase and cupboards but no other records are found. Whilst the search is going on Mr Logan has telephoned Plank's solicitors with the result that Sam speaks to them over the telephone and is told that James Logan will swear an affidavit confirming that he has no knowledge of what is going on, undertaking that any other records which come to light will be immediately handed over, and that Plank would not in any way use any information which may have been obtained relating to the process. Sam along with all others concerned then leave the premises and go straight to Sid's house: as they leave they hear Kevin Jones being fired by James Logan.

Commentary: Execution

See below after Step 8.

STEP 8

It is now 4 p.m. Sam and the others arrive at Sid's house. Mrs Diamond answers the door and Hannah Tubby explains why they are here and asks if Sid is available. Mrs Diamond says he is at the supermarket. Hannah nevertheless explains that Mrs Diamond is obliged to give them access which she does and they are shown into Sid's study. A thorough search reveals a folder containing copies of the documentary records together with the missing original pages and a further number of diskettes. A list of the documents and disks is made in triplicate and just as it is completed Sid arrives home. He is told what has happened, given the list and the parties then leave.

Commentary: Execution and Advising a Client who has been 'Anton Pillered'

Practice Direction (Mareva Injunctions and Anton Piller Orders) [1994] 1 WLR 1233 stipulates that where the premises are likely to be occupied by an unaccompanied woman then the supervising solicitor should be a woman or accompanied by a woman. By choosing Hannah as the supervising solicitor Sam has already catered for that possibility.

What now follows is a brief commentary on how to go about advising a client who has been served with an Anton Piller order, what the solicitor should look out for as the search takes place and what remedies are available to the defendant who has been wrongly Anton Pillered.

When the defendant's solicitor receives notice from his client that he has been served with the order then it is vital that an undertaking is obtained from the plaintiff's solicitor that no execution should take place until he has arrived at the premises. The defendant may delay the search for up to two hours whilst waiting for his solicitor and legal advice. This period may be extended if the supervising solicitor agrees.

Once the defendant's solicitor arrives at the premises then he must explain to his client the effect of the order, in particular that if the defendant chooses not to comply with the order then he may be in contempt of court, one of the penalties for which is imprisonment.

The defendant's solicitor should then study the plaintiff's affidavit, checking that it discloses a cause of action and there is no non-disclosure. The order should be checked to see that it identifies the correct parties (for example, where the defendant is one of a group of companies) and likewise that the address stated in the order corresponds to the premises' address. Additionally, the order will specify the maximum number of people who may be present and the items that may be seized.

One of the defences that may be raised is that of privilege against self-incrimination, i.e., that the defendant will incriminate himself in criminal proceedings if the search takes place. This defence is no longer available for cases involving the infringement of intellectual property rights (see s. 72 of the Supreme Court Act 1981) and has also been curtailed by s. 31(1) of the Theft Act 1968. The other option open to the defendant is to apply for the order to be set aside, though this application should not be undertaken lightly. The application should be made at once supported by an affidavit.

If the search is carried out then the guidelines laid down in *Columbia Pictures* v *Robinson* [1986] 3 All ER 338 should be adhered to, namely that:

(a) a record should be kept of what is removed and a copy provided to the defendant (or other person in control of the premises) and no items should be removed until that person has had an opportunity to check the list;

(b) only the items specifically covered by the order should be removed;

(c) where ownership is in dispute the materials should be returned to the defendant's solicitor pending trial on the undertaking that they are kept in safe custody.

Once execution has taken place the supervising solicitor should prepare his written report, supplying a copy to the plaintiff's solicitors and filing a copy with the court. The plaintiff's solicitor should then serve a copy on the defendant.

Conclusion

Hannah Tubby prepares a report the following day which she files with the court and gives Sam a copy. Sam then serves this on Plank Ltd and Sid Diamond. Within a matter of days and without a statement of claim being served the matter is compromised by Plank Ltd's managing director, James Logan, swearing an affidavit confirming what Sam had been told by their solicitors and agreeing to meet Hawthorn's costs. Kevin Jones also swears an affidavit which confirmed he did this all off his own bat and had intended to use it to impress his bosses. Finally, Sid Diamond, having instructed lawyers, swears an affidavit confirming that he had copied documents and improperly removed them but that he had no other records and undertook to the court that he would not, for a period of six months, contact or obtain employment with any of Hawthorn's competitors nor disclose any of the information to any other party, that he had not given the information to any one other than Kevin Jones, and that he was very sorry. He also agreed to pay Hawthorn's costs.

Commentary: *Inter Partes* Hearing

The return date is Friday 11 April: it should normally be as soon as possible and no longer than seven days before the matter is brought back before the judge for an *inter partes* appointment, at which time the defendants can be heard. In our case by the time of the return date this settlement has been reached and the order is therefore discharged. On the basis of the affidavits then being filed and the undertaking given to the court, the parties eventually agree an order dismissing Hawthorn's claim but ordering the defendants to meet Hawthorn's costs.